JN154599

Cultural Politics around East Asian Cinema 1939–2018

Cultural Politics around East Asian Cinema 1939–2018

Edited by

Noriko Sudo
Takeshi Tanikawa

Kyoto University Press

This English edition published in 2019 jointly by:

Kyoto University Press
69 Yoshida Konoe-cho
Sakyo-ku, Kyoto 606-8315 Japan
Telephone: +81-75-761-6182
Fax: +81-75-761-6190
Email: sales@kyoto-up.or.jp
Web: http://www.kyoto-up.or.jp

Trans Pacific Press
PO Box 164, Balwyn North
Victoria 3104, Australia
Telephone: +61-(0)3-9859-1112
Fax: +61-(0)3-8611-7989
Email: tpp.mail@gmail.com
Web: http://www.transpacificpress.com

© Noriko Sudo and Takeshi Tanikawa 2019.

Edited by Karl Smith.

Designed and set by Sarah Tuke, Melbourne, Australia.

Printed by Asia Printing Office Corportation, Nagano, Japan.

Distributors

Australia and New Zealand
James Bennett Pty Ltd
Locked Bag 537
Frenchs Forest NSW 2086
Australia
Telephone: +61-(0)2-8988-5000
Fax: +61-(0)2-8988-5031
Email: info@bennett.com.au
Web: www.bennett.com.au

USA and Canada
Independent Publishers Group (IPG)
814 N. Franklin Street
Chicago, IL 60610
USA
Telephone inquiries: +1-312-337-0747
Order placement: 800-888-4741
  (domestic only)
Fax: +1-312-337-5985
Email: frontdesk@ipgbook.com
Web: http://www.ipgbook.com

Asia and the Pacific (except Japan)
Kinokuniya Company Ltd.
Head office:
3-7-10 Shimomeguro
Meguro-ku
Tokyo 153-8504
Japan
Telephone: +81-(0)3-6910-0531
Fax: +81-(0)3-6420-1362
Email: bkimp@kinokuniya.co.jp
Web: www.kinokuniya.co.jp
Asia-Pacific office:
Kinokuniya Book Stores of Singapore Pte., Ltd.
391B Orchard Road #13-06/07/08
Ngee Ann City Tower B
Singapore 238874
Telephone: +65-6276-5558
Fax: +65-6276-5570
Email: SSO@kinokuniya.co.jp

The publication of this book was supported by a Grant-in-Aid for Publication of Scientific Research Results (Grant Number 18HP5263), provided by the Japan Society for the Promotion of Science, to which we express our sincere appreciation.

All rights reserved. No reproduction of any part of this book may take place without the written permission of Kyoto University Press or Trans Pacific Press.

ISBN: 978–1–925608–86–1

Contents

Figures — vi
Tables — vi
Photos — vii
List of Contributors — viii

Introduction *Noriko* S<small>UDO</small> — 1

1. Film Control in the Japan Film Law (*Eiga-ho*)
   Atsuko K<small>ATO</small> — 10
2. "Me-istic Nationalism" in Films Promoted by the Japan Self-Defense Forces: Focus on *Midnight Eagle* as an Example *Noriko* S<small>UDO</small> — 36
3. Collaboration between U.S. Film Industry and U.S. Government for Film Distribution in the Republic of China *Takeshi* T<small>ANIKAWA</small> — 58
4. WWII Film Production in Chongqing: *The Japanese Spy* *Yanli* H<small>AN</small> — 82
5. Factors in the Establishment of the Animation Industry in Postwar Japan *Tomoya* K<small>IMURA</small> — 100
6. Virtuous and Depraved: Portrayals of Women in North Korean Cinema *Benjamin* J<small>OINAU</small> — 115
7. Dual Language, Dubbed Cinema: An Enlightened Colonial Subject in *Homeless Angels* *Youngjae* Y<small>I</small> — 157
8. Double-edged National Imagery: From *The Daughter of the Samurai* to *My Japan* *Takeshi* T<small>ANIKAWA</small> — 184
9. The Mysterious Popularity of Japanese Films in Taiwan in the 1950s and '60s *Mamie* M<small>ISAWA</small> — 203

Personal Names Index — 233
Subjects, Film Titles and Geographical Names Index — 234

Figures

6.1 Total produced movies 125
6.2 Corpus analyzed by periods 125

Tables

1.1 List of proposed film laws 19
3.1 The number of American movies screened in
    1945–1949 (Shanghai) 72
6.1 Diachronic trends in our corpus 146

Photos

3.1	Michael Bergher (from Eiga Nenkan)	63
3.2	Advertisement of American films in *Shen Bao* (申報)	71
4.1	*The Japanese Spy*	91
4.2	*The Japanese Spy*	91
4.3	*The Japanese Spy*	92
4.4	*The Great Dictator*	92
4.5	*The Japanese Spy*	94
4.6	*The Japanese Spy*	94
4.7	*The Japanese Spy*	96
4.8	*The Japanese Spy*	96
7.1	*Tuition Fee* (left), *Homeless Angels* (right)	158
7.2	*Homeless Angels*	163
7.3	*Homeless Angels*	170
7.4	*Homeless Angels*	171
7.5	*Homeless Angels*	175
8.1	Advertisement of Towa Shoji & Co., Ltd. (Year Book of the Japanese Motion Pictures 1936)	187
8.2	The last sequence at Manchuria of *Der Tochter des Samurai*	189
8.3	Advertisement of JO Studio, Ltd. (Cinema Year Book of Japan 1936–1937)	193
8.4	Scenes from *My Japan*, which ends with a close-up of Kanto Army soldier, taken from *Der Tochter des Samurai*	197

List of Contributors

Yanli HAN (Chapter 4)
Associate Professor at the Graduate School of Arts and Sciences, University of Tokyo. She specializes in Asian film history and Chinese language films. Her major publications include "Beyond National Cinema: Overseas Chinese Cinema and National Identity", Koyosha, 2014. "Beyond 'Japanese Cinema'", Kurosawa Kiyoshi ed., *Japanese Cinema is Living No.8* (January 2011), Iwanami Publisher, pp. 165–178. "The Yellow Face behind the Camera", in Fujii Jinshi ed., *A Collection of Essays about Modern Hollywood Cinema* (April 2008), Jinbunsyoin Publisher, pp. 121–143, 2007.

Benjamin JOINAU (Chapter 6)
Doctor of Cultural Anthropology specialized in Korean Studies. He is an associate researcher of the Center of Korean Studies (CRC) at EHESS, Paris, and assistant professor at Hongik University, Seoul. He has been living and working in South Korea since 1994. His Ph.D. thesis has analyzed the regimes of otherness in Korean cinema. Through the hermeneutics of cinema and now of urban materials, he is exploring representations and practices in the Korean public sphere (regimes of visibility/invisibility in cityscapes, urban agriculture micro-practices, semiology of spatial forms, etc.). He has published several articles and books in French, English and Korea. Personal Website: www.benjaminjoinau.com.

Atsuko KATO (Chapter 1)
Part-time lecturer at Gakushuin Women's College, specializing in Japanese modern history. She is the author of *Sodoin taisei to eiga* (Tokyo: Shinyosha, 2003). Her most recent article is "Rebuilding of the Censorship System in the Drafting Process of the Film Law," *Media History*, Vol. 28, 2010.

Tomoya KIMURA (Chapter 5)
Part time lecturer at Tamagawa University and Meiji Gakuin University, specializing in animation studies, especially at the point of industrial history. His major refereed paper is Shougyou animation seisaku ni okeru "souzou" to "roudou": Touei-Douga kabushikigaisya no rousihunsou kara (ed., in Japanese, Creation and labor in the production of commercial animation film: The trouble between labor and management in Toei animation studio, *Socio-Culture Studies*, Vol. 18, The Association for the Socio-Culture, 2016).

Mamie MISAWA (Chapter 9)
Professor at the Department of Chinese Language and Culture, College of Humanities and Sciences, Nihon University. She has published two monographs: *The Screen under Colonial Rule: A study on the movie policy of the Colonial Government of Taiwan* (Taipei: Qianwei, 2001, Chinese), and *Between "the Empire of Japan" and "the Motherland China," Collaboration and border-crossing of Taiwanese film activists in the colonial period* (Tokyo: Iwanami, 2010, Japanese; Taipei: National Taiwan University Press, 2012, Chinese), one co-edited volume: *Radio, Movie, Television: Inter-relationship of audio-visual media in East Asia today* (Tokyo: Seikyusha, 2012, Japanese), and one single edited volume: *Propaganda Films in Colonial Taiwan: Research on Newly Discovered Films* (Tokyo: University of Tokyo Press, 2017, Japanese). In English, she has written two chapters (Chapter 5 "The Production of Imperialized Bodies: Colonial Taiwan's Film Regulations and Propaganda Films" and Chapter 6 "The National Anthem Film in the Early 1950s Taiwan") in the book *East Asian Transwar Popular Culture: Literature and Film from Taiwan and Korea* edited by Pei-yin Lin and Su Yun Kim, forthcoming from Palgrave.

Noriko SUDO (Introduction & Chapter 2)
Professor at the Faculty of Contemporary Social Studies, Media Course, Chikushi Jogakuen University. She specializes in cultural politics and media studies. She worked as a program director at NHK from 1991–1993 and as a freelance TV producer from 1993–2002. Her Ph.D. thesis analyzed the interdependent relationships between Japan's Self-Defense Forces and media companies. Her major publications include *Jieitai Kyouryoku Eiga:*

Kyomo Ware Oozora ni Ari kara Meitantei Konan made (in Japanese, The JSDF Films: From Kyomo Ware Oozora ni Ari to Detective Conan, Otsuki Shoten, 2013), *Higashi Ajia no Kurieitibu Sangyo: Bunka no Poritikusu* (ed., in Japanese, Creative Industries in East Asia: Politics of Cultures, Shinwasha, 2015), *Manga Kenkyu Nyumon Ouyouhen* (multi author collaboration, in Japanese, Introduction to Manga Studies Applied Version, Chapter 9 "Cultural Policies," Gendai Shokan, 2018).

Takeshi TANIKAWA (Chapter 3 & 8)
Visiting professor of film history and popular culture studies at the Graduate School of Political Science, Waseda University (Tokyo), and a well-known freelance cinema journalist and film critic for more than two decades. After working for Nippon Herald Film Co. for eight years as publicity staff and marketing director, he has worked both in academia and journalism. His thesis won the prestigious First Kyoto Film Culture Award in 1999, which later become his dissertation for a PhD in sociology at Hitotsubashi University (2001) and was published by Kyoto University Press as *American Films and the Occupation Policy* (2002).

Dr. Tanikawa's recent publications as author/editor include *Border-crossing Popular Culture: From Li Xianglan to Takki* (in Japanese, 2009), *Spreading Subculture:Personalizing Passion and Healing Style Evolution* (in Japanese, 2009), *The Occupation-Period Periodical Materials Compendium: Popular Culture Series, Vol. 1–5* (in Japanese, 2008–2009), *All About Post-WWII 'Chushingura' Films* (in Japanese, 2013), *Kouraiya Three Brothers and Their Movies* (in Japanese, 2018). His current projects include *Baseball and the Occupation of Japan: America's Pastime as a Tool to Promote Social Values*, forthcoming from McFarland & Co, Inc.

Youngjae YI (Chapter 7)
Researcher at Center for Cross Cultural Studies in Sungkyunkwan University, specializing in film studies and Asian film history. Her major publications are *Teikoku Nihon no Chōsen eiga* (in Japanese, Korean Cinema in Imperial Japan Teikoku Nihon no Chōsen eiga, Sangensha, 2013), *Toransu/nashonaru akushon eiga: Reisenki Higashi Ajia no dansei shintai, bōryoku, māketto* (in Japanese, Transnational Asia Action Film: Male Corporeality, Violence, and Market in the Cold War Era, University of Tokyo Press, 2016) and *Modern Korea at the Crossroads between Empire and Nation* (ed., in Korean, Checkwa hamke, 2011).

Introduction
Noriko S<small>UDO</small>

This book is about the interdependent relationships between the film industry and the state in East Asia. In recent years, as East Asian popular culture has drawn attention in various fields of sociology, history, media studies, and many more, countless panels and papers about them have been presented in conferences and symposia. Unfortunately, however, too many of them analyze pop culture with insufficient context, neglecting historical background, the influence of media companies, and changes to industrial structures. Such studies about movies focus on archival records of famous directors, characteristics of characters, and subtle niche subjects. They seem to regard a film as just a work of art, which is created by an individual or a small team. But of course, there are many more people required to make a film, making it a very different art form to, for example, writing a novel. We must recognize that a movie is a product of "the film industry".

In addition, when we think about popular culture, we must consider the state's influence, both direct and indirect. Most states in the world try, more or less, to control cultures by national policies. When considering these kinds of policies, first we should ask whether it is external or internal. External cultural policy are those with which a nation plans to introduce its own culture to others, both to enhance its prestige and to wield influence in the target countries. Such policies are typically connected with economic policy, especially cultural (or creative) industries promotion policy. Recent examples are "Cool Japan" policy, the government-led Korean Pop Culture boom, and so on. Internal cultural policy promotes traditional culture, civic non-profit art activities, and domestic cultural industries. And quite often, it tries to manipulate what people do by various regulations and some national thought.

A second way to distinguish cultural policies is between those for art promotion and those for political-economic benefit. Most scholars of Cultural Policy Studies seem only interested in art promotion, regarding art and culture as an a priori good. They seem to think that governments *should* support art and culture apolitically and unequivocally, and fail to recognize that culture has long been an "arena of struggle" cultivated by states and cultural industries.

Efforts to explain the relationship between cultural industry and state are highly controversial and fiercely debated. One of the most exciting and challenging writings on the topic comes from the Frankfurt School of critical theory. Adorno and Horkheimer criticized the Culture Industry (Kulturindustrie) because it conspired with the government to normalize the transformation of power, capitalism and culture.[1] They argued that the capitalist mass culture industry would commodify and standardize all artforms, which would, in turn oppress individuality and critical thinking. According to them, mass communication is one-way and functional, and the culture industry is an unrivalled indictment of the banality of mass culture.

There are many objections to this type of mass culture theory. One of the most antagonistic views is provided by Cultural Studies. For Adorno and Horkheimer, "culture" was high culture. They tend to consider people to be completely manipulated by mass media and capitalism. Although they highlight the reproduction of social classes, cultural studies are apt to insist on the positive and active functions when people accept and consume mass culture or subculture. They argue that the influence of the media is not as direct and uniform as critical theory assumes; instead, people enjoy various cultures cleverly in their own ways.[2]

Political economy, however, finds these cultural studies wanting,[3] arguing that cultural studies is so interested in texts that they neglect production, distribution, and consumption. We may say all three theories have shortcomings. First, as cultural studies pointed out, the Frankfurt School was overly focused on the world controlled by capitalists' strong power, which they perceived as unassailable. Second, the cultural studies position is too optimistic, neglecting the powerful structures of the media conglomerate interfacing with the government. If it is true that people "decode" media contents in manners unintended by the information transmitters,[4] they seldom examine the business strategy of media companies targeting people themselves. And most of all, their studies are more interested in an ideological analyses than the real experiences of consumers and lack of the detailed analysis for the aims and functions of cultural industry. As for political economy, it over emphasizes production.

Grossberg[5] and Murdock[6] insist on the importance of bridge-building between cultural studies and political economy, a stance we also embrace. Because six of eight participants of this co-authored book have experience working in media companies, we know both the importance of texts and representations in movies, and the controlling power of production companies, media, and governments. So when we analyze films, we cannot help taking nationalism into account to a greater or lesser extent. We seek to demonstrate this through accumulating concrete analyses rather than arguing theories.

In this book, we treat films as political economic products, mixtures of government policy and industrial motives, rather than mere works of art or media commodities. We examine the East Asian film industries from the 1930s to the 2010s pursuing their own economic-political goals by cooperating, negotiating and conflicting with states. Our conviction is that a film's cultural-politics is formed by the interaction of the state's principles, the film companies' speculation and audience preferences.

Historically, governments became overtly engaged with film companies during times of war. In this book, four chapters deal with circumstances around movies during WWII. Atsuko Kato explores the "Film Law" implemented in Japan in 1937. The law aimed at controlling the industry under the exigencies of the Sino-Japanese War. It was severely criticized after the war for robbing the industry of the freedom to make films. The Bureau of Police Affairs began to monitor the social influence of films, and altered its policy from "negative" control based on censorship to a "positive" policy for ethnic cultivation in areas such as production, distribution, and exhibition. Prior to the passage of the film law, the market dominance of the Toho film company had severely affected the domestic motion picture scene. Through a critical analysis of the diary of Mikio Tatebayashi, a key staff member of the bureau, we know the "Film Law" was constructed through econo-political bargaining between the government and the film companies.

This law constructed 80 years ago tells us that government policies and corporate profits were directly connected. If we focus only on political content and influence of laws, we will overlook economic aspects such as hidden deals by government officials and private companies or hard struggles and shrewd management against the government by movie people.

Takeshi Tanikawa considers two Japan-German co-production propaganda movies released in the same year that the Film Law was enacted. One of the main purposes of the co-production by the Empire of Japan and Nazi Germany was to introduce Japanese culture to the German people. Japan wanted to help them to understand why Japan needed Manchuria, and Germany wanted to validate the alliance. Though the aim of the production was to show friendly relations between Japan and Germany, two top directors from each country clashed immediately after start of the shooting and couldn't work together. So, as a result, two versions were produced. One was the German-Japanese version *The Daughter of the Samurai* (1937) directed by Arnold Fanck and the other was the English-Japanese version (international version) *Atarashiki Tsuchi* (1937), which means "new land," a metaphor for Manchuria, directed by Mansaku Itami. The ironic truth is that the Japanese audience preferred the Fanck version.

This is well known but another fact is not so famous, that is, the U.S. government sponsored film *My Japan* (1945) used many scenes from *Atarashiki Tsuchi* for representing feudalistic, fanatical, and cruel aspects of The Imperial Japanese Army. The paper mainly focuses on the differences of impressions of the same visual images in different contexts. Although a movie is made with a specific agenda, we may take the same images in quite contrary ways, depending upon background assumptions and prejudices. It is quite telling that enemies and allies used the same images for their own indoctrination purposes.

By analyzing another type of propaganda film, we question what defines a "national cinema". Youngjae Yi focuses on *Homeless Angels* (1941) directed by Ch'oe In-Kyu in Korea under Japanese rule. This film describes transformations of Korean juvenile vagrants into Japanese imperial subjects. From the late 1930s, Korean males had undergone a drastic identity crisis, faced with the new possibility of becoming "Japanese" imperial soldiers. Of course, as they were not accorded the same social status as ethnic Japanese people in the imperial hierarchy, there was a double standard of nationality and the re-masculinization of colonial males was limited.

According to Yi, initially this film was strongly recommended by the Press Section of the Japanese Korean Army, but then failed to pass censorship in Mainland Japan. The Japan version of the film was severely abridged and dubbed in Japanese "national" language. We can see the deep relationship between domination and native language from the fact that the imperial authorities deprived their new citizens of their mother tongue.

In China, The Manchukuo Film Association was also established in 1937 by Japan for educating the colonial people about the ideals and benefits of The Great East Asia Co-prosperity Sphere. Around the same time, anti-Japan propaganda movies were produced in the temporary capitals Wuhan and Chongqing, exposing the barbarous activities of the Japanese Imperial Army to the international community. The Chinese Nationalist Party regarded films as weapons of external propaganda and used them to win foreign sympathy. Yanli Han focuses on one of these movies, *The Japanese Spy* (1943) dramatized from a book written by Amleto Vespa, who came from Italy and lived in Manchuria for many years as a spy. The film called "China's first international epic" took four years from planning to release and involved immeasurable costs in Chongqing, which was perpetually facing the threat of air raids.

Han points out that film censorship in Chongqing was quite severe. Some scenes were cut because "they would corrupt public morals." During the war, all governments tried to remove frolic content, including love scenes, from movies, and as a result, people were starved for entertainment. In *The Japanese Spy*, the exotic scenes of a licensed quarter, dance halls, and coffee rooms were joyful and longer than necessary, providing degenerate images of the Japanese Army and thus appealing strongly to the Chinese audience. At the same time, the scenes of civilians dressed in Kuomintang army uniforms fighting against the Japanese Army, as per Chiang Kai-shek's demands, were bitterly criticized. The movie was not praised either at home or abroad. It is obvious that even authorities cannot easily control people's minds.

Three chapters are concerned with the postwar or Cold War. Tanikawa's other chapter considers the American film business in China, especially in Shanghai, the largest movie city after the war. Hollywood film industry seems to have maintained a strong interest in the Chinese market since the 1920s when the proportion of overseas markets increased. After WWII ended, eight major Hollywood studios had outposts in China, competing to promote American film import and distribution businesses in order to redevelop the Chinese market, and asking the U.S. State Department for support. A motion picture is a rich cultural product, rather than simply entertainment, and an effective tool for diplomacy because the more popular, for example, American movies became, the more influence the U.S. had on Chinese people.

But these businesses failed following the establishment of the People's Republic of China and American movies were withdrawn from China for a long time. One of the reasons of this failure is that China's import duty for foreign films was notably increased in 1948 related to the massive inflation after the war. In this paper, we can see a strong association between the film industry's business strategy and government cultural policy, even though the main reason American films were withdrawn from China was economic, not political.

In Taiwan, another economic-political circumstance appeared. Japanese movies were very popular and received with great enthusiasm in the 1950s–60s, only a little more than a decade after WWII. Mamie Misawa examines the seeming "pro-Japanese" phenomenon in the Taiwan cinema market by analyzing archival resources such as reports by the local police in Taiwan, as well as surveys conducted by the Japanese embassy and the United States Information Service. It was quite curious that Taiwanese people seem to have totally forgotten about the Japanese colonization and the trauma of war; the Nationalist government allowed the import of Japanese motion pictures while promoting the policy of "de-Japanization."

The "pro-Japanese" phenomenon arose from the cooperation and joint promotion by the two governments of Japan and the ROC, who shared an "anti-communist" policy supported by the U.S. The twisted phenomenon that the Taiwanese audience welcomed and enjoyed Japanese cinema products was fostered by their own marginalized social standing after the war. Furthermore, "pro-Japanese" expressions can ultimately be interpreted as a kind of bottom-up de-colonization (de-Japanization) through pre-existing consumer appropriation mechanism.

Owing to special demands of the Korean War, Japan staged a successful economic comeback, declaring it should "no longer be termed postwar" in the economic white paper of 1956. People were enjoying a new era of high-economic growth and mass media were rapidly developing, commencing with the launch of TV stations in 1953. Tomoya Kimura focuses on the inauguration of Toei Doga Co. (Toei Animation) by using the documentary evidence. At the time, Japanese TV stations needed many programs other than American dramas and cartoons. According to this paper, there were three reasons for founding a new animation studio. First, they planned to supply as many educational films as swiftly as possible. Second, they were expected to make TV advertisements, albeit there were no plans for animated TV series, yet. The third purpose was export of Japanese films in Japanese government bureaucrats' interest. Especially, President Hiroshi Okawa eagerly desired to export Japanese animation and the educational film section lead the way to the company's establishment.

We can see that there are deep ties between the development of the Japanese animation industry and the economic revitalization of Japan after WWII. Around that time, Japan was hungry to get dollars by selling her own products for economic growth. The Japanese film business peaked in the late 1950s, with more than 1.1 billion ticket sales in 1958 and 547 films produced in 1960, both records which still stand today. Toei Animation was established in this period, clearly representing the conditions and the history of the Japanese film industry.

After the war, Japan had prioritized its economy under the shelter of Article 9 of the Constitution which prohibited any direct military investment. Especially in the 1980s, the Japanese people were enthusiastically enjoying a hedonistic life. In other East Asian countries at that time, China was struggling to recover from the damage of the Cultural Revolution and its complicated 3-way relationships with the Soviets and U.S. In South Korea, people were fighting for democratization under military governments and suffering tensions with the U.S., Japan and North Korea. Two chapters deal with this era.

Benjamin Joinau considers women's image in North Korean movies, which we can scarcely see and study. Kim Jong-il, the former supreme leader of the Democratic People's Republic of Korea, regarded cinema as a "weapon" to educate people in Juche philosophy, which is the state ideology meaning self-reliance. In the typical "Socialist realism" movies, there is often a strong male hero onto whom Kim is projected, who saves a "stray" woman and puts her back on the "clean" and "correct" way of life based on Juche. In spy and war movies, most women from South Korea are double agents and various clichés are employed identifying South Korea with negative female characteristics such as prostitution and decadence.

Motherhood and toughness of female characters are also very important elements in the North Korean world vision. Kim Jong-suk, the mother of Kim Jong-il, has been transformed into an icon combining an ideal mother with a Resistance fighter. So it is obvious that the North Korean films clearly represent their national images seeing their Great and Dear Leaders to be models for fighting against capitalist imperialism. From our "capitalist" point of view, they should be quite old-fashioned propaganda movies, but it might also be true that they have certain influence on North Korean people.

In Noriko Sudo's paper, which examines the films officially promoted by Japan's Self Defense Forces, we can see another type of propaganda cling to capitalism and the interdependence of the military section of the government and film industry. The JSDF established in 1954 had existed like some shady organization for a long time because people were fed up with the torments of war and had shared a certain peaceful attitude under the influence of so-called "postwar education". However, after around 1990 when socialist countries collapsed and the economic bubble burst, the social mood turned more conservative and the JSDF gradually increased its presence.

Since 1964, except for the 1970s–80s, the JSDF has promoted about 40 entertainment movies, and many armored vehicle operations under the direction of commercial film directors. As all the JSDF films are entertainment movies, the most important thing for the film companies is box-office success. So, the balance between politics and economic ambition is delicate, because the audience tends to avoid political expressions and, at the same time, the members of the production committee eagerly thirst for the military support to decrease the costs for huge sets or computer graphics.

As the JSDF films are produced by agreements of military institutions and media industries, they are quite different from old propaganda movies. They are more subtly nationalistic and convey a sense that self-sacrifice for the nation is a natural way of being. For example, the main character of *Midnight Eagle* (2007), who sacrifices himself to prevent a bomb exploding, says, "I don't care about the country…but as a father, let me save my son's life." It implies that private interests are ultimately synonymous with public interests, even if motivations do not seem to be nationalistic at first glance. This paper also argues the influence of consumerism and neo-liberalism on contemporary nationalism.

The relationship between East Asian countries has not been so good and remains troubled even now, and they have always been influenced by the foreign policy of the United States. On June 12, 2018, President Donald Trump and Kim Jong-un met in Singapore to negotiate the limitation of nuclear weapons. In East Asia, hereditary leaders in each country are holding the reins of power and struggling to maintain a balance among national and international matters. Politics, economics and cultures are twisting together in ever more complicated ways, and we have to cope with difficult modern/postmodern problems without much ado.

In such difficult times, films remain as potent for propaganda as they used to be, while at the same time, they are strong tools for resistance. Cinema is both national/ethnic and global/local at all times. When we analyze films sociologically, it is much more important to consider political-economic issues than artistic elements. Film has a long history as a means of government propaganda since WWII, and film companies have sometimes cooperated with and sometimes been regulated by national or local governments. Importantly, film industry people all too commonly make it a priority to earn money regardless of any political stance. The film history and the cultural policies in East Asia will give us many points for developing a new theory of Cultural Politics.

Notes

1. Adorno, W. Theodor & Horkheimer, Max, *Dialectic of Enlightenment*, Stanford University Press, 2007 (1947).
2. Hebdige, Dick, *SUBCULTURE: the meaning of style*, Routledge, 1979. Fiske, John, *Understanding Popular Culture*, Routledge, 1989.
3. Garnham, Nicholas, 'Political economy and cultural studies: Reconciliation or divorce?' *Critical Studies in Mass Communication,* Volume 12, Issue 1, 1995.
4. Hall, Stuart, *Encoding and Decoding in the Television Discourse*, Culture, Media, Language. Working Papers in Cultural Studies, 1972–1979, ed. by Centre for Contemporary Cultural Studies. London: Routledge, 1980 (1973), pp. 128–138.
5. Grossberg, L. 'Cultural studies vs. political economy', *Critical Studies in Mass Communication*, vol. 12, 1995, pp. 72–81.
6. Murdock, G., 'Across the great divide: cultural analysis and the condition of democracy', *Critical Studies in Mass Communication*, vol. 12, 1995, pp. 89–95.

1 Film Control in the Japan Film Law (*Eiga-ho*)

Atsuko KATO

This study analyzes the process through which the Film Law was formulated, examining the legislative proposals drafted at each stage. It demonstrates that the Film Law differed from traditional policies for arts and culture. As well as prescribing censorship, which was not new, the Film Law included a new type of business control. This was grounded in the idea that business control would put the film industry on a sound footing, to produce better quality films. To this end, the censorship provisions were not simply continuing observances of conventional ministerial ordinances, but were constructed anew with a view toward business control.

Until the 1990s, much of the research pertaining to films rendered one-sided evaluations of the Film Law, arguing that it was a bad law under wartime conditions that usurped freedom of speech with tightening censorship. To be sure, the registration system and script pre-censorship, which accompanied the Film Law, had a considerable impact on film production, increasing the burden on those involved. However, assessing the Film Law only by its effect on films is to miss its true significance. The Film Law was completely different from the laws controlling films up to that point, and it included provisions not found in other laws related to the arts or culture. The underlying concept of control expressed in the law strongly reflected the economic policies formulated during the Sino-Japanese War. Although some critics have argued that the Film Law was a simple imitation of the Nazi Spitzenorganisation der Filmwirtschaft, Mikio Tatebayashi, an administrative official in the Home Ministry's Police Bureau and a key figure in the drafting of the proposed Film Law, denied this claim, pointing out that the law referenced the relevant policies of Germany, Manchuria, Italy and other foreign countries as well as Japanese policies for various industries.[1]

While addressing economic factors, such as the market and industry, as well as existing laws and regulations, this paper elucidates the distinctive concept of control under the Film Law by highlighting the changes in opinions by government ministries in the process of drafting the proposed legislation. We will examine the legal character of relevant provisions with regard to five points: the business licensing system, decree authority, registration system, pre-censorship system, and recommendation system. These points have been considered in previous research, but primarily as case studies from after enforcement actually took effect. Akira Iwasaki, a film critic at the time the law was passed, and Tadao Sato, who authored a history of writers and works, emphasized how strengthened censorship placed pressure on those engaged in production.[2] The Film Law undoubtedly restricted activities of free expression, but the market and management perspectives were insubstantial in these studies. Studies by Peter B. High and Takahisa Furukawa clearly articulated the concept of control and followed the changes in discussions which occurred in the preparation of drafts of the proposed legislation.[3] However, the legal characteristics of control were not considered in these studies. In Japan, the indoctrination of the national populace through film was not executed by state-operated companies, but through a market where motion-picture companies conducted commercial activities. It is thus not possible to meaningfully inquire into film control policy without considering economic factors such as the industry and markets. The Film Law was the "first piece of cultural legislation" in the area of motion-pictures, and its enactment was the first experience that the Legislative Bureau and Ministry of Justice had with this type of legislation, in comparison to the Home Ministry, the Ministry of Education, and the Ministry of Health and Welfare, which were the competent ministries.

The Film Law governed Japan's film industry until the end of World War II. This study clarifies the concept of control in the stages of drafting the proposed legislation to establish a foundation for analyzing the film control practiced thereafter both within and outside Japan, and for examining continuity with post-war arts and culture policies.

There were two statutory law systems governing the film industry in Japan until 1925. One provided for the safety and sanitation of theaters, and the other concerned censorship of film contents. Both were enacted at the prefectural level, so standards varied by region. The Censorship Regulations for Motion Pictures or "Films" (*Katsudo shashin "firumu"ken'etsu kisoku*) in 1925 brought national censorship uniformity under the Home Ministry's Police Bureau (Naimusho keihokyoku). In the 1930s, against the backdrop of Japan's deteriorating position in the international community and the rapid development of its motion picture industry, the concept of a "national film policy" emerged, holding that the government should protect and develop films as an industry. The Film Law (*Eiga-ho*) was enacted in 1939 to implement this concept through specific controls (promulgated in April and effective in October).

The Film Law was a specific course of action for dealing with issues in the film industry at that time which the government felt needed to be addressed. It was a measure designed to bring the industry closer to the government's ideal of how films and the film industry should be structured. The Film Law was an attempt to realize these ideals through the legal system. To clarify the historical status of the Film Law, it is necessary to outline the concept of film control at the time. This paper will do just that based on analysis of the draft proposals and enactment process. To be certain, a law does not necessarily exert actual control. For instance, with film censorship, the discretion of the censor can result in the flexible operation of the law, to some extent. Nevertheless, an awareness of the issues presented at the time, the concept of control expressed in the proposed legislation, and an analysis of the bill's drafting process is necessary to establishing the foundations of film control in Japan.

Film law content and characteristics

The Film Law gave jurisdiction to the Ministers of Home Affairs, Education and Health & Welfare. The law comprised 26 articles including punitive provisions. Its purpose was stated in Article 1: "The purpose of this law is to promote the quality of film and the sound development of the film industry so that films can contribute to the nation's cultural development." The content of the law can be summed up in the following eight points, according to function.[4]

The first is a licensing system for film businesses. A person who engaged in the business of producing or distributing a film required a license from the relevant Minister. The license would be revoked if the person violated the Film Law, the Film Law Enforcement Ordinance, or performed an act which harmed the public interest.

Second is a registration system for people engaged in film production. Only people who had successfully passed the Skill Review Committee test could be registered to pursue the occupations of director, actor and cameraman.

Third were provisions pertaining to censorship. There had always been censorship of completed scripts and completed films, but the Film Law introduced pre-censorship of scripts as well as completed films. Script pre-censorship was conducted only for theater films (i.e., those intended for cinema screenings). Notification was required for scripts and matters relating to production no less than 10 days prior to the commencement of filming. Changes would be ordered if necessary. Completed films were censored by the Home Ministry's Police Bureau. Films would not be permitted to be shown on the screen for public consumption unless they were approved by the censors.

Fourth is the limitation on the number of foreign films which could be shown in ordinary theaters; no more than 50 per year. This provision was included with the important aim of saving foreign currency during the Sino-Japanese War.

Fifth, the law stated that the competent minister could issue decrees limiting the type and number of films to be produced, coordinating distribution, as well as preventing defective equipment and unfair competition when necessary in the public interest. This provision conferred powerful control authority on the government.

Sixth, there was a system in which the Ministry of Education could endorse outstanding films, and prize money would be awarded to the producer. Japanese laws until then basically could be characterized as stipulating prohibitions; it was unprecedented for it to prescribe legal provisions by which a government agency would reward outstanding works with prize money.

Seventh was a system for the compulsory showing of cultural films. Cultural films were films other than theater films and concerned politics, national defense, education, scholarship, the arts, industry, health and other such themes. Such films were endorsed by the Minister of Education. When a commercial film was screened in a cinema, it was mandatory to also show a cultural film. Later, news films were added to the lineup.

Eighth, there were provisions restricting the scope of screen times, screening methods, and audience size. The length of time for one showing was set at no more than three hours. Ratings were determined by the

Ministry of Education. Films which could be viewed by children under the age of 14 were classified as general audience films and anything else was considered not acceptable for a general audience.

The Film Law was called, at the time of its enactment, the "first piece of cultural legislation." There had long been laws pertaining to the preservation of historic sites and national treasures, but these focused on works of art, cultural assets, historic remains and other physical objects and places. The Film Law was the first law enacted in regard to the production of culture (films). It had several distinguishing features not found in previous laws concerning the arts and culture.

The print media was governed by the Publication Law and Press Law. But, in the field of public entertainment, the establishment of objective standards is difficult; hence, great importance is attached to legal interpretations which vary depending on individual circumstances. Discretion is afforded those who enforce the law. Prefectural ordinances and ministerial ordinances, which allow relatively flexible operation and revision, had been the governing legal ordinances. The enactment of the Film Law elevated control over film to the level of national policy, and solved an important legal issue facing film censorship: apprehension that censorship by the Home Ministry would be declared unconstitutional.

In 1927, the Supreme Court defined moving pictures as being printed matter: matter that is printed on film. This definition enabled producers of obscene films to be prosecuted for violating the Press Law. The Home Ministry, however, maintained that moving-picture film only manifested its primary function after being fed through a film projector and shown on a screen and therefore the film itself did not function as printed matter. So completed films were not censored in accordance with the Press Law, but rather with the Censorship Regulations of Moving Pictures or "Films" (*Katsudo shashin "firumu" ken'etsu kisoku*).[5] However, Article 29 of the Constitution of the Empire of Japan provided that printed matter shall be regulated with the limits of law. So, the Supreme Court definition opened the possibility that censorship by ministerial ordinance rather than by law could be held unconstitutional.[6]

Furthermore, at the time, to prevent films which had been cut by censors from becoming public, it was customary practice for the Home Ministry to seize them without any legal basis. There was an "unspoken rule" between the Home Ministry and film companies. When the Home Ministry asked to submit certain parts of the films, films companies did so.

Such confiscation was, strictly speaking, against the Constitution, but it was performed for a long time as a customary practice in order to avoid any violation of the property protection clause in Article 27 of Constitution of the Empire of Japan. Article 27 provided that measures necessary to be taken for the public benefit shall be any provided for by law, and, ultimately, the validity of regulation based on the Censorship Regulations of Moving Pictures or "Films," which is a ministerial ordinance issued by the Home Ministry, would be called into question. For that reason, in practice, censors adopted a method in which pressure would be put on the film maker by not affixing the seal of approval, if the film maker refused to allow the cut film to be seized.[7]

The Film Law grounded the Home Ministry's censorship in law, and concerns about unconstitutionality dispelled. Although managers of motion-picture companies feared that their company activities might be restricted by the new law, they also hoped that it would provide recognition that films are a "culture of the national population" for the benefit of the state and society. In Japan there were no financial subsidies such as those afforded by the Reich Film Credit Bank in Germany. The Film Law legitimized the position of films in society, which, it was hoped would increase the availability of funding from banks.

Also, previous film controls dealt separately with matters such as censorship, theater management and other areas, but the Film Law covered both the production of films and the film business, including the separate functions of production, distribution and public performance as well as all of the necessary processes for a film to be dispatched publicly. The Film Law made it possible to assert control over any part of this process, or all of it. This model was a response to the situation in Japan in the latter half of the 1930s, where leading companies exercised oligopolistic control over the film market through the unification of production, distribution and public performance.

The Film Law was a comprehensive control statute which integrated two opposing characteristics of enforcement: censorship and guidance / assistance. In addition to the Ministry of Education's endorsements mentioned earlier, the requirement of showing cultural films extended assistance to that part of the industry, and effected a national film policy, by which the government protected and developed the film industry. Furthermore, it is noteworthy that the methodology used for achieving soundness in the film industry was the economic control policies launched during the Sino-Japanese War, through which entire industries were managed by the government controlling the number of companies and creating fair competition among companies so as to ensure production yields. From a contemporary perspective, it would be hard to argue that managing the number of companies and making competition fairer would be an effective way to put the industry on a sound footing. Nor would many contemporaries accept that such measures would be effective in improving the quality of feature films. Nevertheless, at the time the Film Law was enacted, the idea of war-time economic control, which had been applied to coal, steel and other important industries as well as the manufacturing industry, was believed to also be effective for films. This degree of control was not seen in laws related to the mass media or the arts or other culture during the same period.

Process leading to enactment of the film law

The enactment of the Film Law was prompted by a change in the Home Ministry's film control policy towards a national film policy. And, behind this was intense competition in Japan's film market in the 1930s.[8]

With the passage of the "Proposition Concerning Establishment of a National Film Policy" in February 1933, the concept of "national film policy" in which the state should not only censor films, but should also provide guidance and assistance to actively protect and develop domestically produced films gained wide currency within the Home Ministry, the Ministry of Education, and the film industry. The enactment of a control law had been studied ever since a national film policy had been advocated in late 1935, but it remained only an idea, and its necessity was tenuous. In Japan, the film industry had rapidly industrialized since the 1920s. In the 1930s, production, distribution, and performance were integrated in five major motion-picture companies (Shochiku, Nikkatsu, Shinko, Daito and Toho), which held a virtual monopoly on the Japanese market. There were also many small businesses engaged in each of the areas of production, distribution and performance. Since the mid-1930s, four companies, Shochiku, Nikkatsu, Shinko and Daito, were locked in fierce opposition with Toho, a new competitor which had entered the market. A decline in the quality of film production resulting from this intensified competition was regarded as problematic, while the five companies sought to secure distribution networks and viewers by competing on producing quantity. However, at the time, the Home Ministry's Police Bureau took the position of protecting and developing Japan's film industry as a whole, and did not intervene in the competition among companies.

However, the Sino-Japanese War in July 1937 prompted the Home Ministry and other government agencies and ministries to acknowledge the social influence of film. New policies were adopted implementing active control through which guidance would be provided with the aim of utilizing films to indoctrinate the national populace. In the world of motion pictures, the popularity of films about the Sino-Japanese War had risen, and low-budget quickly-produced films were on the increase, but the Home Ministry's Police Bureau was critical of many of these films, and demanded that motion-picture companies make "qualitative improvements." The term "qualitative improvement" had a double-meaning: it meant improving the artistic quality of the films and it meant that works be produced with content that conforms to the intentions of government ministries and agencies. Government ministries and agencies prioritized the latter meaning when using the term. In other words, they demanded films which addressed the present situation and played a role in mobilizing the public. The Home Ministry held informal discussions with people involved in films and strengthened censorship, but "qualitative improvement" was not achieved. As the declining quality was a result of the intense competition among the film companies, this competition needed to be addressed to achieve "qualitative achievement." There were limits, though, to how far censorship and enforcement using stopgap measures based on ministerial ordinances could achieve results. Hence, a comprehensive control policy was necessary, including provisions for positive controls. On November 24, 1937, the Home Ministry's Police Bureau decided to set about working to enact the Film Law.

Distinguishing features of the legislation drafting process

The drafting of the proposed Film Law began in November 1937, and the text was finalized on March 4, 1939. Currently, twelve distinct legislative proposals have been identified. A comparison of the drafting process and each proposal on the basis of text revisions and notes is presented in Table 1.1. The legislative proposals were drafted principally by Tatebayashi and other bureaucrats at the Home Ministry and Ministry of Education.

Divided broadly, (1)–(4) are proposals drafted by the Home Ministry and Ministry of Education to put the control concept into a substantive text. (5)–(7) are measures for finalizing the text, including comments by the Ministry of Justice. And, (8)–(12) reflect revisions made following Legislative Bureau deliberations. Here, the distinguishing characteristics of each measure will be examined separately, and the process of constructing the Film Law will be clarified.[9]

Drafting of the proposed Film Law first began with the work of breaking down the control concept into statutory law form. In the first draft, the control concept was partitioned and consolidated by area, and necessary items were enumerated in detail for each item. In the third draft, the provisions were reconstituted according to function by dismantling the sector-based configuration and numbering them. The order of clauses was finalized in the third draft, and a framework for the Film Law was probably formed during the fourth draft, in which an explanation was given to the director of the Police Bureau.

The proposed Film Law, which had already been reviewed by the Home Ministry, was submitted to a review committee on December 21, 1938, and was reviewed by the Ministry of Justice. The fifth draft includes notations about Justice's deliberations.

The sixth draft followed further rigorous review of the issues brought to light in its predecessor. This draft underwent the longest review process, from December 26~28, 1938 until January 18~20, 1939. The proposed measure was being compared with other laws currently in effect. Potential problems if the legislation passed, and ways of addressing such issues were also studied.

A clean copy of the wording finalized in the sixth draft was prepared and submitted to a review committee at the Home Ministry on January 27. The seventh draft reflects the deliberations which took place there. Other than the articles and clauses about which issues were raised, revisions were limited to amending wording and terms, and there was no significant change in the sentences. Then, on January 30, a typed version based on the seventh draft was prepared.

In sum, drafts 1~4 are the initial formations of the proposed legislative framework, while drafts 5~7 flesh out that framework and arrange it properly, adding the Ministry of Justice's perspective. Articles and clauses were drafted assuming implementation, taking into account existing laws, introducing what might be called a bird's-eye perspective to the drafting

Table 1.1: List of Proposed Film Laws

No.	Name of Proposed Law	Dates Used	Purpose
(1)	"Strictly Confidential: Outline of Proposed Film Law (Provisional Title)"		
(2)	(Proposed Film Law)		
(3)	"Strictly Confidential: Draft of Proposed Film Law (Provisional Title)"		
(4)	"Confidential: Draft of Proposed Film Law (Provisional Title)"	Nov. 21–22, 1938	1st explanation to Police Bureau Director Review Committee
(5)	"Draft of Proposed Film Law (Provisional Title)"	Dec. 21, 1938	
(6)	"Strictly Confidential: Proposed Film Law (Revisions: 13, 12 and 23)"	Dec. 26, 1938–Jan. 20, 1939	Coordination of opinions among Home Ministry, Ministry of Education and Ministry of Justice
(7)	"Proposed Film Law"	Jan. 27, 1939	Home Ministry Review Committee
(8)	"Proposed Film Law (14, 1, 30)"	Feb. 27–Mar. 1, 1939	Legislative Bureau deliberations
(9)	"Proposed Film Law"	Mar. 2, 1939	Arrangement of provisions by Legislative Bureau
(10)	"Strictly Confidential: Proposed Film Law"		
(11)	"Proposed Film Law"	Mar. 3, 1939	Additional revisions by Legislative Bureau
(12)	"Film Law"	Mar. 4, 1939	Approval by Legislative Bureau

Source: Created based on Atsuko Kato: "Motion Picture Regulations during the Sino-Japanese War: A Study of Laws Pertaining to the Film Industry [in Japanese]," Shigaku-zasshi, Vol. CIX, No. 6; Collection of the National Archives of Japan: "Tanemura-shi keisatsu sanko shiryo, Collection No. 64 [in Japanese]." Included in (4E-15-15 Hei 9 Kei No. 745); and Collection of the National Archives of Japan: "Tanemura-shi keisatsu sanko shiryo, Collection No. 102 [in Japanese]." Included in (4E-15-4 Hei 9 Kei No. 781). (1)–(9), (11), (12) are included in "Tanemura-shi keisatsu sanko shiryo, Collection No. 64."; (10) is included in "Tanemura-shi keisatsu sanko shiryo, Collection No. 102."

Notes: Numbers have been added by the writer for division. Names of proposed laws are based on the names written on the cover of each bill (if touched up and corrected, then the touched up and corrected name). For numeral ②, a provisional name has been given as no name was written on the cover sheet of the original document. The dates when (1)–(3) and (10) were used were unknown, so the arrangement was determined based on the state of revisions made to provisions.

process. The provisions were then put into proper order through repeated reviews, including the Ministry of Justice, and the most appropriate terms, expressions and sentences for expressing the concept of control were adopted as a final version of the provisions were worked out.

The typed version, which was prepared on January 30, was debated in the Legislative Bureau. The eighth draft is annotated, describing in detail the deliberations in the Legislative Bureau which took place between February 27 and March 3. Numerous provisions and terms were amended as a result of the Legislative Bureau deliberations, but the greatest change was an addition to Article 1 to clarify the purpose of the law.[10]

As we have seen, the Home Ministry's Police Bureau sought not only the authority to conduct censorship, but also to provide guidance and assistance in order to make the most effective use of films in disseminating propaganda and educating the public. To this end, the Bureau wanted the power to issue orders to film businesses to improve their structure of production, distribution and performance. However, the Legislative Bureau pointed out that this sort of guidance and assistance was a departure from law enforcement, and was not compatible with the principal duty of the Police Bureau.

Tatebayashi and the rest of the staff hastily drafted a new provision indicating the purpose of the Film Law and inserted it as Article 1. Tatebayashi made it clear that the Film Law differed from conventional control over films that centered around censorship, and, he stated, this provision would herald the sense of the Film Law being the "first piece of cultural legislation."[11] The insertion of Article 1 sought to demonstrate that the Film Law was different from the Publication Law, Press Law and other previous media control laws, and to reflect the idea that the role of the Home Ministry's Police Bureau should change during the Sino-Japanese War.

After three days of deliberations in the Legislative Bureau, the ninth draft includes the March 2nd adjustment of provisions. The eleventh draft includes further revisions written in red or penned onto the clean copy of notes made in reference to the ninth draft. The twelfth draft is a clean copy of number 11. Based on the structure of Article 1 and the manner of the revisions, the tenth draft is likely to have been a memorandum for people concerned with this legislative proposal which was prepared after the ninth.

Drafts 8~12 are the legislative proposals prepared in the final stages, where adjustments were made aimed at submitting the measure to the Imperial Diet. Many of the matters reviewed at this stage were carried over from the preceding stage in which the provisions had been finalized, and additional revisions to the wording of provisions were also made. Through this lengthy process, the Film Law was located within the legal system, and its proper arrangement verified the legislation's validity as a governing law for the administration.

Points of contention in drafting the legislative proposals

The key intent behind the Film Law was the qualitative improvement of films. In the process of drafting the proposed Film Law, two methods were considered for achieving qualitative improvement.

One concerned the processes through which films were produced and distributed. What would be sought was restructuring the motion-picture industry such that companies would be capable of taking the public interest into account when setting works in motion. Competition would be maintained to the degree necessary to ensure that outstanding films would be produced. Severe competition would not be permitted to prevent films from being released. This strongly reflected criticisms of the commercialism of motion-picture companies at the time.

The other was promotion of the distribution of outstanding films. If the film industry were an ordinary industry, the quality of the products could be improved through technological development. In the case of films, however, quality is not a simple technological issue, but a much more subjective, aesthetic issue. Furthermore, regardless of any official criteria, a film would not enter distribution or performance routes unless it could be expected to do well at the box office. So, it was necessary to construct a system for outstanding works to be produced and delivered to the audience.

In the process of drafting the Film Law, many items were considered and configured to realize either or both of these two methods. In this section, taking into account the separation of stages in the preceding section, five items which were reviewed in the process of drafting the proposed Film Law will be analyzed for their points of contention: the business licensing system, decree authority, registration system, pre-censorship system, and recommendation system. The business licensing system and decree authority sought to develop a healthy process for producing and distributing films. The registration system, pre-censorship system, and recommendation system were intended to promote the creation of outstanding films.

To explain the final control concept of the Film Law, we will compare two documents prepared during the same time period. The first of these documents, "Survey of Legislative Precedents, Terms and Related Laws," excerpts existing laws which are similar or related to each provision of the Film Law proposal. Despite it not being dated, we can infer on the basis of the order and content of the articles to have been prepared during the period of the sixth draft.[12] The second document, "Article-by-Article Commentary on the Film Law," is a detailed commentary of each provision including the reasons for enactment, discussion of terms, referenced laws and so on. Similarly, its exact preparation date is unknown, but the articles correspond to the typed version prepared on January 30, 1939. It is believed to have been prepared as an explanatory document to accompany the proposal to be submitted to the Imperial Diet.[13]

Business licensing system

The business licensing system is peculiar to the Film Law, not found in laws pertaining to the arts or culture. It was established for production and distribution. The ostensible purpose of the licensing system was to limit the number of businesses, but the ultimate purpose was to facilitate business integration. The motivation and intent varied across the different aspects of the film industry, though. With regard to production, the aim was to limit the number of businesses to avoid overproduction, as well as ensuring adequate government guidance and supervision. In distribution, though, the aim was to consolidate company-specific distribution. The first draft of the legislation pointed out that while most film distribution businesses in Japan operated under combined management with film production businesses or in an extremely close relationship between the two, they were not necessarily ideal organizations. This draft stated that these operations should be placed under the control and supervision of the government to be steadily maintained and rationally improved through the business licensing process. It noted that the unsupervised unification of distribution in Manchuria and Italy had brought severe confusion to their respective film industries.

In July 1938, Tatebayashi envisaged the consolidation of production and distribution businesses, but concluded that consolidation of the production businesses would be difficult because of strife between Toho and the other four companies, and therefore decided to focus on consolidating the distribution business.[14] In fact, when film production was brought into the total war management system in 1941, distribution networks were unified in consolidation with performance halls. But, when the Film Law was enacted, simplifying distribution was one of the central challenges of film control policy.

Control techniques for ordinary industries were invoked as legal precedents for the licensing system that would deliver business consolidation. At issue there were the scope of the licensing system and the standards for license revocation.

The licensing system assumed that motion-picture companies were private. However, at the time, there were numerous instances of government agencies and prefectures producing movies. Hence, defining the scope of a production business was problematic. The stages of planning, filming and editing were considered to be the essential elements of production, and a person who engaged in any of these was deemed to be a production business. This did not include government agencies, but public institutions and public interest corporations were deemed to be included in the legal interpretation of the term, and provisions were written in such a way as to not exclude persons with no commercial interests.

The revocation of licenses was addressed in the next clause. Three conditions were considered: 1) cases in violation of the Film Law or any laws or regulations consequent upon the Film Law, 2) cases of management uncertainty, delinquent financial standing, or instances deemed to be too inappropriate to permit operations to continue, and 3) acts that harm the public interest. At the time, there were many small and mid-sized businesses. There were also cases where even major firms' operations were not stable, such as Nikkatsu, which had an impact on market stability. So, it appears that these three conditions were considered sufficient to eliminate these uncertainties. The second of these three points posed a particular challenge, so management uncertainty was defined to mean, for example, a situation where production could not continue due to the loss of a human or physical equipment, or in which distribution was not possible due to an inability to obtain finished films. Delinquent financial standing meant, for instance, a situation where operations could not be continued due to bankruptcy or other such reason.[15] The Home Ministry insisted on including economic conditions in the licensing standard, but the Legislative Bureau pointed out that the term "management uncertainty" could not be used in this case.

The authors turned to the Automobile Manufacturing Business Law to resolve this issue, which had been formulated by the Ministry of Commerce and Industry. The Automobile Manufacturing Business Law deemed automobile manufacturers over a certain size to be authorized businesses, and sought to protect and develop authorized companies. Three companies, Nissan Motor Company Limited, Toyota Motor Company, and Diesel Motor Industry Company Limited (today, Isuzu Motors Limited), were authorized companies. Japan Ford and Japan GM had been excluded from the authorized companies and withdrew from Japan in 1939. The effect was that the Automobile Manufacturing Business Law provided the foundation for the domestic automobile industry to develop with just a small number of Japanese companies. The main text of the Automobile Manufacturing Business Law does not specify licensing standards. Instead, they were stipulated by an enforcement order, because, at the time the legislative proposal was being deliberated, decisions had not been reached on Toyota's and Nissan's candidature to become authorized companies.[16] The Ministry of Commerce and Industry explained that these provisions were not aimed at dealing out punishments for violations, but was rather to promote harmonious and impartial implementation of the business.[17] The concepts underpinning this law for controlling the manufacturing industry by protecting and developing a few companies, was introduced into the proposal for the law governing film, an artistic and cultural industry.

In the end, the economic conditions for license revocation were not included in the legislation. This may be largely due to the Legislative Bureau's ruling discussed above, but also because the production and distribution businesses included many public institutions and public interest corporations, which had non-commercial purposes, as well as small individual operators. It would have been difficult to apply the term "management," which assumed a commercial enterprise of a certain scale. Nevertheless, there was scope within the Film Law for a competent minister to implement a licensing system, and to exercise even tighter control over the business aspects of films. The foundation for that was the decree authority.

Decree authority

On the cover of the fifth draft, a note can be seen: "Scalpel for treating cancer (showing Five Scouts in all theaters)." The film *Five Scouts* (Gonin no Sekkohei) was released by Nikkatsu in 1938. It was one of the few films released in cinemas depicting the Sino-Japanese War which received a commendation by the Home Ministry. It was well-received, earning the number one spot in the "Kinema Junpo" rankings.[18] A provision was instituted for the mandatory showing of cultural films, but this memorandum about *Five Scouts* goes further, indicating an idea for applying decree authority to the demand to show one particular film in all theaters. In other words, the decree authority would not only eliminate elements which were deemed negative, but also promote factors which appeared to be positive in improving the national culture and developing a healthy and sound film business.

The "Survey of Legislative Precedents" document referenced laws which pertained to trade, machine tool manufacturing, automobile manufacturing, petroleum, electricity, raw silk exports, and gold mining. These laws stipulated that demand and supply could be coordinated by order of a competent minister. However, with the exception of raw silk exports and gold mining, adjustments could be made to supply and demand when the government or minister determined that such was necessary for the public interest. The fifth draft of the Film Law legislative proposal stipulated that demand and supply could be coordinated to be conducive to the improvement of the culture of the national population. However, the sixth draft is annotated to indicate that the term "culture of the national population" is "not well-defined." This is assumed to have been added by the Ministry of Justice.

The decree authority could also exercise initiative over businesses. After confirming that the purpose of the Film Law was to contribute to improvement of the national culture and sound development of the film business, the "Article-by-Article Commentary on the Film Law" explained that, to achieve these objectives, the foundation of the film business would be subjected to considerable change. Furthermore, it stated that there was no other choice but to tolerate such changes from the perspective of the state and the public, and observed that decree authority could issue orders spanning a considerably broad range for this very reason.[19]

In the seventh draft, a notation states "Corporate mergers are impossible…have agreements formed." The claim that the foundation of the film business is to be subjected to considerable change seems to suggest corporate mergers, but the seventh draft ruled them out. It was nevertheless possible for the competent minister to issue powerful orders pertaining to an extensive range of matters, such as quantitative restrictions, distribution adjustments, equipment improvements, preventing unfair competition and so on.

The licensing system was created as a method for consolidating the production business and unifying the distribution business. The establishment of decree authority made it legally possible to put film production and distribution on a sound basis. However, no matter how "sound" the process might be made, "qualitative improvement" cannot be achieved unless there are outstanding films to be distributed. The registration, pre-censorship and recommendation systems were established to provide for the creation of excellent films.

Registration system

The registration system would only allow directors, actors and cameramen who sat for and successfully passed a test and then registered through a company to be engaged in film production. This provision was unprecedented in laws concerning the arts and culture. Behind this provision was an intensifying confrontation between Toho and four companies: Shochiku, Nikkatsu, Shinko and Daito. The four companies had formed an accord which, among other things, stated that any person involved in production with one of the four companies could not appear in another company's productions without the consent of the original company. The four companies invited Toho to join the accord, but Toho refused. Toho had been headhunting actors and directors from the others, so the relationship between Toho and the other companies rapidly deteriorated.

In the first draft, the purpose of the registration system was explained as being to homogenize the capabilities and skills of the businesses, to ensure adequate education and guidance for registrants, to stabilize the economic position of registrants and improve their skills. The examination covered the applicant's academic background, skills, experience, conduct and other aspects. However, the fourth draft noted that since most applicants are registered if they apply, it might be difficult to improve the quality of personnel by means of registration alone. At this point, the registration system was largely idealistic, a problem that the Home Ministry was aware of. However, in the fifth and sixth drafts, aptitude as a performer and similar qualities were recognized as important for film control, and the registration system was developed with abstract conditions which were difficult to explicate in the law.

The registration system in the proposed Film Law included not only job-related qualifications, or skills and experience, but also an examination of the individual's personality and ideological beliefs. Laws governing notary publics included similar personal criteria. The conditions for revocation in such cases included an act which violated professional obligations or a loss of dignity, which might undermine the integrity of the system of notary publics. The "Article-by-Article Commentary on the Film Law" noted that people involved in the production of films were role models for young people, and, regardless of the fact that the influence of their words and behavior was far reaching, problems pertaining to conduct and ideology had been observed. It also recognized that society is lenient toward such behaviors, which posed a problem for films in achieving their mission as an "art for the national populace." Therefore, it explained, provision was made for revoking registration.[20] In the end, the registration system of the Film Law excluded inappropriate persons from the abstract objective of making film an "art for the national populace," which was a fundamentally new legal concept.

Pre-censorship system

The proposed Film Law would replace the existing system of censoring completed films, while introducing new provisions for script pre-censorship. Script pre-censorship was set up as a notification system, which required neither approval nor authorization according to the law. This was different from censorship, which required authorization, in that, in principle, the censor could not question the content of the work as long as notification had been given. Nevertheless, although this was a literal interpretation of the law, in practice, the legislative proposal treated the notification system as pre-censorship, and a system of censorship was established in which intervention by the Home Ministry in the substance of works came to be taken for granted.[21]

The first draft provides commentary on the pre-censorship system, outlining two justifications. First, censoring scripts in advance would reduce the amount of footage to be excised and disposed of in film censorship. Second was to enable the Home Ministry to actively insert "scenes demanded by the state" in pre-censorship. In this system of control censorship would not only delete unacceptable content but would also provide positive guidance to reflect the state's demands in the content of the work.

In the second through fourth drafts, a concept of control is seen in which censors' approval of a completed film may be withheld or an application rejected where the substance of the pre-censored script differed from that of the completed film. However, the fourth draft was marked with a comment that script pre-censorship did not restrict censorship of completed films. In the fifth draft, it appears that attempts were made to separate script pre-censorship and completed film censorship. This did away with problems in legal theory concerning mutual constraints on script pre-censorship and film censorship. For example, if a film was produced and submitted for censorship without having given the required advance notification, the fact that notification had not been given would be punished, but the film would nevertheless undergo censorship. At the same time, the Home Ministry would be able to refuse to censor or cut a film for which changes had not been ordered during pre-censorship of the script. The "Article-by-Article Commentary on the Film Law" explained, though, that because pre-censorship is an enforcement action, the Home Ministry would not be able to actively insert "scenes demanded by the state."[22]

Following the separation of script pre-censorship and completed films censorship, this comment appears to make a definite statement about the character of script pre-censorship once again, presumably in response, as mentioned earlier, the Home Ministry's Police Bureau, whose principal duty was enforcement, providing positive guidance.[23]

Legally, the notification system required more than a simple advance declaration; the company was required to submit a complete business plan. The "Survey of Legislative Precedents" referred to laws concerning the automobile manufacturing business and gold mining business. Both laws state that, when necessary, the government was empowered to order changes to the business plans. The automobile manufacturing law stipulated that business plans were to be approved by the government, but the gold mining law did not. The drafts of the proposed Film Law adopted legal wording similar to expressions found in the latter.

After the Film Law took effect, the notification system operated, in effect, as censorship. Since the notification system and censorship of completed films functioned for the most part in tandem, both were ordinarily referred to as "censorship." Censorship of completed films was conducted in accordance with the Film law and related laws, but censors exercised considerable discretion, and guidance was provided as a matter of course. In the end, the law was a mere legal framework and did not severely restrict censorship, but the refusal to grant the Home Ministry authority for providing positive guidance in the pre-censorship system could be viewed as a significant retreat from the perspective of legislative technique.

The Film Law's censorship system cannot simply be seen as a product of enhanced censorship during the Sino-Japanese War. In the stages of drafting the Film Law, the censorship system was not simply reproduced, but was reconstructed towards comprehensive control over films based on a new concept of control that took into account the distinctive characteristics of film. In the case of printed matter, basically, the content of the manuscript remains unchanged in the product sold, but, in the case of film, even if the actors' lines and cues are performed exactly as scripted, the way images are constructed may create a meaning entirely different from what was in the script. In script pre-censorship, the story and actors' lines were checked in advance, reducing the burden on the censor when the completed film was inspected. In the censorship of the completed film, emphasis was placed on checking cinematic expression. Furthermore, by not binding the censorship of completed films to script pre-censorship, it was possible to maximize flexible control. A detailed check was conducted of the story and actors' lines during the censorship of the completed film as well. Differences in the pre-censored script and the completed films were not always apparent, but this sort of double-checking was contemplated when the legislative proposals were drafted.

It was also important that the script pre-censorship system required the submission of a business plan to facilitate government management of production for the purpose of rationalization, and strongly reflected the economic policies in place during the Sino-Japanese War. However, in contrast to the automobile manufacturers and gold miners, for whom a business plan was submitted annually outlining production volumes and facilities, the script pre-censorship system required a business plan for each and every production. Its main purpose was to monitor the content of the work, in the manner of quality control. The complicated manner in which films were perceived by the Home Ministry and Ministry of Education at the time was reflected in a focus on "quality" while continuing to treat film productions as a "commodity," much like an automobile or piece of machinery.

Recommendation system

Since 1920, the Ministry of Education had had in place a system for recommending films. The Film Law expanded the system by adding prize money. The first draft explained that this addition was because it was natural for the government to provide appropriate encouragement to realize good films. The government's financial assistance provided only a small incentive for films. The films to be awarded prize money were Japanese films whose content contributed to the public welfare, and which demonstrated superior production techniques. Awards were limited to Japanese films to protect and develop domestic film production.

The Education Minister was the competent minister under this provision, but he disagreed with the Ministry of Justice about the provisions concerning awarding prize money. Whereas the Ministry of Education argued that the conferment of prize money was explicitly stated in the legal text, the Ministry of Justice interpreted these provisions to mean only the awarding of commendations. The seventh draft reflects the Ministry of Education's position. Shipbuilding, manufacturing military vehicles, manufacturing synthetic petroleum, developing petroleum resources, gold mining and other businesses were consulted for laws which provided for the awarding of prizes. Of these, laws related to manufacturing synthetic petroleum and gold mining overlapped with the "Survey of Legislative Precedents." But laws for manufacturing synthetic petroleum and gold mining stipulate that subsidies would be provided to enterprises, while the laws for the shipbuilding industry stipulate that protection and assistance was limited to Japanese companies.

However, there were significant differences between the incentives in mining and manufacturing industry laws and those in the proposed Film Law. In the former case, subsidies were given to companies who set up production facilities and engaged in production, whereas, in the case of the proposed Film Law, prize money was to be awarded to those who produced superior films. Furthermore, in the mining and manufacturing industries, facilitating production was the direct purpose, whereas, in the proposed Film Law, prize money would be awarded on the basis of an assessment of product excellence, although it was difficult to apply a mechanical standard to the quality of the product.

Mention of the conferment of prize money was deleted from the seventh draft, but the Ministry of Finance and the Legislative Bureau subsequently enquired about the provision.[24] The Ministry of Finance was skeptical about claims of urgency for the Film Law legislation during the Sino-Japanese War. Nevertheless, the Ministry of Finance agreed on February 23, 1939, to allow the measure through for the time being, but on the proviso that the award system be deleted. The following day, Tatebayashi and others took up the matter with the Ministry of Finance, and came to the understanding that the commendations could be reworded to read "recommendation." On the 25th, the Finance Minister approved the proposed Film Law. However, during deliberations in the Legislative Bureau the following day, the recommendation system was once again raised as an issue. According to Tatebayashi, it was observed that the disbursement of subsidies could be achieved by ministerial ordinances, and that laws were not used to prescribe such subsidies.[25] It appears that the Legislative Bureau maintained that a recommendation system was not compatible with Japan's legal system which, basically, stipulated prohibitions.

In the final drafts, the object of recommendations was amended to be film productions, rather than producers or companies. The Ministry of Justice, the Legislative Bureau and the Ministry of Finance had each indicated that the proposed recommendation system did not accord with Japan's underlying legal precepts, but the Home Ministry and Ministry of Education argued that the proposed Film Law differed from existing laws, as a comprehensive control law which had aspects of both censorship and positive guidance and assistance, and strongly advocated for the inclusion of a recommendation system.

Structural characteristics of the proposed film law

The Home Ministry was at the center of drafting provisions for the proposed Film Law. Comments by the Ministry of Justice and the Legislative Bureau were addressed with revisions.

The business licensing system was prepared with reference to the Automobile Manufacturing Business Law. The idea of intensively protecting and fostering a small number of authorized companies was invoked by the Film Law. The objective appears to have been to repress competition between companies and thus stabilize Japan's film market. A pre-censorship system was adopted to assure the quality of films distributed to the market. The pre-censorship system was set up as a notification system, which enabled it to operate independently from traditional film censorship of finished products. A registration system was prescribed for staff engaged in film productions, drawing on principles in product manufacturing. The inclusion of decree authority gave government authorities a broad range of possible control measures, including quantitative restrictions and distribution coordination. The recommendation system followed the traditional system for cultural works, but policies for encouraging production increases in mining, manufacturing and other producer industries were also referenced for this law, confirming that film works were produced as commodities.

In the proposed Film Law, characteristics can be seen where concepts of industrial control legislation were introduced, while existing film control policy was followed and expanded. Film was the only industrialized area in Japan's entertainment sector, and thus when film production was incorporated into Japan's legal system, concepts for industrial control in mining, manufacturing and other industries were invoked in the proposed legislation. In particular, references were made to provisions promoting entire industries through the protection and development of a small number of companies as well as provisions for adjustments to supply and demand in specific sectors. In provisions for cultural control of the works' social impact, existing laws related to the arts and culture were invoked as well as concepts of industrial control legislation.

The invocation of existing industrial control legislation highlight the distinguishing characteristic of films, which are both a commercial activity and an artistic expression, at the same time. For example, the actors targeted under the registration system differ from factory workers and not only in their labor, but also in that there is social value in being a laborer or an actor. Accordingly, the proposed Film Law sought to manage the whole personality of those working in film, which went well beyond the legal registration systems for industrial labor management. Legal means for encouraging production were stipulated in the recommendation system, but the concept of control invoked sought not only an increase in production volume, but also improvements in the quality of film productions. Hence, when attempts were made to invoke provisions from other industrial control legislation, the Ministry of Justice and the Legislative Bureau pointed out issues with legislative techniques. The Film Law incorporated those aspects of ordinary industrial control legislation aimed at maintaining sound companies and a sound market. However, it also sought to exert a particular type of control in the distinctive motion-picture industry. The disposition toward cultural control markedly effected the drafting of the Film Law. In the process, the Ministry of Justice and the Legislative Bureau formulated better expressions for defining the control concept from existing legislation.

Officials were afforded much discretion in "flexibly" administering the Film Law. This versatility was introduced to the Film Law at the stage where the concept of control was being debated. When the film industry was enlisted to produce films preparing for military action in 1942, Japanese films were to be produced, or "manufactured," amid competition on an appropriate scale, and were to satisfy the market in a systematic manner. This was a type of production management. After 1943, planning guidance, a form of quality control, was practiced by government agencies. The germination of these ideas can be found in the concept of control[26] which arose during the drafting of the Film Law.

There was a global trend in the 1930s and 1940s toward national film control policies. Behind these tendencies were the economics of establishing and expanding film markets in various countries, as well as the political and social factors of international relations and changing concepts of art and culture as nations militarized. Films are distributed in the global market but are also heavily reflective of the distinctive characteristics of the regions and ethnic groups who produce them. Occasionally, films are used to represent the state. Detailed comparative reviews of control legislation in other countries is important in considering the relationship between global and domestic standards in regard to film control concepts.

Notes

1 Tatebayashi Mikio. "Eigahoan zakkan," *Nihon Eiga*. March 1939 edition.
2 Iwasaki, Akira. *Nihon Eiga Shishi*. Tokyo: Asahi Shimbunsha, 1977. Sato, Tadao. *Nihon Eigashi 1~4*. Tokyo: Iwanami Shoten, 1995.
3 High, Peter B. *Teikoku no Ginmaku*. Nagoya: The University of Nagoya Press, 1995. Fururkawa, Takahisa. *Senzika no Nihon Eiga: Hitobito wa Kokusaku Eiga wo Mitaka?* Tokyo: Yoshikawa Kobunkan, 2003.

4 Okudaira Yasuhiro, "Eiga no kokka tousei," in Shohei Imamura et al, eds., *Koza nihon eiga 4: senso to nihon eiga*, Tokyo: Iwanami Shoten, 1988.
5 Yanai Yoshio. *Katsudoshashin no hogo to torishimari.* Tokyo: Yuhikaku, 1929, pp. 505–510.
6 Okudaira Yasuhiro, "Ken'etsu seido," in Ukai Nobushige et al, eds., *Koza nihon kindai ho hattatsushi* 11, Tokyo: Keiso shobo, 1967.
7 Torigoe Jukuji, *Jitsumu shugan hoan keisatsu kenkyu.* Tokyo: Shokado shoten, 1929, pp. 270–271.
8 Regarding the political and social background behind the Film Law and the deliberations within the government, see Kato Atsuko, *Sododin taisei to eiga.* Tokyo: Shinyosha, 2003, pp. 28–48.
9 For details about the documents used for explanation and legislative measure numeral 12, see Kato Atsuko, "Stipulation of the Control Concept Appearing in the Drafting Process of the 'Film Law,'" *Cultural Policy Research* (*Bunka seisaku kenkyu*), Vol. 2, 2008.
10 For details of Legislative Bureau deliberations, see Atsuko Kato, "Motion Picture Regulations during the Sino-Japanese War: A Study of Laws Pertaining to the Film Industry," *Shigaku-zasshi*, Vol. CIX, No. 6, 2000.
11 "Held November 8, 1939: Eigaho unyo zadankai shitsugi sokkiroku," Documents of Mikio Tatebayashi, Collection of Setagaya Bungakukan, A-7.
12 Collection of the National Archives of Japan. "Tanemura-shi keisatsu sanko shiryo, Collection No. 102," Included in (4E-15-4 Hei 9 Kei No. 781).
13 Collection of the National Archives of Japan. "Article-by-Article Commentary on the Film Law," (4E-15-4 Hei 9 Kei No. 650).
14 Atsuko Kato, "Motion Picture Regulations during the Sino-Japanese War: A Study of Laws Pertaining to the Film Industry," *Shigaku-zasshi*, Vol. CIX, No. 6, 2000.
15 "Article-by-Article Commentary on the Film Law," op.cit., p. 32.
16 Yeo, Inman. "Was Japan's Automobile Industry Established by the Automobile Manufacturing Business Law? Reorganization of the Automobile Industry Through the Automobile Manufacturing Business Law and Wartime Control Policies." *Keizaigaku ronshu*. Tokyo Daigaku Keizai Gakkai, Vol. 69, No. 2, 2003.
17 Udagawa, Masaru. "Article-by-Article Explanation of the Automobile Manufacturing Business Law." *Keiei Shirin*. (The Hosei Journal of Business by the Faculty of Business Administration, Hosei University), Vol. 39. Number 4, 2003.
18 *Five Scouts* (Go-nin no Sekkohei). Production of Nikkatsu. Directed by Tomotaka Tasaka and starring Bontaro Miake. January 1938.
19 "Article-by-Article Commentary on the Film Law," op. cit., p. 239.
20 "Article-by-Article Commentary on the Film Law," op. cit., p. 52.
21 For the process of reconstructing the censorship system, see Atsuko Kato, "Rebuilding of the Censorship System in the Drafting Process of the Film Law," *Media History*. Vol. 28, 2010.
22 "Article-by-Article Commentary on the Film Law," op.cit., pp. 77–78.
23 "Motion Picture Regulations during the Sino-Japanese War: A Study of Laws Pertaining to the Film Industry." op. cit.

24 *Sodoin taisei to eiga*, op.cit., pp. 58–63.
25 "Held November 8, 1939: Eigaho unyo zadankai shitsugi sokkiroku," op. cit.
26 The Film Law did not specify *what* to censor, but *how* to censor. The details of censorship were regulated by the Enforcement Regulations of the Film Law. Please refer to; Kato Atsuko," Rebuilding of the censorship system in the enacting process of 'Film Law,'" *Media shi kenkyu* (Media history), Vol. 28, 2010.

2 "Me-istic Nationalism" in Films Promoted by the Japan Self-Defense Forces: Focus on *Midnight Eagle* as an Example[1]

Noriko Sudo

Introduction

This chapter examines one of the films officially promoted by Japan's Self-Defense Forces, henceforward "JSDF films". We focus on *Midnight Eagle* released in 2007, which promotes "self-sacrifice for the nation" as an implicit behavioral value without calling for any explicit public service. In this chapter, we name this subtle ideology "me-istic nationalism" and reveal it to be an outgrowth of neo-liberalism and economic developments in Japan from the 1990s to the present. This chapter will demonstrate how the JSDF's political goals have correlated with this contemporary situation. We focus on *Midnight Eagle* because the main character who sacrifices himself for the nation is a civilian who clearly declares that he is *never* concerned about national security. This makes this new nationalism quite different from classic nationalism. Furthermore, the film interweaves political-economic conditions with this contemporary expression of nationalism in such a way as to mutually reinforce each other.

We take a cultural-political approach with close attention to economic factors. This approach differs from a typical representative approach, as economic circumstances are accorded more importance than directorial technique or cinematography. First, we examine how the JSDF decides to support commercial films and the kind of movies they have supported until now. Second, we look at the film production committee[2] of *Midnight Eagle*, the scale of the JSDF's support, and the box office. Third, we analyze the plot in detail and discuss the idea of self-sacrifice in *Midnight*

Eagle. Finally, we point out problems when such sacrifice is influenced by economic-political issues.

There are scarcely any studies focusing on the economic-political dimensions of JSDF films. Aaron Gerow perhaps comes closest, analyzing contemporary Japanese war movies, *Lorelei*,[3] *Samurai Commando: Mission 1549*,[4] *Aegis*,[5] and *Otoko-tachi no Yamato*,[6] all released in 2005. He says "such films may express the kind of "healthy nationalism" that political conservatives heartily advocate, desiring that Japan finally become a "normal nation," that is, one with no restrictions on its military power."[7]

Gerow analyzes these movies in detail and points out the contemporary nationalism in Japan as well as the complicated relationship between Japan and the U.S., but he pays little attention to their production background. And he does not mention JSDF support, although *Aegis* and *Otoko-tachi no Yamato* are both JSDF films. Moreover, he ignores the political mechanisms of the film production committee, which has no small influence over the content of the movies.

Films are not only artworks but also commercial products subject to careful cost-benefit analyses. So when we analyze films, we must consider the profit motive as well as artistic efforts. It is also important to consider political issues, since the film industry is quite responsive to them. For example, the film industry had no interest in movies depicting the JSDF in 1970s and 1980s, as most Japanese people at that time were repelled by the military and militarism. By contrast, in 2013 when they had got used to the "active" JSDF and rising nationalism, three JSDF films were released and did well at the box-office. One is a quite popular animation "Detective Conan", the English title is *Case Closed: Private Eye in the Distant Sea*,[8] which describes international terrorism on the SDF ship Aegis. Another is a film version of the bestselling novel *Library Wars*[9] and the final is *Eien no Zero*,[10] another film version of a top-selling novel, the drama of a zero pilot.

The JSDF films

Before analyzing *Midnight Eagle*, let us explain JSDF films. In 1954 the Self-Defense Forces Act came into force and in 1960 the administrative vice-minister of the Defense Agency (Now the Ministry of Defense = MOD) issued an Official Notice,[11] which established a standard for subsidizing commercial films dealing with military themes, including cases of disaster-relief or training. So, "JSDF films" in this section means films promoted under this Notice.

Movies are ranked based on the degree of contribution to the publicity of the JSDF in the Notice. "A-rank" films are those determined to contribute "extremely" well to the JSDF and can be provided the following support: 1) research in education and training, 2) use of the facilities and equipment of the JSDF, 3) technical training, 4) use of films made by the JSDF. "B-rank" films are judged to contribute "fairly" and can get "minor" support. "C-rank" films are ineligible for subsidies.

The support is provided in the name of military training, so not only personnel but also many kinds of weapons are made available at no cost to the filmmakers. The JSDF supported various movies with F-15 flights, battleship maneuvers, and many armored vehicle operations under the direction of commercial film directors according to the above Notice. Film companies and producers accept these subsidies because it saves them huge sums for movie sets and computer graphics that would otherwise be required. Few Japanese people are aware that the military hardware in these films is funded by public taxes, though, or that the film companies allow the JSDF to censor their projects directly or indirectly in exchange for its support.

In the 1960s, so-called "propaganda movies," in which self-defense officials played active roles as main characters, were made one after another.[12] However one of the opposition parties criticized the arrangement in the early 1970s, and the practice ceased for about 20 years. The end of the Cold War, though, triggered the JSDF's resumption of subsidizing commercial films. From 1989 to 2017, about 40 JSDF movies[13] were produced and promoted.

JSDF subsidized films are not always war movies. One-third of the films are special effects monster films like *Godzilla*[14] and *Gamera*, while many others are disaster or fantasy pictures aimed at adolescents and children. The heroes and heroines of these movies are not always self-defense officials and the JSDF takes a backseat role in many films. The main characters seem to be more subtly nationalistic than the typical "propaganda films" made in WWII, conveying a sense that self-sacrifice for the nation is not exceptionally honorable and admirable, but simply a natural way of being.

Midnight Eagle is quite uncommon in the JSDF films in that the main characters all die defending Japan even though it is not about Kamikaze pilots. More curiously, too, the hero clearly announces that he is *not* dying for his country. This bizarre nationalism that denies nationalism is typical of contemporary expressions of nationalism. We will examine this "nationalism without mentioning the nation" through *Midnight Eagle*.

Historical background

During the 1980s, during the period when the JSDF was not supporting films, important political-economic changes occurred. In 1979, Margaret Thatcher became the Prime Minister of Great Britain and promoted a new nationalism. "Thatcherism", a combination of nationalism and neo-liberalism, was echoed in "Reaganomics," the social and economic policy pursued by the U.S. President Ronald Reagan. The policies by Prime Minister Yasuhiro Nakasone, who came to power in 1982, were influenced by these international trends. Nakasone proceeded to privatize the national railways in 1987 as I will discuss in more detail below. The political style of the time was described as "small government" that wields "big power". This political-economic policy is called neo-liberalism, which has been severely criticized by many scholars such as David Harvey,[15] Antonio Negri and Michael Hardt,[16] Maurizio Lazzarato,[17] and so on.

From 1989 to 1990, the Cold War effectively ended with the collapse of the Soviet Bloc. Neo-liberalism quickly expanded into the former socialist countries. In Japan, Emperor Hirohito died, and the Japanese calendar changed from the "Showa" to "Heisei" era. Since Japanese think in terms of epochs rather than a continuous timeline, this change of eras helped memories of WWII to recede into a more distant past. In 1991, after the first Gulf War, the Maritime Self-Defense Force was sent to the Persian Gulf to clear underwater mines. This was the first overseas mission for the JSDF,[18] which was banned by the Constitution from participating in foreign wars. The government attempted to justify the action by explaining that Western countries were dissatisfied with Japan's monetary contributions of a "mere" 13 billion dollars to the Gulf War. The international demand that Japan contribute men and materials unleashed the JSDF's pent-up desire to take a more active role in world affairs. JSDF support and promotion of commercial films resumed with this new world order after the Cold War.

In 1995, three events reinvigorated the JSDF: the Great Hanshin Earthquake on January 17, the Aum Shinrikyo sarin gas attack in the

Tokyo subway on March 20, and the 50th anniversary of the end of WWII on August 15. The JSDF image was enhanced by daily media images of troops conducting search and rescue operations after the earthquake. Likewise, the Ground Self Defense Forces, including the chemical weapons corps, were seen taking the lead in the response to the Aum Shinrikyo attack. Both events were framed in such a way as to encourage the public to look favorably upon the JSDF's attempts to protect them. While most Japanese people were unhappy about the Gulf War intervention in 1991, attitudes began to change following these two major disasters in 1995.

As the public got used to mass media images of the JSDF, the JSDF saw an opportunity to further enhance its image through the film industry. The main character of *Gamera 2: Attack of Legion*[19] (1996) is a JSDF officer in the chemical corps, an obvious attempt to capitalize on the positive image of the JSDF created by the Sarin Incident.

When the 50th anniversary of the end of WWII was commemorated on August 15, Prime Minister Tomiichi Murayama[20] issued a statement, which among other things, addressed the rising neo-nationalism in Japan. The relevant part of the statement is as follows:

> During a certain period in the not too distant past, Japan, following a mistaken national policy, advanced along the road to war, only to ensnare the Japanese people in a fateful crisis, and, through its colonial rule and aggression, caused tremendous damage and suffering to the people of many countries, particularly to those of Asian nations.[21]

Prime Minister Shinzo Abe repeated this condemnation of the invasion of East Asia in his statement for the 70th anniversary of the war, but this self-criticism irritates the right wing and fuels a tendency toward historical revisionism and deflecting criticism from the Japanese military. As this neo-nationalist movement was gaining momentum in the 1990s, the JSDF increased its range of activities, as mentioned above.

On September 11, 2001, synchronized terrorist attacks occurred in the United States. American nationalism erupted in response, and under the slogan of the "war on terror," the U.S. bombed Afghanistan and then invaded Iraq, although the latter had little if anything to do with the terrorist attacks. U.S. President George W. Bush called Iraq, along with Iran and North Korea, an "axis of evil." This increased tensions on the

Korean peninsula, and in December 2001, North Korea engaged in a gun battle with the Japan Coast Guard, resulting in the scuttling of a North Korean covert operations vessel. Since 2003, North Korea has ratcheted up its provocative nuclear weapons program.[22]

Under these political conditions, legislation to deal with military emergencies was hastily revised in 2003 to 2004. These contingency bills easily passed the Diet in an atmosphere in which military attack against Japan were clearly envisaged, with the shocking memories of the 9/11 attacks in the background, and an increasing acceptance of neo-nationalism since the late 1990s.

Beyond Japan, nationalist sentiments grew stronger across East Asia at that time. Japan has had tense relations with South Korea since the beginning of the Takeshima (Dokdo) Island Dispute in 2004; there were numerous anti-Japanese demonstrations in China in 2005; and at the time of writing, at least seven ballistic missiles have been launched from North Korea into the Japan Sea. The kind of social anxiety produced by these incidents is reflected in *Midnight Eagle*.

Outline of *Midnight Eagle*

Midnight Eagle was directed by Izuru Narushima. It was released in both Japan and the United States in 2007. Universal Pictures Japan (UPJ, now NBC Universal Entertainment Japan LLC) had invested in the film as one of the co-producers, earning it a rare-U.S. release for a Japanese original live-action film. The world premiere was held in the Egyptian Theatre in Hollywood, and the film was distributed to the American film market. It was also screened as an opening movie at the 20th Tokyo International Film Festival.

Many popular actors and actresses were cast, and 1000 million yen (U.S.$9 million) was pumped into this film, twice the average budget for a Japanese film at the time. Many companies seek to produce JSDF-subsidized films, which have grown in popularity due to funding and the promotion of TV companies. *Midnight Eagle* is part of this trend. It was co-produced by 12 companies, including 6 affiliated with the TV Asahi Group.[23] The film was promoted through a series of TV and radio ads as well as a great deal of printed publicity in Asahi newspapers.

A quick summary of *Midnight Eagle* is as follows. The U.S. stealth fighter "Midnight Eagle", equipped with a special bomb, has been captured by terrorists (though not explicitly stated, the implication is that they are North-Koreans) and then crash-landed in the Japan Northern Alps in winter. Nishizaki (Takao Osawa), a freelance photographer, just happened to witness the flash from the crash and begins to investigate the event, climbing through the deep mountain snow with Ochiai (Koji Tamaki), a newspaper reporter. At the same time, Keiko (Yuko Takeuchi), Nishizaki's sister-in-law who works at a magazine, came into contact with one of the escaping terrorists and helped Nishizaki as we shall see. Meanwhile, a JSDF commando team sent in by the government to recover the bomb has been wiped out in a gunfight. This leaves Nishizaki, Ochiai and Saeki (Eisaku Yoshida), a valiant JSDF officer, to fight a heroic battle against the terrorists in the blizzard. Finally, disaster is avoided by the protagonists sacrificing themselves to interrupt the terrorists' scheme. The promotional copy for the movie was: "The largest-scale mountain suspense action movie in Japanese film history!!"

Midnight Eagle was fully supported by the MOD, which about 10 months before the release had been promoted from agency-level to ministry-level. Fighter jets, tanks and other technical units were deployed in making this movie. According to an interview with the MOD,[24] they supported this film because:

> The theme of this movie is to express a JSDF official who sacrifices himself for the defense of his family and his country Japan. We can represent the conditions and efforts of the JSDF to a wide segment of the Japanese people. And, because not a few popular actors are in the cast, we will be able to introduce our actions especially to the young generation and women. The film production committee will also make a TV program about the movie. In addition, the actors will enter the army for a trial period in order to prepare for their roles and report their experiences in various media including their blogs.

Against expectations, however, *Midnight Eagle* totally died at the box office. The film company data reported to the MOD in mid-May 2008 shows box office receipts of about 760 million yen (U.S.$6.8 million), much less than the budget. The cinema attendance was only 620,000. Before the release, the film was promoted in 55 magazines, several TV programs promoted the film, a photo exhibition was held at four Mitsukoshi department stores and the producers collaborated with a confectionery maker to sell special chocolates, but none of their efforts paid off. In the U.S, the film was released in three cities at three theaters[25] for three weeks, but the final box office was only $7,056.[26]

Sacrifice by civilians

The most remarkable point in the story of *Midnight Eagle* is the sacrifice made by civilians. As indicated above, the men who fought to save Japan from foreign soldiers were two civilians and one JSDF officer. While the latter may have been duty-bound, Nishizaki and Ochiai were not compelled to self-sacrifice by official obligations, but did so as a result of their personal sentiments.

Nishizaki and Ochiai head up the mountain to get a scoop, but after getting caught in the fight, they become aware of their opportunity to save their country. They are represented as "ordinary Japanese people" who are neither overly strong nor patriotic. Nevertheless, they fight and sacrifice themselves on their own initiative, without orders from the government. In other words, nationalism is not imposed upon them. In Benedict Anderson's terms, they were not expressing "official nationalism."[27] So, why did they make the extremely nationalistic self-sacrifice for the nation?

The main answer is "family." Nishizaki has a son and his wife is dead. If the bomb explodes, his son might be in danger. So he acts only for his son. Of course, he also wants to save many other Japanese people, but the most important thing for him is his son's life. He makes these feelings explicit when he says; "I don't care about the country…but as a father, let me save my son's life." He has previously abandoned his career as a successful battlefield photographer because it kept him from being at his wife's bedside when she died. The last refuge of his identity is his role as "father". Grounded in the paternalistic ethic that a father must save his family, he is drawn into a nationalistic mission without being especially interested in the consequences for the state. Yet this personal and private attitude strongly resonates with nationalist sentiments.

In contrast, Ochiai does not seem to have a family, so he has neither a personal nor a political motivation to save anyone. Nevertheless, he rushes toward the dangerous battlefield even more enthusiastically than Nishizaki. He is a civilian and has no reason to risk his life in this fight.

But he refuses the excuse of getting his scoop pictures to his office, missing a chance to go down the mountain, and takes a bullet to protect his colleague. He dies smiling with no hatred for the enemy and no animosity toward the government; he was satisfied that he had done the right thing. He murmurs, "I didn't run away this time," referring to a previous failure to track down a political cabal.

These two characters' nationalistic attitudes are quite personal, selfish even. They are not interested in any national cause or benefits, but merely their own satisfaction. But, of course, the implication is that private interests are ultimately synonymous with public interests, even if motivations do not seem to be overtly nationalistic. The civilians self-sacrifice in the spirit of a suicide mission is this film's "tear-jerker" moment. In Japan, being able to bring the audience to tears is commonly taken as indicative of a good quality film. But when they cry because the main characters made the extreme self-sacrifice, we should suspect a strong political ideology, as tears of sympathy reflect the audience's preparedness to sacrifice for the nation, if only by proxy.

Another form of sacrifice can be seen in the women behind the lines helping the men fighting at the front. This promotes the idea that people on the "home front" should keep a "stiff upper lip", not complaining or blaming the government if a loved one dies for the sake of the nation. The last scene of *Midnight Eagle* is Keiko and Nishizaki's son returning to ordinary life and living together happily. There is no bitterness or sadness. They seem to have easily overcome their hard luck and even appear somewhat proud of their family's death. Incidentally, Keiko was not actually "behind" the lines for the entire film; she got caught in a gunfight in town and had no choice but to shoot a gun.

In films about the WWII period, challenges and difficulties contribute to a sense of national coherence. According to Ruth Benedict, one characteristics of Japanese war movies is that the family who loses a husband or father tries to live bravely without him.[28] This is quite an ideological and problematic trait. Yet, this contemporary JSDF movie persists in portraying the survivors as accepting their loss as a private matter. They do not blame the government for causing their suffering. Instead, they try to get over it personally. Although there are no explicit expressions of nationalist ideology in *Midnight Eagle*, it makes some seriously errant suppositions about human motivation.

Sacrifice by soldiers

While Nishizaki, Ochiai, Keiko and her niece are portrayed as "model civilians", Saeki embodies the ideals of the JSDF, sworn to the mission of saving the nation and its people. As mentioned above, *Midnight Eagle* received JSDF support because it depicts a JSDF officer who courageously embarks on a dangerous mission to save his comrades, civilians and the nation. He is tough, and an expert marksman. He can knock off enemies from a distance like shooting fish in a barrel. He stays cool under pressure, giving us a sense of security.

Shortly before the final scene, Saeki tells Nishizaki about his wife, her pregnancy, and the expected child. In this scene we learn that Saeki is not only an excellent JSDF officer, but also an ordinary Japanese man. Like Nishizaki, his self-sacrifice is also as a "father" struggling to save a daughter whom he has never seen. He is not only an exemplary JSDF officer, but also an exemplary father, and an exemplary citizen. Eisaku Yoshida's performance of the role of Saeki was well received; even people who bitterly criticize the quality of the film typically speak well of Saeki.[29]

However, the other JSDF soldiers are remarkably weak. The JSDF commando team sent into the Japan Northern Alps is completely wiped out, accomplishing almost nothing, and the fighter planes sent to help them are rendered ineffective by a snowstorm. On the film's website, many have commented on their miserable weakness. We might read this to mean that they want the JSDF to be stronger in the future. Making the JSDF appear weak has had the effect of making the public yearn for a stronger JSDF.

Midnight Eagle also portrays the complicated relationship between Japan and the U.S. It is a U.S. stealth fighter equipped with what might be a nuclear weapon that has been captured by terrorists. That is, it was the U.S. armed forces that made the fatal mistake. In the film, the prime minister says "I'm very sorry that there are some confidential matters we didn't know," is a reference to the three non-nuclear principles which prohibit such weapons in Japan.[30] The implication is that the U.S. brought an illegal weapon into Japanese territory, lost it to terrorists, and burdened the Japanese people with the task of fighting the terrorists and trying to recover it. As the prime minister says in the film, "an incident has happened in our country, so we must settle it by ourselves." These words express a double-meaning: first, irritation with the U.S. armed forces taking liberties and, second, dissatisfaction with the nation's military restrictions under Article 9 of the Constitution.

It is quite different from "the pro-American [Japanese] patriotism", which Naoki Sakai mentions.[31] He points out some of the ambiguities in the right-wing position in Japan: they have defined the benefit of the U.S.-alliance in terms of a pro-American-anti-Soviet stance since WWII, but since the Cold War, they are left with only the pro-American leg to stand on, which seems to leave Japan in a subservient role. So Sakai describes pro-American patriotism as really strange and bizarre. In the process, the film expresses an anti-American patriotism, which has been living underground during the post-war era.

Taro Aso was reported to have said, "In these days, I saw a preview of a Japanese movie named *Midnight Eagle* whose story is that Japan covers for the failure of the United States. This kind of scenario would be really hard to imagine in an earlier time."[32] Aso, who became prime minister soon thereafter, hinted at both his satisfaction with the depiction of Japan as an equal in the military partnership with the U.S. and his repugnance at any hint of subservience in the relationship. This not too subtle anti-American message is an interesting aspect of a movie supported by the JSDF, which is in many respects characterized by its pro-American stance.

Although, the main theme of this movie is not rejection or criticism of the U.S. but the anxiety facing Japan in an emergency; the suspense builds on the question of whether Japan can resolve the situation promptly and properly—even though its American ally cannot be relied upon. *Midnight Eagle*'s producers too obviously insist on the Japanese "defense-only" doctrine, which can also be seen in *Samurai Commando: Mission 1549* and *Aegis*. For example, lines like "No war and no military forces must be in this country" and "We are not military forces but self-defense forces" are inserted in the dialogue quite unnaturally. In this sense, the JSDF's ambivalent situation of regulation and mission is highlighted in the fiction of JSDF supported films. So let us turn now to how the enemies who impose this kind of dilemma onto this anti-military military force[33] are depicted in this movie.

Midnight Eagle implies that the terrorists are North Korean, although "North Korea" is never mentioned in the movie. One hint is when "some Asian spies" break into the U.S. Yokota base, and Nishizaki murmurs "No, they're not JSDF officers because they didn't speak Japanese," and again when one of the government officers says that an undercover agent has "escaped from his country." A more direct clue is provided when the Chief Risk Management Officer explains the case to the Prime Minister, pointing out a particular name on the list of agents: the Japanese name "Kanamoto Sou," which is a typical Korean-Japanese family name. So the audience should be clear that the terrorists are North Korean. *Midnight Eagle* was released soon after the North Korean nuclear issue became a serious concern, and while images of North Korea as a "dangerous rogue state" were produced daily in the mass media.

Another typical image of North Korea in this film is the mention of "the undeveloped country which is very poor and isolated from the world". The secret agent Hirata is one of the main roles. He is the only enemy agent who has dialogue. He certainly seems to be dangerous, yet he is patriotic enough to sacrifice himself in service to his impoverished country. As it were, he is not a figure of disgust and dread, but one deserving of sympathy, a "poor ordinary North Korean person suffering from oppression."

This kind of representation "looks down on" the North Koreans. We can see this most clearly in the depiction of Hirata's girlfriend. When she steals Keiko's camera, which contains shots of her and Hirata, she feels elated by her success, even though the memory card has been removed from it. Keiko and her young colleague share meaningful smiles because Hirata's girlfriend does not know the high-tech digital camera is useless without the memory card.

There is another scene in which Keiko provides shelter to Hirata and his girlfriend, caring for them like their "elder sister". In this scene, the terrorist couple is "protected" by their enemy, a Japanese woman. The suggestion here is that ordinary people who have been brainwashed by a dictatorial ideology are not to be blamed but rather to be redeemed. This is the same logic underpinning George W. Bush's call for the liberation of Iraq as he launched the Iraq War with a "shock and awe" bombing campaign.

This relationships between the strong and the weak is a stereotypical plotline in movies of this kind. Naoki Sakai refers to this perspective as a "missionary's standpoint."[34] Analyzing *The Deer Hunter* (1978), he argues that the Americans act like "missionaries," eager to take care of and teach the "natives" whether they want help or not. And sometimes helping the enemy means destroying him. One of the most famous lines to come out of the American-Vietnam War was, "We had to destroy the village in order to save it." This scenario presents typical power relations when they romanticize a conquering man and a conquered woman.[35] In *Midnight Eagle*, the "victor" Keiko, acts like a missionary, guiding the "vanquished" North-Korean terrorists to safety. After their relationship has deepened, Hirata hands Keiko the chip which contains the secret code to defuse the bomb, suggesting that the problem is resolved through Keiko's patient and warm-hearted charity toward her enemies.

Hirata dies saying, "you can save your country by this chip." Here the chip means patriotism. Hirata submits his patriotism to the noble Japanese duty to save the nation. Handing over the chip expresses an unspoken message: the sacrifice for the nation is superior to a particular mission because only the nation is ultimately sovereign. Hirata, an exemplary North Korean patriot, is revealed to be a model Japanese citizen, one who faces his enemy to protect his country, the way one *ought to* act. In the end, Hirata kills himself to protect his girlfriend and Keiko from their pursuers, a somewhat bizarre identification between sacrifice for family and friends, with the ultimate goal of saving the sovereign nation.

The problem of sacrifice

As we have seen, many men die in *Midnight Eagle*. Near the end of the movie, when Nishizaki and Saeki decide that their only option is to detonate a napalm bomb, which will kill themselves along with their enemies, Saeki says, "See you over there" to Nishizaki. He might mean "See you in heaven" but it recalls another well-known expression: "See you in Yasukuni"[36] invoked by Kamikaze suicide bombers during WWII.

Tetsuya Takahashi argues that the rhetoric that presents hideous and tragic death in battle as sacred and sublime is the logic of Yasukuni, as well as the logic of the Holocaust and of contemporary Japanese sacrifice.[37] In many films, including *Midnight Eagle*, the victim's death is neither painful nor miserable because such a sacrifice is intrinsically beautiful. In the final moment, just before the napalm strikes, the brilliant golden light of the rising sun shines on the wrecked Midnight Eagle, and Nishizaki turns his face towards the light and smiles. Then the monitor in the office of the prime minister, which has been connected to the cockpit of the Midnight Eagle where Nishizaki and Saeki have been defending themselves at all costs, goes blank. We can imagine their death symbolized by the blank monitor.

Takahashi also points out that rather than the government, the people themselves embrace and propagate the Yasukuni logic.[38] When many people die in battle, the government concocts a "national story" that "consecrates" them as sacred victims for defending and developing the nation. It thus presents their death in a way that helps their family to recover from sadness, emptiness, and ambivalence. Furthermore, by invoking sympathy with the war dead and the bereaved, they reinforce a collective tendency to think "we must follow them," thereby strengthening the validity of sacrifice.[39]

Of course, the persuasive power of the nation-state is not as absolute as Takahashi suggests; very few Japanese people would happily give their lives for the state. But for the Self-Defense Forces, preparedness for such sacrifice is a basic prerequisite.

"The Stance of the JSDF officials," the JSDF's official guidelines since 1961, emphasizes the importance of completing one's mission even when faced with crisis. They also state that the basis of the JSDF spirit is "the sanity of nation." Similarly, the National General Mobilization Act of 1938 stipulates that a sense of nation or national spirit includes sacrifice for the nation. So it appears that the Japanese national spirit of WWII remains alive, if less explicitly, in contemporary JSDF doctrine. From this perspective, JSDF officer Saeki is the archetypal Japanese: he accomplishes his mission to defend his family and his nation despite all obstacles, even at the ultimate cost to himself.

"The Stance of the JSDF officials" also states that the JSDF spirit consists of "correct" love for one's own ethnicity and homeland. "Nation" is one of the most difficult concepts to define, but for the JSDF, the identity of the nation-state has been equated with ethnicity. The Constitution of Japan defines the nation as the totality of its citizens, but the government clings to the specter of an ethnically homogeneous nation.

In an official commentary on the constitution in 1985, a Ministry of Justice officer, Kiyoshi Hosokawa commented, "Our country has been a homogeneous nation consisting of only one language, only one culture, and only one history ever since national unification was achieved in ancient times."[40] Japan lost its Korean and Taiwan colonies and the puppet state of Manchuria when it was defeated in WWII and immediately abandoned those people who were not ethnically Japanese but had been recognized as Japanese citizens before the new constitution came into effect. By forgetting the history of colonial occupation, the Japanese government sought to perpetuate the myth that Japan is a racially and culturally homogeneous nation.

In JSDF movies like *Midnight Eagle*, as well as in the "JSDF Stance", the difference between "nation" and "ethnicity" seems to be intentionally blurred. "A Japanese" must be a citizen of Japan and must therefore be of the Japanese race. Unsurprisingly they completely ignore Zainichi Korean[41] people, new migrants from South America, and others.

Most JSDF films present standardized notions of patriotism and sacrifice based on such old-style racism. In other JSDF films, the enemies are of different races rather than the other nations and Japanese people are compelled to fight against them. In these cases, distinctions between the categories of the Japanese people, Japanese citizens and the Japanese race are less explicit, if no less apparent.

Takao Osawa, who plays Nishizaki in *Midnight Eagle*, explained on the stage of The Tokyo International Film Festival that, "I tried to act not as a hero but as a real ordinary Japanese man."[42] Why was he conscious of "being Japanese" even though "Japaneseness" was not demanded in the script? What type of people does he imagine? This reflects the most alarming way that racism and nationalism are slipped into the Japanese way of thinking.

Such nationalism is quite different from the "official nationalism" through which the government takes the initiative to define national identity. Osawa's image of ordinary Japanese people does not derive from formal state-education, but is propagated in the national consciousness through the repetition of images presented in the mass media. In this kind of nationalism, the value of loyalty is understated and "being Japanese" provides an unobtrusive connection with other Japanese people. This kind of Japaneseness is not seen as overtly political because it appears to be natural and intrinsic.

The contemporary nationalism we find in *Midnight Eagle* is not so much a public as a private sentiment. The characters have no sense of responsibility to contribute to their society or country, thinking only about themselves and their family. Yet, although their self-sacrifice is selfishly motivated, the outcome is exploited by the government. Unintentionally, if not unknowingly, private sacrifice turns into public sacrifice and ultimately national sacrifice. Underlying all of this is a deep-seated consciousness of "being Japanese."

"Me-istic nationalism"

This kind of private nationalism can already be found in the old Japanese propaganda movies during WWII. Toshiya Ueno points out an important difference between Western and Japanese propaganda films of the 1930s and '40s. Western war movies exaggerated and caricatured the enemy's savagery and atrocity, whereas Japanese war propaganda movies focused on the endurance and solidarity of Japanese soldiers and civilians in the face of difficult situations.[43] When Japan's impending defeat became apparent, solidarity was almost entirely defined by the collective endurance of hardships. But, this ideology is no longer relevant in the contemporary situation. Nationalism today is defined by a thoroughgoing consumerism.

Motoaki Takahara draws on Rika Kayama's idea of "petit nationalism,"[44] which he defines as an innocent effusion of patriotism. Takahara raises questions such as "Are they really right/left?" He identifies two types of nationalism; the unity requested by the government for national development, and that embraced by isolated anxious people who are thrown into a fluid society.[45] Takahara concludes that the conservative homogeneous nationalism focusing on a high-growth economy has already disappeared, replaced by a more pluralistic and self-centered nationalism because the labor market is increasingly precarious in the neoliberal economy, in which people do not collaborate but compete with one another. Takahara's analysis highlights the relationship between global social change and contemporary nationalism.

Midnight Eagle clearly depicts this new type of nationalism. Nishizaki's family is almost broken; his wife died from disease and his only son has been taken in by his wife's sister. He is not struggling for money, but nor does he belong to any company or association; he is somewhat rootless. In the Japan of the 1980s, "a freelance photographer" would have implied upward mobility, but in the 2000s, it portrays precarity. In this sense, he really is an ordinary man living in an uncertain and precarious society. By chance, he dies in a national crisis; but perhaps he was inexorably drawn into this situation by a tacit nationalism which speaks to individual anxieties of contemporary life. In other words, insecurity drives him to latch onto any available identity—even if it is a false one.

Shintaro Nakanishi expands on the concept of "petit nationalism" to categorize the nationalism of contemporary young people as "virtual nationalism"[46] which is different from the traditional nationalism that was prevalent after WWII and is entirely unaware of the politics of national issues. According to Nakanishi, the young generation's immersion in consumerist culture, a mixture of anti-statism and neo-liberalism, fuels their hatred of politics. In the hyper-consumerism of Japan, culture is just another consumable, not something that grows inherently out of one's own lived-experience.

Importantly, Nakanishi correlates consumerism and the younger generation's discomfort with overt nationalism. Young people appear to be rich and free; but they can only construct their identities from "commodities" because they have been compelled to identify as consumers since birth. This is a form of alienation, stemming from the commercialization of national issues, which mixes up the "Japanese people", "Japanese race" and "Japanese nation". The political implications of the words "race" and "nation" are shunned by consumers, who are nevertheless easily swayed by the "non-political" and cultural implications of the terms "Japanese people" and "Japanese culture," which are taken-for-granted as obvious, comprehensible, and even fashionable.

We can see this in the tag-line from a TV commercial for JR Tokai (JR Central: Central Japan Railway Company) in 2009 when, anticipating the 1,300th anniversary of the establishment of Japan's old capital, Nara Heijo-kyo in 2010. The ad's tag-line was "Now, come back to Nara again". This ad is notably similar to the old Japanese National Railways "Discover Japan" campaign in 1970 and the "Exotic Japan" campaign in 1984. "Again" in the 2010 ad implies the "re"-discovery of Japan by the Japanese people themselves. It is an invitation to "consume" Japan and the Japanese as a commodity, rather than to live as a Japanese.

Akira Asada calls this kind of commercialization of Japan "J-recurrence."[47] Nakanishi calls the phenomenon "J-lization" or "J-nationalism."[48] In both cases, the use of the letter "J" infers the nation-state Japan or the Japanese nation has already been commodified. Hiromichi Ugaya observed that the letter "J" was scattered all over Japan, as in "JR" and "JT" (Japan Tobacco Inc.) in the late 1980s following the Nakasone Cabinet's call for "the bottom line of the post-war politics."[49] Nakasone, the first significant Japanese politician to advocate neo-liberalism, understood the commodification of Japan itself to be the basis of the new nationalism.

Consumption is *a priori* personal. Consumers are basically selfish. Especially in Japan, people appear to have regressed from a mature "egoism" to a more childish "me-ism." Rather than discerning between those things that are desirable and those which are not, Japanese youth tend to indiscriminately gobble up everything in sight, identifying themselves as consumers rather than as citizens in this mass-consumption society. For contemporary people who form their identities through consumption, purchasing certain goods and services helps to establish their individual identity as part of the national collective. Nationalism has been repackaged to appear as an individual's consumer choice. Reflecting the infantile nature of this process, we call this identity constructed by consuming national goods "me-istic nationalism."

Takao Osawa performed his internalized image of the "ordinary Japanese man" Nishizaki. Eisaku Yoshida portrayed an image of a do-right JSDF officer Saeki. Both are motivated to self-sacrifice in *Midnight Eagle*. The audience watching this movie might identify with the images of ideal Japaneseness; consuming these images and might reproduce them. We might see them all performing the roles of customers and purveyors of me-istic nationalism. In this process, nationalism is promoted by these movies without directly calling attention to the nation-state. Unlike typical WWII propaganda films, the nation-state is not foregrounded here as sacred, but provides, instead a naturalized background. In representing the extreme act of self-sacrifice as ordinary and mundane individual choices, the JSDF films promote nationalism as an ordinary commodity.

As the JSDF increases its involvement with the major mass media companies to make and promote such films, me-istic nationalism becomes ever-more pervasive. In his study of the J-pop cultural phenomenon, Ugaya observed that what appears on the surface to be three separate industries, the interrelationships between pop music, advertising agencies, and television companies in fact form a single compound industrial structure sharing human resources, budgets, and information.[50] We can see a similar formation in the contemporary Japanese film industry, centered on the film production committee. When the JSDF is involved in producing films, the structure integrates with the military-industrial complex. The aim of this complex is to earn as much money as possible while encouraging obedience to authority. People can actively consume anything, while being rendered passive and thus powerless to political matters.

In neo-liberal society, the ideology of equality is reframed to create competition rather than co-operation. Everyone, including the elderly and disabled people, must compete with one another while confronting hardship individually. According to Nakanishi, in contrast to statism or the mobilization of traditional collective ideologies, we are witnessing the triumph of individualization; an internalization of the neo-liberal ideology of self-responsibility in consumer society which underpins me-istic nationalism.

Conclusion

In this chapter, we examined *Midnight Eagle*, a film officially supported and promoted by the Japan Self-Defense Forces, to analyze the contemporary nationalism that it expresses. The film depicts several self-sacrifices, all of which share the characteristic of portraying private issues as more important than public issues. Even though the self-sacrifice ultimately serves the nation, that is of secondary importance. "Being Japanese" significantly defines the characters' identities, but this consciousness is not overtly imposed by the government. Rather, it is formed by mass media images and the meanings attached to commodities and internalized by people who remain unaware that these images and meanings have been subsidized, and sometimes formulated by the government. This is what we are calling "me-istic nationalism".

"Me-istic nationalism" emerged in the context of the ever expanding neo-nationalism and neo-liberalism of the late 1990s. Neo-nationalism in Japan combines traditional xenophobia with bitter memories of WWII while neo-liberalism is a significant contributor to the collapse of social democracy. The "Japaneseness" expressed in "me-istic nationalism" is inseparable from traditionalist notions of the "Japanese people", "Japanese race" and "Japanese nation," arrogantly defending its new orthodoxy.

In the 21st century, borders between politics, economics, and culture are rapidly dissolving as their inter-relationships become ever more complex. Under these conditions, analyzing any aspect of culture requires in-depth consideration of the political-economic background, which today means paying attention to the influence of neo-liberalism. The JSDF films are blatant examples of this situation, with *Midnight Eagle* clearly communicating that sacrifice for the nation may be done for quite personal reasons.

Notes

1. This chapter has been based on Chapter 8 of my book *Jieitai Kyouryoku Eiga: Kyomo Ware Ozora ni Ari kara Meitantei Konan made*, Otsuki shoten, 2013, pp. 192–213. And it has also been retouched substantially with the report delivered at 2nd Flying University of Transnational Humanities in Hanyang University (Korea), June 25–29, 2011 and 2017 TEEP (Taiwan Experience Education Program) Winter Camp at National Chiao Tung University (Taiwan). The choice of "me-istic" rather than the more usual "ego-istic" will be explained at the end of the chapter.
2. The "production committee method" of funding films with the pooled resources of film production companies, publishing houses and ad agencies became common in Japan after 1990. As the copyright is jointly owned by these committees, small production companies consigned to produce the films receive only small payouts. By JETRO *Japan Economic Monthly*, May 2005. (http://www.jetro.go.jp/en/reports/market/pdf/2005_33_r.pdf) (3/2/2013)
3. Director: Masatsugu Higuchi, Production Committee: Fuji Television Network, Toho, Kansai Telecasting, King Records.
4. Director: Masaaki Tezuka, Production Committee: Kadokawa Pictures, Japan Film Fund, Nippon Television Network.
5. Director: Junji Sakamoto, Production Committee: Japan Herald Pictures, Bandai Visual, Geneon Entertainment, IMAGICA, Tokyo FM.
6. Director: Junya Sato, Production Committee: Toei, Kadokawa Haruki Corporation, TV Asahi, Toei Video, Asahi Broadcasting, Hiroshima Home Television, Kyushu Asahi Broadcasting, Hokkaido Television Broadcasting, Nagasaki Culture Telecasting, Kagoshima Broadcasting, The Asahi Shimbun Company, Tokyo Metropolitan ASA Association, The Niigata Television Network 21, Chugoku Shimbun, The Kitanippon Shimbun, Toei Animation, GEO, Tokyo FM, Genkishobou, SUNBOOK, Toei Agency.
7. Gerow, Aaron "Fantasies of War and Nation in Recent Japanese Cinema" "Japan Focus" Posted February 20, 2006. http://www.japanfocus.org/-Aaron-Gerow/1707 (5/17/2018).
8. Director: Koubun Shizuno, Production Committee: Shogakukan, Yomiuri Telecasting, Nippon Television Network, Shogakukan-Shueisha Productions, Toho, TMS Entertainment.
9. Director: Shinsuke Sato, Production Committee: Tokyo Broadcasting System Television, Kadokawa, Toho, J Storm, Sedic International, Chubu-Nippon Broadcasting, WOWOW, The Mainichi Newspapers, Mainichi Broadcasting System, Hokkaido Broadcasting.
10. Director: Takashi Yamazaki, Production Committee: Toho, Amuse, Amuse Soft Entertainment, Dentsu, ROBOT, Shirogumi, Abe Shuji, J Storm, Ohta Publishing Company, Kodansha, Futabasha Publishers, The Asahi Shimbun Company, Nikkei, KDDI, Tokyo FM Broadcasting, Nippon Shuppan Hanbai, Gyao!, Chunichi Shinbun, The Nishinippon Shinbun.
11. "Bugai Kyoryoku Eiga ni Taisuru Boueishou no Kyouryoku-jisshi no Kijun ni tsuite" (The standard for subsidizing commercial films) http://www.clearing.mod.go.jp/kunrei_data/a_fd/1960/az19600818_00160_000.pdf (5/17/2018)

12 Some films can be officially confirmed by interviews with MOD: *Kyo mo ware oozora ni ari* (1964), *Jet F104 dasshutsu seyo* (1968), Other films are confirmed by the journal of the Diet: *Yokaren monogatari – Konpeki no sora tooku* (1960). Others considered by some film critics to be promoted by SDF are yet to be confirmed. We will research these films in a future study.
13 A list of movies released in 1964–2011 were officially confirmed by MOD in 2012. However, as many documents have been lost, it is possible that more films might have been promoted.
14 The most popular recent JSDF film is *Shin Godzilla* (2016) deploying state-of-the-art JSDF armory and positively portraying officers. The film earned 8.75 billion yen ($74 million) at the box office and was celebrated across the media for a long time in Japan. The box office in North America was only 0.21 billion yen ($189,000), though, despite a large number of Godzilla fans there.
15 Harvey, David. *A Brief History of Neoloberalism*, Oxford University Press, 2005.
16 Hardt, Michael and Antonio Negri. *Declaration*, Argo Navis Author Services, 2012.
17 Lazzarato, Maurizio. *The Making of the Indebted Man: An Essay on the Neoliberal Condition*, Joshua David Jordan (translator), Semiotext(e)/Intervention Series, 2012.
18 In this regard, however, the special minesweeping corps participated in a UN mission in 1950, organized by maritime safety officials and civil mariners.
19 Director: Shusuke Kaneko, Production Committee: Daiei, Nippon Television Network Corporation, Hakuhodo, Fujitsu, Nippon Shuppan Hanbai.
20 The 13th party leader of Socialist Party of Japan, and its first Prime Minister since the Katayama Cabinet in 1947–48.
21 Ministry of Foreign Affairs of Japan HP http://www.mofa.go.jp/announce/press/pm/murayama/9508.html (5/17/2018).
22 U.S. President Donald Trump and Kim Jong-un, the leader of North Korea, met in June 2018 in Singapore to discuss denuclearization, but the despite much fanfare, the outcome remains unclear.
23 UPJ, Shochiku (production, distribution, exhibition), Geneon Entertainment, TV Asahi, Asahi Broadcasting, Nagoya Broadcasting Network, Hokkaido Television Broadcasting, The Niigata Television Network 21, Kyushu Asahi Broadcasting, IMAGICA (image development, editing), USEN (music distribution), Destiny (production).
24 For this study, interviewing and browsing documents in MOD was allowed three times on June 30, 2011, September 6, 2011 and February 27, 2012.
25 Imagine Asian Theater in New York, Sundance Kabuki in San Francisco, and Imagine Asian Center Theater in Los Angeles.
26 IMDB: Box Office"Middonaito Iguru" http://www.imdb.com/title/tt0997167/business (5/17/2018).
27 Anderson, Benedict. *Imagined Communities*, new edition, Verso, 2006 (1984)
28 Benedict, Ruth. *The Chrysanthemum and the Sword: Patterns of Japanese Culture* (With a new foreword by Ian Buruma), A Mariner Book, Houghton Mifflin Company, 2005 (1946) p. 194.
29 Referring to the comments by viewing public on web. (5/5/2010)

30 The fact is that there have been some agreements to carry nuclear weapons in Japan as Prime Minister Abe affirmed in 2014.
31 Sakai, Naoki. *Nihon, Eizō, Beikoku* (Japan, Image, the United States – Community of Sympathy and Imperial Nationalisms), Tokyo: Seido-sha 2007. p. 222.
32 *Nikkei Business*, 2007/12/, Nikkei BP, pp. 44–45.
33 Fruhstuck, Sabine. *Uneasy Warriors: Gender, Memory, and Popular Culture in the Japanese Army*, University of California Press, 2007.
34 Sakai, ibid. p. 89–90.
35 ibid. p. 154.
36 The Yasukuni Shrine located in Tokyo commemorates soldiers who died in wars after the Meiji era. As this shrine is one of the symbols of Imperial Japan, it has been a contentious political matter among China, Korea and Japan. Each year, people take note of whether the prime minister visits it or not on August 15.
37 Takahashi, Tetsuya. *Kokka to Gisei*, NHK books, 2005, p. 29.
38 ibid. p. 57.
39 ibid. p. 98.
40 Houmu-shou Minji-kyoku nai Houmu Kenkyu Kai (A study group at Civil Affairs Bureau of Ministry of Justice) edited, *Kaisei Kokuseki-hou/Koseki-hou no Kaisetsu* (Commentary on amended Nationality Act and Census Registration Act), Kin-yu Zaisei Jijou Kenkyu-ka, 1985, p. 8.
41 Zainichi Koreans are ethnic Koreans residing in the Japanese "homeland," many of whom are second- or third-generation migrants.
42 goo blog "WOWOW Tokyo Kokusai Eigasai 2007 (The 20th Tokyo International Film Festival) Soshuhen November 6 (7/19/2012) http://blog.goo.ne.jp/wowow-tiff/e/fcd321e2a38b772ae5ef9ac64b44b406
43 Ueno, Toshiya. *Tasha to Kikai*: Shimizu Akira else *Nichibei Eiga-sen*, Seikyu-sha 1991, p. 112.
44 Kayama, Rika. *Putit-Nationalism Shoko-gun*, Chuko-Shinsho Laclef, 2002.
45 Takahara, Motoaki. *Huan-gata Nationalism no Jidai*, Yousen-sha, 2006, pp. 9–42.
46 Nakanishi, Shintaro. *Shakai wo Hakudatsu sareta Wakamono no Virtual-Nationalism,* Yuibutsuron Kenkyu Nenshi Vol.8, 2003, pp. 98–124.
47 Asada, Akira. *"J-Kaiki" no Yukue*, Voice March 2000, pp. 58–59.
48 Nakanishi, Shintaro. *Kaika suru "J-Nationalism"*, Sekai February 2006, pp.104–111.
49 Ugaya, Hiromichi. *J-Pop towa Nanika*, Iwanami-shoten, 2005 p. 19–23.
50 ibid. p. 93.

3 Collaboration between U.S. Film Industry and U.S. Government for Film Distribution in the Republic of China

Takeshi TANIKAWA

Introduction

This discussion aims to clarify how the development of American movie business in China was planned during World War II, implemented after the war, and failed amid political and economic chaos. The discussion is based on analyses of U.S. government documents as well as Chinese materials and considers the close cooperation between the U.S. film industry and the State Department.

Some important studies have been done in related fields; notably Kristin Thompson, *Exporting Entertainment: America in the World Film Market 1907-1934* (BFI Publishing, 1985), and Kerry Segrave, *American Films Abroad: Hollywood's Domination of the World's Movie Screens* (McFarland, 1997). However, Thompson only explores the prewar period, while Segrave's global perspective provides only a limited description of China. Generally, published English-language studies are based exclusively on English documents, though several examine both U.S. government documents and materials from the motion picture industry. Similarly, most papers by Chinese researchers tend to draw solely on Chinese materials. Recent publication like Ying Jin Zhang; (ed.), *Cinema and Urban Culture in Shanghai, 1922-1943* (Stanford University Press, 1999), or Gang Bian Chen, *The Cultural Consumption History of Film on Shanghai Nanking Road* (China Film Press, 2011) examine both English and Chinese sources, but there have been no studies comparing the postwar American movie business in China with the situation in Japan of the same period. That is the objective of this discussion.

In the 21st century, the U.S. film industry is once again looking at China as a potentially huge overseas market. They cannot draw a blueprint for continuing to dominate the global film industry without China, which now enjoys significant economic growth, although there are problems such as illegal filming of screens in movie theaters and rampant bootlegging unauthorized copies.

While it is correct to say that this is a "renewed interest" in the Chinese market, it is also safe to say that Hollywood's perspective remains unchanged since the 1920s, when it first began expanding into overseas market.

In China, many research papers written relatively soon after the withdrawal of the American film industry from the local market maintained that its failure was due to Chinese people rejecting the contents of the films, recognizing that they were ideologically problematic. They interpreted the event as a defeat for cultural imperialism and reclamation of films for the Chinese people.

Official archives in Beijing, Shanghai, and Nanjing denied my requests to film-related official documents from the Republic of China period (1945–1949). I was informed that access to these documents was temporarily suspended, but was not given any reasonable explanation for suspensions. In Hong Kong, I could only find old film fan magazines. The archives in Shanghai had limited materials filed by the authorities from the magazines at that time. This paucity of available materials might reflect an official view that the modern history of China began with the creation of the People's Republic of China in 1949, when they broke the fetters of imperialism.

Recent studies by Li Daoxin and Wang Chaoguang, however, are much closer to my perspective, recognizing that the main reason for the withdrawal of the American film industry was economic, rather than political.[1]

My research focuses on the war-time preparations to re-establish the American motion picture industry in the Far East, how these plans were implemented after the war, and the close cooperation between the U.S. motion picture industry and the U.S. government in occupied Japan. This research was the basis of my PhD dissertation and a subsequent book.[2]

The American motion picture industry has succeeded in the Japan market but failed in China. The reason behind these different outcomes is the question to be discussed. More specifically, why did it fail in China? There is no doubt that the political situation provided substantial obstacles, and it is tempting to conclude, as many Chinese researchers have that American motion pictures were obstructed by the Chinese government because they contain too many description of corruption or degradation which might be negative influences on Chinese audiences. My argument is that we must focus instead on economic factors. Most specifically, it was the combination of runaway inflation, and tough negotiations with Chinese government officials and the Central Bank of China, that led to the American motion picture industry and the U.S. Department of State withdrawing from the Chinese market.

Motion pictures are an expression and purveyor of culture, rather than "mere" entertainment. Culture is an effective tool for diplomacy, something of which both the American motion picture industry and the U.S. government were well-aware. If the American motion picture industry were profitable in overseas markets, its success would provide the U.S. an opportunity to assert powerful cultural influences on the people of those countries. In other words, it would have both significant economic and political benefits.

To discuss a case study, especially a failed case, is significant enough for studying American cultural diplomacy of today. The following sections focus on the prewar and wartime periods, the postwar situation, and withdrawal of American motion pictures from the Chinese market after the establishment of Peoples' Republic of China.

Conditions until the war ended

Asia as a market for the U.S. film industry

Just before World War I, in the early 1910s, a new industry was born in the wake of invention of the new communication medium: motion pictures. In these times of peace, the movie business became well-established. The buying and selling of films as "goods" transitioned into the buying and selling of the rights to screen them. The *contents* of the films, rather than the films themselves, became "soft" commodities throughout the world.

Destruction of the European film industry during the World War I, the mass-migration of its people to Hollywood, and increasing demand in the U.S. for news reports from the battlefields all contributed to the American film industry's conquest of the global film industry after the war. But in the early 1910s, before the war, the dominant movie business across Asia was Compagnie Générale des Établissements Pathé Frères Phonographes & Cinématographes (C.G.P.C). In 1911, the American consul in China pointed out that "A well-known French company had a practical monopoly on the market" with offices in Hong Kong, Singapore, and other major cities in the easternmost countries.[3]

The rapid growth of American movies after the war brought significant changes in Asia. A 1921 consular report from Hong Kong found that "practically all the pictures shown are of American manufacture."[4] Another report states that "about 450 foreign films had been shown in China during 1926, with 90% being American; the Chinese had made 57 films that year."[5] There were not enough movie theaters in China at that time, though, for it to go beyond "A potentially-promising market."

After the medium evolved from silent movies to "talkies" with the release of *The Jazz Singer* (1927) the situation remained largely unchanged. According to a report in 1934, 67 Chinese films were made in the previous year, only 14 of which were talking pictures. In contrast, 300 American films were screened in China that year. Despite the fact that Hollywood's eight major studios[6] maintained offices in Shanghai and other cities in China by this time, only 20% of the population of China – urban dwellers in large maritime cities – could afford to pay the admission charges.[7] Kerry Segrave, film historian and the author of *American Films Abroad: Hollywood's Domination of the World's Movie Screens*, introduces a 1934 report by Wilbur Burton about China in which he claimed it was not from missionaries, gunboats or businessmen that the Chinese learned about the West but "it is from the cinema… particularly the United States' films."[8]

Coinciding with the birth of the film industry and Hollywood coming to dominate the Asian market was a period of great political transformation in China, beginning with the Xinhai Revolution in 1911. There is no need to go into details about this period, but a brief summary of significant events is warranted: transition from the age of rival warlords, which continued after the death of Yuan Shikai in 1916, to national unification by the Nanjing Nationalist Government in December, 1928; the Manchurian Incident in September, 1931 and the establishment of Manchukuo the following year; the outbreak of Sino-Japanese War following the Marco Polo Bridge Incident in July 1937; the conquest of Tientsin and Shanghai by the Japanese military; the relocation of Chiang Kai-shek's Nationalist Government to Chungking in November 1937; the Japanese conquest of Nanjing (and the Nanjing Massacre) and the formation of the Wāng Zhàomíng government with Japan's support in December 1937; the start of the Pacific War at Pearl Harbor in December 1941; and the Nationalist Government in Chungking (The Republic of China)'s declaration of war against Japan, Germany, and Italy. The major Hollywood studios' Japanese branch offices which had been established in the 1910s–30s (Columbia Pictures was the last opening its branch office in 1933), were closed by the freeze of American assets in July 1941 and their Chinese branch offices were almost all relocated to Chungking with Chiang Kai-Shek's relocation of the capital.

It's worth noting that during World War II, the American film industry willingly and openly cooperated with the U.S. government. Many filmmakers worked in various capacities for the country's war effort. The Office of War Information (OWI) played an important role as the U.S. government's liaison with the American film industry, and many filmmakers were directly employed as OWI staff.

Toward the end of that period, Michael Bergher played a vital role in re-establishing the American film industry in postwar China and occupied Japan. Before the war, Bergher worked as a general manager at Columbia Pictures' Tokyo branch office, its headquarters in the Far East, and during the war he worked in Chungking as Chief Film Officer of OWI. As will be discussed, OWI documents in the U.S. National Archives and Records Administration reveal that upon winning the confidence of the general managers of all eight major studios in Chungking, Bergher finalized a concrete proposal for resuming the importation and distribution of American films across the Far East after the war. This proposal was approved by the U.S. government and implemented as official policy.

During the war, OWI assigned intelligence collection tasks not only to former American film company staff, but also those who had worked in the Far East prior to the war, as well as many locals who had worked with them. It also prepared various preliminary plans for the forthcoming postwar situation. Some of those plans became official doctrines at OWI's Overseas Operation Branch in Washington D.C. Upon receiving approval

Photo 3.1 Michael Bergher (from Eiga Nenkan)

from the China experts in the U.S. State Department, OWI staff was to execute these plans in cooperation with the staff of the embassy to be established after the war.

OWI's preparation of the film policy for China during the war

By May 1945, OWI had established ofices in Chungking, Tsingtao, Kunming, and Yunnan in China. Its plans for after the war, were to establish further offices in Guangdong, Shanghai, Hankou, Tientsin, Manchuria and Taiwan.[9] Among the policies for China, the information policy was approved as "Guidance for OWI Informational Work in Unoccupied China" dated October 24, 1944 and "Long Range Policy Directive for China" dated January 15, 1945. George E. Taylor, a Deputy Area III Director of Overseas Operation Bureau, signed the latter document. This implies that he was the official responsible for the information policies among OWI's policies for China at least at the time of signing the document, the time that the actual postwar period was about to begin.[10]

This master plan states that "Among films specially prepared for China, the most effective for our purposes should be documentaries dubbed in Chinese, inasmuch as our themes can be most effectively portrayed in them" and "On the whole motion pictures carry the most impact and it is therefore of the greatest importance to select those commercial films which most nearly carry out our purpose." Based on experience, the plan also outlines three points to keep in mind when selecting commercial films for the Chinese market:[11]

1. Persons selecting films for China must keep in mind the fact that the Chinese censor will pass foreign films according to his own criteria rather than ours. Observation in the field shows that Chinese censors as a general rule will object to films which deal with (a) imperialism, (e.g., *Drums*, *Gunga Din*); (b) ghosts or spirits, (e.g., Topper series); gambling, highway robbery, (e.g., *Tip-Off Girl*); techniques of jail breaking, (e.g., *Blackwells Island*); excessive cruelty, or films which present the Chinese in a bad light (e.g., Harold Lloyd's *The Cat's Paw*).
2. Films which will appeal most strongly to a Chinese audience, on the basis of box-office records, include Technicolor pictures, especially those with plenty of action or fantasy, spectacles of the De Mille type with extensive pageantry, South Sea or Tarzan stories, and action pictures generally.
3. Types of films which are not popular include propaganda plays, (e.g., *This Land is Mine*), and films containing extensive dialogue which is difficult both to understand on the part of English-speaking Chinese and to keep up with in translated form when shown to the audience on slides adjacent to the screen.

Although "Long Range Policy Directive for China" was dated on January 15, 1945, there is an earlier policy document dated December 22, 1944, titled "Operational Guidance for the Distribution of O.W.I. Documentaries and Industry Films in the Far East." This document was drafted by Michael Bergher and Louis Lober, Chief of OWI Overseas Motion Pictures Bureau. The document covered all major areas in the Far East including the Philippines, China, Manchuria, French Indochina, Thailand, Taiwan, Japan, Korea, Dutch East Indies, Burma, and Malaysia. It provided detailed plans in preparation for the moment after the Japanese were defeated such as how informational education films produced by OWI (these became CIE films in Japan) and feature films made in Hollywood were to be distributed, how staff were to be deployed, and how equipment was to be prepared and transported. The proposal nominated Bergher as Chief Motion Picture Officer, responsible for Motion Picture Officers who handled operations in close cooperation with the military. It also suggested Central Motion Picture Exchange (CMPE) be established to centrally distribute feature films made in Hollywood in both the U.S. occupied areas and other areas in Asia which were to be released from Japanese domination.[12]

We can conclude that this proposal was approved from the fact that Bergher's title appears in subsequent documents as "Chief Motion Picture Officer." Further evidence that this proposal became the U.S.'s official motion picture policy for the Far East can be seen in the fact that Bergher, who transferred to the State Department after the OWI's abolition, was dispatched to occupied Japan to establish CMPE, and took command.

An earlier version of "Guidance on Pictures and Features for the Far East" dated October 13, 1944 had included sections on each country and region, within which were headings advising "What should be done" and "What should not be done." In the sections discussing China, under the heading "What should be done " in films was the advice to: 1) show that Chinese have entered into many phases of our national life, and have been successful, 2) show physical problems involved in getting supplies to China, and 3) show Russia as a cooperating member of United Nations and America is cooperating with Russia and urges other nations to do the same (Examples: postwar planning conferences, military cooperation, and lend-lease). In contrast, the following things should not be done: 1) emphasize Chinese students in U.S., 2) use religious subjects, Chinese are very tolerant but disinterested, 3) use women's (or men's) fashion pictures, and 4) show too much factory mass production materials.[13]

China was considered to be the best prospective market in the Far East (along with Philippines and Thailand) for the OWI's subject matter. The guideline policy stated that "Occupied China, because of the size of its population, will probably be a major scene of our activity, whatever may happen there militarily."[14]

Subsequently, as a motion picture policy specifically for China, another of Bergher's proposals, dated May 15, 1945 was circulated. This one included a detailed discussion of the situation facing film distribution:

> Due to the difficulties encountered in transporting prints to China and within Free China, all local American distributors sell their products to the exhibitors on an individual basis, picture by picture. As a result, the

distribution of our documentaries and newsreels heretofore proved highly inadequate. New arrangements have been made with the distributors in Chungking whereby OWI will distribute United Newsreels and documentaries to various exclusive Chinese theaters. The OWI will continue to assist the American distributors in bringing their features into China from India.

It is also clear from Bergher's records and a letter to Bergher dated May 14 from the Film Board of Trade that all eight major studios with Chungking offices were signatories to this distribution agreement. Republic Pictures, which did not have a branch office in Chungking, was excluded.[15]

In sum, specific and detailed Hollywood film distribution policies for postwar China were prepared as official OWI policy documents by Michael Bergher, who had been involved in the distribution business in Japan and other Asian countries prior to the war. These policies were approved by the State Department, and implemented after the war. This is clear evidence that the American film industry and the U.S. government worked closely together to establish and expand the Chinese market for American films, but the role of former film industry executives in drafting the policies to expand the Chinese market might also suggest that they used their wartime government positions to garner the government's support for their postwar commercial activities.

Development of the postwar American film distribution business

Resumption of the American film distribution business

Following the end of the war on August 15, 1945, temporarily established wartime departments and bureaus were consolidated. OWI was abolished by a presidential decree dated August 31, which was effective from September 15. Michael Bergher was transferred to the State Department, dispatched to occupied Japan, established CMPE, and relaunched the American film industry in Japan, after a four-year hiatus, by screening *Madame Curie* (1943) and *His Butler's Sister* (1943) on February 28, 1946.[16]

Soon after setting the CMPE on track, Bergher handed it over to Charles C. Mayer of Motion Picture Export Association of America

(MPEA), temporarily returned to the U.S., and was interviewed by *Variety*, a film industry magazine on August 14. In the interview, he stated that Japan under U.S. occupation is no longer a difficult environment for American film studios as it had been prior to the war, but China would become a more lucrative market because of the following factors: 1) plenty of money to go into new construction, 2) vast growth in population despite war ravages, and 3) Chinese government is sponsoring film theatres on a considerable scale, and that government leaders look on pictures not only as good business but as a medium for enlightening the people. The article noted that the population of Shanghai alone had grown: "Before the war, it had 2,000,000 people. Today, it has upwards of 4,000,000" and mentioned that Bergher would return to Shanghai as Universal's Far East chief, by the end of August 1946.[17]

On April 13, four months earlier, *Motion Picture Herald*, another film industry magazine, stated "The Motion Picture Export Association will begin immediately to operate in 13 countries: Austria, Bulgaria, Czechoslovakia, Hungary, Netherlands, Netherlands East Indies, Poland, Rumania, Russia, Yugoslavia, Germany, Japan and Korea." It also mentioned that four other trouble spots would be excluded: Spain, France, China and Denmark. It also stated that

> The China Film Society is continuing the Japanese monopoly in China. Further, as an example of current problems, the Export Association had to negotiate for a formula for film rental remittances. It was reported that Chinese exhibitors had reported fictitious charges which reduced box office receipts on which rental percentages were figured by nearly 75 per cent.[18]

Among the problems in China reported by *Motion Picture Herald*, remittance of their earnings was of critical importance. Carl E. Milliken, a vice chairman of Motion Picture Association (MPA), received a telegram from Shanghai Film Board of Trade, informing that Central Bank of China was intentionally delaying the remittances and sales figures for five of eight major studios. These were scheduled to be remitted in July, but there seemed to be no prospect for remittances to the other three studios. Milliken wrote to George R. Canty, an Assistant Chief of Telecommunication Division (later, the Division of Commercial

Policy) in the State Department and Francis Colt de Wolf, a Chief of the Division, explaining that

> The companies are at the moment greatly concerned about the failure of the Chinese official authorities to comply with the 1945 agreement with respect to remittances due to the companies since July 1. As previously advised, it is hoped that the Embassy will bring strong pressure to bear on the Chinese government to complete the remittances for 1945 promptly.[19]

Before joining the MPA and becoming a Hollywood film industry executive, Milliken was a governor of Maine. He had significant influence on the U.S. government's attitude towards the film industry. However, regardless of Milliken's influence in Washington, the Chinese government was a tough negotiator for the American Embassy in China, negotiating on behalf of the State Department.

Motion Picture Herald pointed out another problem; the Chinese Film Society was continuing the Japanese monopoly in China. Specifically, this seems to refer to the Nationalist Government seizing Japan's imperial project for movie organizations such as China Film Company (Zhongying) established in Nanjing in June 1939 by Nagamasa Kawakita following a request by the Imperial Japanese Army; China United Productions Ltd (Zhonglian) established in Shanghai in April 1942; and China Film United (Huaying) established in May 1943 based on the Wang government's "Uniform Act on Motion Picture Business" and built a new film industry system as China Film Company (Zhongdian).[20]

The American film industry (MPA/MPEA) considered the China Film Company to be the local equivalent of CMPE established in Japan and tried to resolve the issue through diplomatic channels. Milliken wrote to Canty of the State Department that:

> China Film Company has been spreading word among exhibitors that it has secured exclusive rights to distribute American motion pictures in China. We would appreciate your cabling, at our expense, requesting the diplomatic representatives of our Government in Shanghai to reassure American representatives of motion picture interests by advising them that no such arrangement has been made and would not be considered for a moment.[21]

But in February, 1946, Secretary of State received a telegram from Chungking stating "Central Cine Service (China Film Company) is not a Govt. monopoly organization. It is merely a commercial agency for the distribution of films" and confirmed that each film studio could freely conduct their business.[22]

But any relief the Hollywood studios experienced was short-lived. On March 1, 1946, the Chinese government announced quotas for American films to restrict imports by limiting the length of films to be distributed. The studios responded by petitioning Milliken between July and November, asking him to defuse the situation. Every time, Milliken attached a copy to another letter to Canty, encouraging the government to resolve the situation. The first petition was from MGM (Leow's International) and it was strongly worded, saying:

> A violent protest should be made through our State Department. After all the help China received from the United States in recent years, I feel that it is outrageous for them to impose any kind of restriction on American merchandise, particularly a commodity which does not conflict in any way with local production. If the Chinese Government feels that a restriction based on footage imported will reduce their dollar obligation, they are greatly mistaken because the earnings of films are based on quality and not quantity of prints.[23]

Subsequently, letters of protest were sent from 20th Century Fox, RKO, and Columbia Pictures to the State Department via Milliken. Canty forwarded these letters to the American Consulate in Shanghai to use in negotiations, but the Chinese Government maintained their hardened attitude.

In August, a copy of a telegraph from the American consulate in Guangdong to the American embassy in Nanjing was sent from Woodbury Willoughby of Division of Commercial Policy in the State Department to Milliken, telling him that the Chinese government announced the implementation of the film censorship on June 3. According to the copy, the system was that "A censorship fee of $2,500 is charged for each 9 reels or part thereof and an electricity charge of $6,000 is made for the screening of the picture before the censorship officials and a fee of $1,500 for the official certificate issued for the film."[24] No evidence of the film industry's response to this announcement was found in State Department documents, but it is notable that the U.S. State Department willingly and immediately notified the film industry about the Chinese government's policy, which would reduce earnings by the Hollywood film industry.

Characteristics of the American film distribution business in China

Such problems plagued the resumption of American film distribution in China. At the same time, though, quite separately from Chinese government officials, the Chinese film industry was expressing a desire to learn techniques from American movies in order to develop movies in their country. For example, in the first issue of *World Movie Industry* published in October 1945, immediately after the war, Xu Xizhen wrote "It is the first time in four years and let's see how foreign films are evolved. Learning a high level of techniques of the motion picture arts from those Hollywood films and other foreign films is a critically important task for filmmakers in China."[25]

A survey of American film screenings from 1945 to 1949 by Li Daoxin and arts students at Peking University, who examined the movie advertisements in *Shen Bao*, concluded that the distribution of American films increased significantly in Shanghai from the end of war though 1946. More specifically, 21 American films were advertised in November 1945, 136 in January 1946, 169 in February and March, and 202 in April and May. The researchers also examined the length of each film's screening, finding that of 169 films screened in February and March, 42 films (24.9%) had screen run of five days or less, 79 films (46.7%) screened for 5-10 days, 29 films (17.2%) screened for 11–20 days, and 19 films (11.2%) screened for more than 20 days. It is noteworthy that of the 169 films, seven were in color, and six of those seven were among those films that screened for more than 20 days.[26]

In occupied Japan, CMPE did not distribute Technicolor films initially because it was too expensive. However, although very few Russian films were permitted to screen, Agfa Color films such as *Kammennyi Tsvetok* (A Stone Flower) (1946) and *Skazanie o Zemle Siberskoi* (A Tale of Siberia) (1948) made a strong impression on Japanese audiences. The competition from such films, prompted CMPE to screen feature-length color films, beginning with the animated *Gulliver's Travels* (1939) and the musical *State Fair* (1945) in April and September 1948, respectively.[27] One-hundred and fifty American films had already been screened in Japan

Collaboration between U.S. Film Industry and U.S. Government in China 71

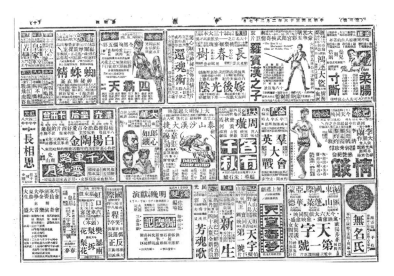

Photo 3.2: Advertisement of Hollywood films in Shen Bao (申報)

since the end of the war when the first color Hollywood film was shown, and 203 films had been screened when the second one was screened. When compared to the situations in Japan, it is apparent that the U.S. Film Industry was making a stronger effort to capture the China market with color films, heeding the advice that "Films which will appeal most strongly to a Chinese audience, on the basis of box-office records, include Technicolor pictures" as discussed in the preceding section.

Although the extent of the penetration of the broader Chinese market is unknown, the rapid market expansion in Shanghai, considered to be the corner-stone of the American film distribution business, was encouraging, and the Hollywood film industry had high expectations. Michael Bergher, as discussed above, moved to Shanghai as soon as the business in Japan was back on track, and MGM, the largest of the eight major studios took aggressive action. MGM launched a monthly magazine *METRO NEWS*, in August 1946 to promote their own films. Tom Farrell, MGM China's General Manager, proudly announced in the second issue that a new MGM-owned movie theater with 2,000 seats would be built in Shanghai within a month and a half.[28] This was probably the Roxy Theatre on Nanjing Road, but the evidence is not clear.

Table 3.1: The Number of American Movies Screened in 1945–1949 (Shanghai)¹

Studio	1945	1946	1947	1948	1949	Total
Warner Brothers	—	123	73	63	1	260
20th Century Fox	—	153	79	75	—	307
Paramount Pictures	17	151	60	14	—	242
Universal Pictures	63	170	66	66	—	365
Columbia Pictures	3	83	30	29	—	145
United Artists	48	24	24	—	—	96
MGM	2	122	36	3	—	163
RKO	1	55	25	22	—	103
Eagle-Lion Films	6	30	32	25	—	93
Total	140	911	425	297	1	1,774

Note. ¹ Shanghai Film History' Editing Committee, ed., Shanghai Film History (『上海電影史』), Shanghai Social Science Publishing (上海社会科学院出版社), 1999, pp. 596–597.

The withdrawal of American movie studios from the PRC

Throughout the prewar, war, and postwar years, the reception of the American films screened in Shanghai, was considered to be indicative of how they would be received across China. Hence, in the immediate postwar years, when it was difficult to acquire prints for screening in China, films were screened in Shanghai first and then sent to other large cities such as Beijing, Tientsin, etc. Therefore, all the American films screened in China were considered to have been screened in Shanghai.[29]

Table 3.1 indicates the number of American films screened in Shanghai during the period 1945-1949. This Table is an excerpt from *History of Movies in Shanghai* compiled in 1999. This data is sufficient to see the rapid expansion of American films after the war until 1949 when they withdrew as well as the conditions of their scale down.

As we can see, the number of American films screened in 1946 increased more than 600% on the previous year, but decreased by half in 1947, by another 30% in 1948 and in 1949, only one film was shown.

Note, however, that the source of this data is not indicated in *History of Movies in Shanghai*, but it might be the advertising data from *Shen Bao* as previously discussed. If that is the case, we must recognize that *Shen Bao* was discontinued on May 27, 1949, so the figures for that year may not be accurate. In the following paragraphs, I will outline the situation until their ultimate full withdrawal.

On September 17, 1946, Dr. W. Y. Lin, Director of Foreign Exchange Examination Department, Central Bank of China informed eight American motion picture distributors by letter that the "bank was prepared to remit only 15% of distributors net 1946 earnings at the official rate, the balance to be frozen." The eight major studios replied through the Film Board of Trade that this was "Inequitable and cannot be accepted," insisting that the "Bank's offer would allow them a remittable amount of less than five cents United States currency per each top price ticket sold (CN dollars 4,000) which amount would not justify the investment and continued operations of their respective offices in China."[30]

A high rate of inflation in the postwar Chinese economy was perhaps an even more significant problem than having their remittances frozen. According to a letter dated May 18, 1946 to the Secretary of State from the American consulate in Tientsin, "The 10% increase in the amusement tax was imposed by the Municipal Finance Bureau" in Tientsin. The letter also stated:

> Other costs have risen sharply since January 1, such as advertising by 300%, light and power by 1000%, together with increases in the salaries of employees, printing, et cetera. However, income has remained at fixed levels in Chinese National currency, the value of which has decreased in buying power, whether for local goods and services or for United States currency in which film distributors must meet a high percentage of their expenses.[31]

Rapid inflation, of course, also affected the exchange rate between the U.S. and China. The official exchange rate between the Chinese and the U.S. governments until March, 1946 was 20 Chinese Dollars = 1 U.S. Dollars but according to a letter from Gerald M. Mayer of MPA to George R. Canty of the State Department dated September 23, 1946, "The 15% exchange basis is based on 2020 Chinese Dollars to the U.S. Dollars from March to July of this year, and on 3350 Chinese Dollars to the U.S. Dollars from August to the present date."[32]

In September 1947, the municipal government in Peiping[33] requested the American consulate to provide films for free of charge every Thursday night and Saturday afternoon for soldiers and police officers' recreation. Nine companies, including the eight major studios (the other is unknown, but was possibly Eagle-Lion Films), rejected this request. The problem was finally reported to U.S. Ambassador J. Leighton Stuart at the end of November, by which time the issue had become a diplomatic problem. This unreasonable request, on top of the problems of inflation and frozen remittances promoted the film industry to temporarily suspend the screening of American film in Peiping, but the move backfired. At a cocktail party in the American consulate on 5 November, Peiping mayor Ho Szu-Yuan said:

> If they do not care much about giving up their market in Peiping, well, we also have nothing to worry about. Local theatres can present Chinese films if they do not have their (foreign) films to screen. Anyway, foreign films are not as indispensable as food is to our living. Moreover, only a very few of the local population view foreign films, and those who completely understand foreign films are fewer still.

The letter reporting this situation concluded: "It can be perceived that foreign films very likely will be off at Peiping."[34]

Behind the mayor's seemingly arrogant attitude, there was a campaign to boycott American films by the fourth estate centered in and around Shanghai, because "American films are corrupt and cause damages to the Chinese people." The magazine 文華 (wén huá), in particular, featured articles expressing this perspective in every issue in 1947.[35]

In 1948, the Chinese government significantly increased the import duty for foreign films. According to a letter to MPA by the Film Board of Trade in Shanghai, dated August 17:

> Whilst on July 28, the cost of importation of a program of 10,000 feet amounted to US$272.00. As of August 7, the cost of importation of the same program amounts to US$800.00. Thus the importation of the above program, including print cost, handling charges, shipping and censorship charges, excluding distribution expenses would now amount to an average of US$1,200.00. The consensus of opinion of the members is that the average earnings of a program in China, based on today's black market

rate of exchange, may amount to about US$2,500.00 [...] We have already unofficially conveyed to the exhibitors that we have stopped importation of films. [...] In view of the urgency of the matter, we would appreciate your directives for our future guidance, as soon as conveniently possible.[36]

Merrill Gay, an Assistant Section Chief of Division of International Commercial Policy in the State Department, replied that

Despite most persistent efforts at Geneva to obtain a concession on the rate of duty applicable to imports of developed cinematographic film the Chinese Government firmly refused even to bind the then existing rate. Therefore, the concession as finally agreed to cover only Chinese Tariff Numbers 656/11-13 and 656/31-39. [...] Thus we are unable to claim that the new tariff rate is a violation of a commitment with respect to the rate of duty.[37]

This resulted in the suspension of exports of new American films to China. Subsequently, the screening of old films quietly continued for a brief period, until rapidly changing political conditions led to the collapse of the Nationalist Government in Nanjing. Chiang Kai-shek transferred the Government to Guangzhou in January, 1949, the People's Liberation Army "liberated" Nanjing and Shanghai in April, and the People's Republic of China was established on October 1.

The PRC government did not take immediate action to suspend screening of American films, but MPA asked the local managers of the eight major studios through State Department via the U.S. consulate in Shanghai whether to completely withdraw their businesses.[38] The local managers replied that "The Shanghai Military Control Council and the Department of Commerce and Industry probably would not give permits to close so long as the companies were financially able to carry on with no total ban on American motion pictures" and "Many of the companies have men which they have employed since the early nineteen thirties. MGM has paid seventeen weeks as termination "advance" but the employees refuse to resign or to accept termination."[39] In other words, it would be very difficult to withdraw.

On December 7, the evacuation of the Chinese Nationalist Government to Taipei was announced. A telegram to the Secretary of State from McConaughy, a staff member of the U.S. State Department residing in Shanghai, dated December 8, explained that they had gotten into a situation where

> 1) Government pressure on MGM-owned Roxy Theatre to show Soviet and Chinese films now strongest, [...] 2) Chinese and Soviet films draw 60 to 70 percent less box office but authorities scoff that education [is] more important than profits, [...] 3) Audience reaction [to] Soviet films [is] not good, 4) Total US remittance by all MOPIX companies since take-over only 10,000 US Dollars and this by subterfuge, and 5) Representatives believe authorities would allow import [of] new films but that prohibitive duty and home office attitude toward lack remittances will prevent import.[40]

The relationship between the PRC government and the U.S. government deteriorated rapidly with the outbreak of the Korean War in June 1950. The Government Administrative Council of the Central People's Government issued five administrative orders such as Provisional Law for Registration for Motion Picture Businesses (電影業登記暫定弁法), Provisional Law for Distribution and Screening Rights of New Films (電影新片頒布上映執照暫定弁法), Provisional Law for Disposition of Old Films (電影旧片清理暫定弁法), Provisional Law for Exporting Domestic Films (国産影片輸出暫定弁法), and Provisional Law for Importing Foreign Films (国外影片輸入暫定弁法) in rapid succession, expelling American films.[41] An association of Shanghai Movie Theaters Guild (上海電影院同業公会) which comprised about 40 movie theaters held an emergency conference on November 11, 1950 and decided to suspend screening of American films in theaters belonging to the association. This was the decisive blow and the American film industry completely withdrew from mainland China.[42]

Conclusion

During World War II, many cities in China were under the control of the Empire of Japan and American companies lost most of their Chinese market along with their Japanese market. Although the American film industry, quietly continued their distribution business in Chungking, a stronghold for Chiang Kai-shek's Nationalist Government, they assumed they would be able to resume developing their business across China after the war and waited for the opportunity while not being able to remit their earnings.

After the war, the eight major studios resumed their film importation and distribution businesses based in Shanghai while asking for support from the U.S. State Department in redeveloping the Chinese market during the reconstruction of war-torn cities. But ultimately, the businesses failed following the establishment of the People's Republic of China and the U.S. movie industry had to withdraw from China for a long time.

This discussion has outlined how the development of American movie business in China was planned during the war, implemented when the war ended, and failed in the midst of political and economic chaos. It also established that the American film industry and the U.S. State Department cooperated and worked closely together (but failed).

This case study of the U.S. film industry's apparent failure in China provides a useful point of comparison with the Japanese case, which I have previously studied. My previous research concluded that the U.S. film industry and State Department cooperated closely to democratize Japan, using American movies as an effective tool. The process helped the American film industry to re-establish a profitable market in Japan.

Chinese researchers seeking to explain the failure of the U.S. film industry maintained that the withdrawal of American films was due to the Chinese people's rejection of the contents of the films. They interpreted this as a defeat for cultural imperialism and a reclamation of films for the Chinese people. But my analysis of U.S. government documents led to another explanation: the U.S. motion picture industry had to withdraw from the Chinese market because of the massive postwar inflation, and the unwavering position of Chinese government officials and Central Bank of China. In other words, it was primarily an economic matter.

Both of these case studies, one successful and one failure, reveals that the American film industry and the U.S. State Department maintained good communication and worked closely together. Although it is unsurprising that a national government would work to protect the profitability of its industries, there is nevertheless something special about the relationship between the American film industry and the U.S. State Department, effectively operating as one body and mind.

Motion Picture Producers and Distributors of America, Inc was founded as a trade association for the major companies in the motion picture industry "to foster the common interests of those engaged in the motion picture industry in the United States."[43] The organization changed its name to Motion Picture Association (MPA) after the war. Its subsidiary organization for exporting films was called Motion Picture Export Association of America (MPEA), and later the Motion Picture Association of America (MPAA). Its web site[44] used to include the statement: "MPA, which was frequently referred to as "a little State Department" from its beginning until today, expanded its area to cover the diplomatic, economic and political stages overseas". This sentence reveals how close the ties were between the American film industry and the U.S. State Department.

Notes

1 Li Daoxin (李道新), *Critical History of Chinese Films, 1897–2000* (『中国電影批評史　1897–2000』), China Film Press (中国電影出版社),2002, Li Daoxin (李道新), *Cultural History of Chinese Films, 1905–2004* (『中国電影文化史 1905–2004』), Peking University Press (北京大学出版社), 2005, Li Daoxin (李道新), *Monographic Study of the History of Chinese Film* (『中国電影史研究専題』), Peking University Press (北京大学出版社), 2006, Wang Chaoguang (汪朝光), *Study of U.S. Films in China during Republic of China Years* (「民国年間美国電影在華市場研究」), Film Art (『電影芸術』) 1st period, 1998, pp. 57–65, Wang Chaoguang (汪朝光), *Study of Market of the U.S. Films in Shanghai* (「戦後上海美国電影市場研究」), Study of Modern History (『近代史研究』), 1st period, 2001, pp. 119–140, Wang Chaoguang (汪朝光), *U.S. Films and Shanghai in the First Half of 20th Century* (「20世紀上半叶的美国電影与上海」), Film Art (『電影芸術』), 5th period, 2006, pp. 37–41, etc. The opportunity of meeting with and exchanging opinions with Prof. Li Daoxin gave me some great insights.
2 Takeshi Tanikawa, *'America Eiga to Senryou Seisaku* (American Films and Occupation Policy)' (『アメリカ映画と占領政策』), Kyoto University Press, 2002.
3 United States of America vs. Motion Picture Patents Co. and others, District Court of the United States for the Eastern District of Pennsylvania, no. 889 (Sept. Session, 1912), vol. 3, pp. 1765, 1968; Kristin Thompson, *Exporting Entertainment: America in the World Film Market 1907–1934*, BFI Publishing, 1985, p. 33.
4 Leroy Webber, 'The Hong Kong Motion-Picture Trade', Commerce Reports, 29 Oct. 1923, p. 294; Thompson, p. 143.
5 Richard C. Patterson Jr., 'The Cinema in China', *New York Times*, 23 Jan. 1927, Sec. 7, p. 7; Thompson, p. 144.
6 MGM, Paramount, 20th Century FOX, Warner Brothers, RKO, Columbia, Universal, United Artists. The first five were previously called the Big 5, while latter were called the little 3.
7 Wilbur Burton, 'Chinese Reactions to the Cinema', Asia, 34:594, Oct, 1934.

8 Kerry Segrave, *'American Films Abroad: Hollywood's Domination of the World's Movie Screens'*, McFarland, 1997, p. 100.
9 OWI Information Plan for China (Draft), May 21, 1945, Central Records of the Department of State: Records of the Division of Chinese Affairs: Subject File 1944-47, Box 4, Lot File 110, RG59, NARA.
10 Long Range Policy Directive for China, January 15, 1945, Central Records of the Department of State: Records of the Division of Chinese Affairs: Subject File 1944-47, Box 4, Lot File 110, RG59, NARA.
11 Long Range Policy Directive for China, p. 12.
12 Operational Guidance for the Distribution of O.W.I. Documentaries and Industry Films in the Far East, December 22, 1944, Records of OWI, Records of Overseas Branch 1942–45, Box 2, "Overseas Branch Motion Picture Branch Jan–Feb 1945" Folder, RG208, NARA.
13 Guidance on Pictures and Features for the Far East, Revised October 13, 1944, Records of OWI, Records of Overseas Branch 1942-45, Box 2, "Overseas Branch Motion Picture Branch Oct–Dec 1944" Folder, RG208, NARA.
14 op. cit.
15 Office of Outpost Representative for China, Memorandum (Copy of letter from Michael Bergher, Chief of Motion Picture Distribution, Area III to Mr. Peters and Mr. Louis Lober regarding Film Operations – China, dated May 15, 1945), Jun 2–3, 1945, Records of OWI, Records of Overseas Branch 1942–45, Box 2, "Overseas Branch Motion Picture Branch, May 1945" Folder, RG208, NARA.
16 Takeshi Tanikawa, *'America Eiga to Senryou Seisaku* (American Films and Occupation Policy)', Kyoto University Press, 2002, pp. 265–305.
17 'China Looming as U.S. Film' Biggest Far East Market; Gov't Lends Hand', *Variety*, Vol. 163, No. 10, August 14, 1946.
18 'Majors Pool Strength to Share Europe and Asia', *Motion Picture Herald*, April 13, 1946.
19 Letter from Carl E. Milliken, Motion Picture Association, to George R. Canty, Assistant Chief, Telecommunication Division, Department of State, March 5, 1946, 893.4061/3-546, and Letter from Carl E. Milliken, Motion Picture Association, to Francis Colt de Wolf, Chief, Telecommunication Division, Department of State, March 11, 1946, 893.4061/3-1146 (Microfilm), RG59, NARA.
20 Yau Shuk-ting, *'Hong Kong – Nihon Eiga Kouryuushi: Asia Eiga Network no Roots wo Saguru'*, Tokyo University Press, 2007, pp. 52–59, pp. 338–345. Yau Shuk-ting, Kinnia, *Japanese and Hong Kong Film Industries: Understanding the origins of East Asian film networks*, Routledge, 2010, pp. 20–24, p. 234.
21 Letter from Carl E. Milliken, Motion Picture Association, to George R. Canty, Assistant Chief, Telecommunication Division, Department of State, October 17, 1945, 893.4061/10-1745 (Microfilm), RG59, NARA.
22 Department of State Incoming Telegram from Chungking via War, to Secretary of State, February 19, 1946, 893.4061/2-1946 (Microfilm), RG59, NARA.
23 Letter from M.A. Spring, Leow's International Corporation, to C. Milliken, Motion Picture Association, June 27, 1946, 893.4061/6-2846 (Microfilm), RG59, NARA.

24 Letter from Woodbury Willoughby, Assistant Chief, Division of Commercial Policy, to C. Milliken, August 12, 1946, 893.4061/8-1446 (Microfilm), RG59, NARA.
25 Xu Xizhen (許席珍), *Forward – Acquiring Higher Standard of Motion Picture Art* (「学取更高的電影芸術水準—代発行辞」). The World of Movies (『世界映画界』) Inaugural Issue, October 1945, Ding Yaping (丁亜平), *Moving Images of China: Chinese Motion Picture Art 1945–1949* (『影像中国—中国電影芸術 1945–1949), Cultural Art Publishing (文化芸術出版社), 1998, p. 264.
26 「影像与影响：" 《申報》与中国電影"研究之二」、Li Daoxin (李道新), *Monographic Study of the History of Chinese Film* (『中国電影史研究専題』), Peking University Press (北京大学出版社), 2006, pp. 249–272.
27 Takeshi Tanikawa, 'Senryouka Nihon niokeru Beiso Eigasen: Soutennenshoku Eiga no Yuuwaku (U.S.–Soviet Cinema War in Occupied Japan: Seduction of Color Films)', *Intelligence*, Vol. 7, pp. 71–80.
28 MGM To Build Theatre Here, *METRO NEWS* (米高梅影訊), Vol. 1 No. 3, September 15, 1946, p. 16.
29 Wang Chaoguang (汪朝光), *Study of U.S. Films in China during the Republic of China Years* (「民国年間美国電影在華市場研究」), Film Art (『電影芸術』) 1st period, 1998, p. 58.
30 Department of State Incoming Telegram from Shanghai via War, to Secretary of State, December 5, 1946, 893.4061/12-546 (Microfilm), RG59, NARA.
31 Letter from M.S. Myers, American Consul General, Tientsin, to the Secretary of State, May 18, 1946, and Letter from M.S. Myers, American Consul General, Tientsin, to Yang Pao-Ling, Esquire, Director, Foreign Affairs Department, Tientsin Municipal Government, April 13, 1946, 893.4061/5-1846(Microfilm), RG59, NARA.
32 Letter from Gerald M. Mayer, Associate Manager, MPA, to George Canty, Assistant Chief, Division of Commercial Policy, Department of State, September 23, 1946, 893.4061/9-2346 (Microfilm), RG59, NARA.
33 Peiping or Beiping (北平) was the name used for Beijing from 1368 to 1403, and from 1928 to 1949.
34 Letter from O. Edmund Clubb, American Consul General, to J. Leighton Stuart, American Ambassador, Nanking. November 28, 1947; Enclosure No.3: Memo of Shih Chih Wan Pao, November 6, 1947,893.4061/11-2847(Microfilm), RG59, NARA.
35 For Example, 清漣, *American Motion Pictures Which Makes the Souls Lost* (「美國電影的迷魂陣」), 『文華』, Vol. 2, No. 14 (第2年第14期) (January 9, 1947), 余平譯, *Hollywood Way of Imperialism* (「好萊塢的帝国主義」), 『文華』, Vol.2, No. 20 (第2年第20期) (February 20, 1947), 李何林, *American Motion Pictures Poisons* (「美国電影的毒害」), 『文華』, Vol. 2, No. 23 (第2年第23期) (March 20, 1947) etc. All these articles are from Shanghai Municipal Archives.
36 Cited in a letter from John G. McCarthy, Associate Manager, MPA to Merrill Gay, Assistant Chief, Division of Commercial Policy, Department of State, August 24, 1948; Letter from Film Board of Trade (China) to Motion Picture Association, August 17, 1948 (Copy), 893.4061/8-2448 (Microfilm), RG59, NARA.

37 Letter from Merrill Gay, Assistant Chief, Division of Commercial Policy, Department of State to John G, McCarthy, Associate Manager, MPA, September 10, 1948 (Copy), 893.4061/8-2448 (Microfilm), RG59, NARA.
38 Letter from W. T. M. Beale, Acting Chief, Division of Commercial Policy, Department of State to Theodore Smith, International Division, Motion Picture Association, October 11; Enclosure 1: Text of Communication to American Consulate General at Shanghai, 893.4061/10-1149 (Microfilm), RG59, NARA.
39 Enclosure 2: Text of Communication from American Consulate General at Shanghai, 893.4061/10-1149 (Microfilm), RG59, NARA.
40 Department of State Incoming Telegram from Shanghai to Secretary of State, December 8, 1949, 893.4061/12-849 (Microfilm), RG59, NARA.
41 Rao Shuguang, Shao Qi (饶曙光・邵奇), *The First Movement in New China: Clean Up Hollywood Films* (「新中国電影第一次運動：清除好萊塢電影」), Film Art (『当代電影』), No. 5, 2006 (2006年第5期), p. 121.
42 Xiao Zhiwei, Yin Hong (萧知纬、尹鴻), *Hollywood in China: 1897–1950* (「好萊塢在中国：1897–1950年」), Film Art (『当代電影』) No. 6, 2005 (2005年第6期), p. 73.
43 http://mppda.flinders.edu.au/history/mppda-history/
44 http://www.mpaa.org/about/history The description was on the site at least until 2004, but then disappeared. The quote above is paraphrased based on the author's memory. But the explanation of MPA on the web page of Japan and International Motion Picture Copyright Association uses the same description. (http://www.jimca.co.jp/about/about_mpa.html). See also Paul Swann, *The Little State Department: Hollywood and the State Department in the Postwar World*, American Studies International, Vol. 29, No. 1 (April 1991), pp. 2–19.

4 WWII Film Production in Chongqing: *The Japanese Spy*

Yanli HAN

Introduction

The author has been investigating the state of film production in film studios managed by the Chinese government from the beginning of the Second Sino-Japanese War in 1937. Two government-run film studios, the Central Film Studio and the China Film Studio, were established to produce so-called national defense films in Wuhan and Chongqing, each of which had been the temporary Chinese government capital for a short period during the war. Soon after these companies were established, Chinese government produced propaganda films became prevalent.[1]

As well as encouraging the Chinese people to develop a fighting spirit, these national defense films told epic tales self-consciously pitched at foreign audiences. In November 1937, the International Propaganda Division was established, with responsibility for all Chinese government overseas propaganda. Its main goal was to "expose (the international community) to the assault of the Japanese Army and gain sympathy from international public opinion."[2] The films were considered to be influential external publicity tools, and at the time when the term "film exporter" came into prominence, showing national defense films abroad was seen to enable "our friends in the world to not be deceived by enemy propaganda, our war of resistance to gain more sympathy, and us to receive greater and more serious support, effectively restraining the enemy."[3]

The Japanese Spy was released in Chongqing in 1943 and is representative of these propaganda films aimed at international audiences. Several local newspapers promoted this film from the time of its production, calling it an "international epic." At the film's premiere, the important government official and military leader Zhang Zhizhong gave a speech stating that "the significance of this film is that it particularly emphasizes international publicity."⁴

The Japanese Spy was inspired by Amleto Vespa's book *Secret Agent of Japan* (1938), based on Vespa's personal experiences. Vespa was an Italian with Chinese citizenship; his Chinese name was Fan-Sibo (範斯伯). He had lived in China for many years as a professional spy, initially working for Zhang Zuolin, the supreme ruler of Manchuria. After the Manchuria Incident in 1931, he became a special agent for the Doihara arm of the Japanese Army. In 1936, Vespa escaped from Manchuria to Shanghai, and the following year, published *Secret Agent of Japan* in English. The book divulged the inner workings of Japan's Manchurian colonization. It was also published in Britain and the U.S. Both Vespa's personal experiences and this book recording them were unique for war-time publications; the book's film adaptation was also considered unique. Based on materials such as newspapers and publications from the time, this chapter begins with an examination of the process of how this unique work was created, and then analyses the context of this Chinese national defense film in detail. .

Amleto Vespa and his book

Harold John Timperley wrote the foreword to Amleto Vespa's book. Timperley was a reporter for the *Manchester Guardian*, a leading newspaper in Britain. This foreword provides many details of Vespa's personal history and the various events that led to the book's publication. Beginning with Timperley's descriptions, this chapter traces the events that led to the creation of this strange book chronologically, while referencing other sources.

Amleto Vespa was born in L'Aquila, Italy in 1888. In 1910, at the age of 22, he went to Mexico. He served as an officer in the revolutionary army and was promoted to Captain. In 1912, he left Mexico and traveled to South America, the United States, Australia, French Indochina, China and elsewhere as a freelance journalist. During World War I, recognizing his knowledge of languages and geography, the Allied Intelligence Agency invited him to join them. His assignment was to follow the Japanese Army, one of the Allied nations at the time. This assignment took him to Amur Oblast, Lake Baikal, and Nikolayevsk-on-Amur, where he developed personal connections with many influential Japanese and Chinese individuals.

After the war in 1920, he received a request from Zhang Zuolin, the supreme ruler of Manchuria or Northeast China (*Dōngsānshěng* in Chinese, including the three provinces of Liaoning, Jilin, and Heilongjiang). He subsequently was employed by Zhang Zuolin's secret military agency. This is the point at which Vespa begins telling the story. Over the eight years until 1928, when Zhang Zuolin was assassinated by the Japanese, "he continued an intense fight for law and order under the most prominent leader Zhang Zuolin using inappropriate weapons."[5] He stated that "I gathered government information and observed the other country's secret military agents. I also hunted down rebels, narcotics, and weapons smugglers, and the white slave traders who were exporting several thousand young Russian women fleeing from the revolution. I also hindered Japanese and Soviet activities."[6] Vespa apparently saw himself fighting on the side of law and order in Manchuria at a time when things were incredibly complex. He was granted Chinese citizenship in 1924.

After Zhang Zuolin's death, Vespa made a living through commercial enterprise for a short while. After Japan established its control over Manchuria on February 14, 1932, Vespa was called by Kenji Doihara and ordered to join Japan's secret military agency (Doihara was its head).

According to Ohara Kaname, former manager of the *Manchuria Daily Bulletin*, there were two main reasons for Vespa being drafted as a special agent by Japan. First, Vespa knew the local conditions and had many influential contacts in Harbin, a prosperous international city at the time, and home – at least temporarily – to many foreign nationals whose support and trust was required to procure military funds. Second, an unregulated anti-Japanese military resistance of more than 100,000 people was persistently attacking the Japanese all across Manchuria. Vespa was an old friend of several of the rebel commanders from his time in the Zhang Zuolin administration, and the Japanese believed that Vespa could be of assistance in forcing the rebels into submission.[7]

Vespa worked for the Japanese secret military agency in Manchuria for four and half years, until the Japanese threatened his family, and he escaped in September 1936. In principle, Vespa was perhaps not resistant to serving as a spy for either Japan or China; however, he writes that he disliked Japan's strategic activities and unjust actions in Manchuria, that he followed orders because he had no other choice. He also felt animosity toward the Japanese because they put his family under strict surveillance, seized his assets, and did not pay him, all to prevent his escaping. But the Japanese had good reason to doubt him, for Vespa was secretly supplying information about the Japanese Army to the anti-Japanese guerilla forces through his former contacts. When Vespa realized that the Japanese knew of his double-dealings, he escaped from Manchuria to Shanghai in the fall of 1936, leaving his family behind. His wife and family were imprisoned in Manchuria but managed to escape, reaching Shanghai more than six months later in February 1937. With his family safe, he commenced writing the book that would expose the inner workings of the Japanese secret military agency.

Vespa's book has fourteen chapters. The first chapter recounts his time in the Zhang Zuolin period, and the last chapter describes the events that led to his escape from Manchuria. Chapters 2 to 13 provide vivid descriptions of Japanese misdeeds in Manchuria, such as the persecution of and atrocities committed against Chinese, Russians, and Jews, the human trafficking and prostitution of Japanese women, the monopoly on opium sales and opium dens, the abduction and ransoming of wealthy citizens, and the deception of the League of Nation's Review Committee. The chapters titles are as follows:

Chapter One	Introduction
Chapter Two	Japanese Occupation of Mukden
Chapter Three	Interview with Doihara
Chapter Four	Duties Assigned
Chapter Five	My Subordinates
Chapter Six	Prostitution and Narcotics
Chapter Seven	Trapped by the Japanese Army
Chapter Eight	Revenge
Chapter Nine	The Lytton Commission
Chapter Ten	Commendations and Entertainment
Chapter Eleven	The Patriotic Irregular Forces and Rebels
Chapter Twelve	Abductions
Chapter Thirteen	Money
Chapter Fourteen	Journey to Escape

Vespa clearly specifies dates, locations, and perpetrators' names. He states, "I have not described anything but real facts in this book. These are the realities I saw with my own eyes, and these are the incidents that I reluctantly took part in almost every time. I haven't described anything other than that."⁸ He insists that this book was entirely nonfiction. Vespa handed over the completed manuscript to Timperley. Referring to what he had just read as "like an unbelievable nightmare,"⁹ after perusing the manuscript, Timperley asked three others to read it – a coworker, a diplomat friend, and Edgar Snow, the author of *Red Star over China* – to judge its authenticity and veracity.

His diplomat friend asked to meet Vespa and spoke to him at length several times.

All three reviewers of Vespa's story believed it to be true. Timperley, who had visited Manchuria as a magazine and newspaper reporter from 1933 to 1935, concluded that "most of Vespa's extraordinary book must be acknowledged as truth."¹⁰

Thus, Amelto Vespa, a secret agent in the Kwantung Army, and a double agent for guerrilla resistance fighters, exposed the strategic operations of the Japanese Kwantung Army after the Manchurian Incident. His criticisms and revelations had great appeal to the international reading public, and thus the book was published in both Britain and the U.S.¹¹ In 1939, it was translated into Chinese and published in Chongqing. In 1946, a Japanese translation was published under the title *A Secret History of the Invasion of China: The Notes of an Officer in the Secret Military Agency*.

Before the "first Chinese international epic" was created

In February 1939, Vespa's book was published by the People's Publishing Company in Chongqing, titled *A Child of God is in China: The Autobiography of One Japanese Spy*.¹² In April of the same year, the government-run Central Production Studios, which had moved to Chongqing, decided to make it into a film. One of the reasons for making this film was that the Chinese version of Vespa's book had been well-received and had become a popular conversation topic. Furthermore, it was also considered to be an appropriate subject for an international propaganda film because the author and many people in the book were European and the story had also been published in English.

After the film was released, Yuan Congmei, the director, thought back on the events that led to the book being selected for production. He said,

> I was surprised that the content (the original work) faithfully presented the facts! Moreover, they were all real things that Vespa witnessed himself. I felt

the need to choose this as the subject matter for publicity, and we decided to make a good film based on the original work.[13]

The Central Production Studios had moved from Wuhan to Chongqing in September 1938, and in April '39, construction of the studio was partially completed. *The Japanese Spy* was one of several films to be made in the relocated studio. In September 1939, construction was completed, and the famous playwright Yang Hansheng completed the script for the film. According to a series of newspaper stories related to the production of the film, the shooting of the studio scenes had been nearly completed by the end of 1940, and in 1941, the film crew began shooting on locations in northwestern China such as in the Shanxi province. The film production appeared to be going smoothly. Predictions of its completion were reported several times, but the completion date kept being pushed back. *The Japanese Spy* was finally released in April 1943. From its inception to completion, it had taken four years to complete.[14]

There were several reasons for this lengthy production period. First, during the war, the conditions for filming were often poor. Chongqing, the capital of the Republic of China at the time, was subject to frequent Japanese air raids, which continuously disrupted filming. The Central Production Studio was directly hit by bombs during air raids in both 1939 and 1941, suffering extensive damage on both occasions.[15] Even on days when there were no air raids, there were regular power outages and irregular currents. And when the Pacific War began, routes for importing necessary goods such as film stock, equipment, and chemicals were blocked.

While such conditions made the production of an epic film such as *The Japanese Spy* seem impossible, the main reason the film fell far behind its anticipated schedule was much more mundane.

Filming in the cosmopolitan city of Harbin, where much of the story is set, was difficult at the best of times. Located in the mountain recesses in China's northeastern region where the weather can become extremely cold, it was very difficult to recruit people from the different nationalities who lived there to perform in the film and recreate the scenes from the book. Even in Shanghai, known as the "Hollywood of the east," no films of this scale were being produced. In the group scenes, there were English, American, and Soviet residents;[16] but there were not enough actors available to perform the roles of all the foreigners who appeared in the book. To overcome this obstacle, special makeup was used for Chinese actors playing the roles of foreigners, including the main character. The foreigners' wardrobe was similarly contrived; overall, it was very difficult to make this film in a regional city during a world war.[17] In the end, to complete this epic film, "four million yuan was spent, and around 10,000 people were mobilized."[18]

The "international epic" was finally released on April 20, 1943 after a very turbulent production process. More than 1000 people attended the premiere, including many important government officials and prominent social figures. As previously mentioned, Zhang Zhizhong, then Minister for Political Training, gave the opening speech.[19] After the official opening, the film was shown in several theaters in Chongqing, attracting full houses for several days. However, this success only lasted a week. The film screenings ceased on 28 April. A newspaper reported that "there was damage to the film while it was being transported, and therefore the screenings were suspended." Another newspaper article on May 17 reported that a "new copy of the film was completed,"[20] but the film's re-release was much less enthusiastically received. The film reportedly was sent to film associations in Europe and America; but, no reports of its overseas publicity reception have been found. Seventy years after the film's release, both in mainland China and Taiwan, *The Japanese Spy* is not highly rated at all.

Advertised from the very beginning as "China's first international epic," "a magnificent national defense film," and "the most important page in the history of Chinese cinema," was *The Japanese Spy* a complete failure as a creative work? As mentioned above, large-scale films were not even being produced in Shanghai, at the time, the center of Chinese cinema until 1937. None of the many private film companies in Shanghai had the type of assets and abilities necessary to mobilize such large numbers of people. In effect, the beginning of the war provided an opportunity to develop China's first government-run film production company. The studios' government support included the ability to borrow military equipment such as machine guns and fighters, and allowed this film with an extraordinary budget and a long production schedule to be made, in the midst of a world war. Although the work was not a box office success, this is probably how it should be remembered in Chinese cinema history.

The production process for this film was a common topic of conversation for several years in Chongqing, being continuously reported about in local newspapers during its long production. For example, from late 1939, after the decision to make the film had been made, several articles seeking temporary actors were published. One article stated:

> we need more than 100 people to play Japanese women, more than 200 people to play Japanese POWs, 6 people to play Russian investigators, 3000 to play the volunteer army, more than 400 people to play Japanese military police, and around 10,000 people to play groups of foreigners or Chinese people."[21]

One month later, another article reported that they "are conducting interviews for more than 500 applicants from the age of 15–40."[22] When the set of a Japanese style red light district was built to shoot scenes in brothels, the film again attracted attention. Several rounds of invitations were sent to invite Chongqing newspapers and government officials, including Guo Moruo – head of the third government office at the time – to come to the set. Each of these events was reported in the newspaper, introducing the scene that was being shot.

After visiting the set, Guo Moruo praised it highly saying that "even Japanese people wouldn't be able to see through" the Chinese actors who played the Japanese prostitutes.[23] Even though it was during the war, stereo-types of Japanese did not necessarily evoke contempt among the Chinese people; instead, these newspaper articles indicate a sense of curiosity about Japanese culture. As mentioned, regular news reports about the film continued for four years, exceeding the text of the film script itself, and becoming an important part of the cultural discourse in the capital of China at the time. Hence, it is safe to assume that this was a popular topic of conversation in Chongqing throughout the long production process.

About the film *The Japanese Spy*

When watching *The Japanese Spy*, we certainly realize that it has a deeply "international character." This is not only because more foreigners than Chinese people appear in the film but also because several shots include English letters or English-language newspapers. Furthermore, the credits include a translation of the director's name in English, "Directed by James Yuan," which was exceptional for a Chinese film.

As previously discussed, though, this film was not commercially successful either within or outside the country. As we will see, its shortcomings were unrelated to the material conditions of the war; but rather because many scenes in the film appear to have had effects rather the opposite of what had been intended for international propaganda purposes.

We can identify three key points in this film through in-depth analyses of concrete examples.

Representation of the Japanese

It was difficult to adapt Vespa's original style into a film; but a more faithful reproduction his original realistic reporting might have helped audiences both within and outside China to understand the situation in Manchuria.

Specific events were generally depicted accurately; but two of the main characters, the head of Japan's secret military agency and the lieutenant in the Japanese military police, were depicted as stupid and comic. This may have been intended to increase contempt for Japan and the Japanese; but unfortunately, these two-dimensional comical depictions lacked authenticity.

Vespa portrayed the head of Japan's secret military agency who tortured civilian Russians and Chinese and the military police lieutenant who indiscriminately committed atrocities in the following way in his book:

> He was a man who was unpleasant to look at, who was stunted to the point that it was funny, and who had bent looking legs. He constantly licked his lips, and to make it even worse, he had an overbite and his teeth stuck out from his lips at a 45-degree angle.[24]

The make-up shown in Photo 4.1 was based on this description; however, the actor delivered his lines and gestures exaggeratedly. A scene not in the original work depicts the military police lieutenant tearing an American flag in half (Photo 4.2). This was inserted to trigger American hostilities, a call to arms to China's allies at the time of filming; but in the Manchuria depicted in Vespa's book, that is, the Manchuria between 1932 and 1936, this was nearly inconceivable.

Photo 4.1: The Japanese Spy

Photo 4.2: The Japanese Spy

Vespa's contemptuous portrayal of the military police lieutenant may have left scope for this representation in the film; nonetheless, the representation of the head of the Japanese secret military agency, and his lieutenant are much more comical, and hence less sinister, in the film than in the original work.

In the original work, the head of the secret military agency spoke nearly perfect English, and Vespa thought that "he had undoubtedly lived abroad for a long time or had lived in America." He was also depicted as a character with "uncommon wisdom." However, in the film, he does not speak English and tells Vespa to speak in Chinese. Moreover, he is depicted as a hysterical person, the opposite of wise. He flies into rages evocative of epileptic

Photo 4.3: The Japanese Spy

Photo 4.4: The Great Dictator

fits, and frequently takes a medicine from his pocket when this happens. Furthermore, the scene in which he smirks as he spins a globe in his hand and talks about the ambitions of the Empire of Japan was clearly intended to associate him with Hitler, who had recently been parodied by Charlie Chaplin in *The Great Dictator* (1940; Photos 4.3 and 4.4).[25] The Chaplin film, however, was a comedy, skillfully using exaggeration to produce a satirical effect. In an epic drama such as *The Japanese Spy*, which claimed to present truth and authenticity, such exaggerated performances were inappropriate.

On an interesting side-note about the roles of the Japanese people in this film, at least four Japanese POWs appear in the credits; next to their names "comrades in the war against Japan" appears in small letters. It is well known that dozens of Japanese POWs from a prison camp in Chongqing were cast (including for the main role) in *The Light of the East* (1940); but it seems that very few are aware that four prisoners of war played minor roles in *The Japanese Spy*.

Expenditure on exotic elements

As previously mentioned, the set for the red-light district scenes attracted great interest in China. The depictions of the dance halls, red-light districts, and places for enjoyment, such as tea rooms, appeared to be longer than necessary. This was intentionally done to emphasize the enjoyment. For example, the scenes portraying the red-light district used long shots that slowly panned from left-to-right showing various groups of people enjoying themselves. These included people drinking alcohol in every room, people applauding dances by Japanese women in kimonos, and people embracing under flowers. Finally, a Japanese youth, who gives a dancer a necklace and proposes marriage to her, is quickly refused. None of this was in the original work, which further fueled the claims that these detailed scenes were excessive (Photos 4.5 and 4.6).

And yet these parts of the film received rave reviews when it was released, with comments such as: "several of the shots in the Harbin Japanese red-light district scenes are as good as European and American films." These reviews also praised the cameraman Wu Weiyun who "had surpassed all of the works that he had been in charge of up to that point and had established an unprecedented technical level for nationally made films."[26] Another newspaper reported that

> many young Japanese women were brought from Japan to Manchuria, and all sorts of drug manufacturers appeared like bamboo shoots after the rain. All sorts of gambling facilities stretched around Northeastern China.
> All of this is included in the opening scenes of *The Japanese Spy*. For the last few days, director Yuan has worked day and night. The scenes in the bars, coffee shops, dance halls, and tea houses have already been completed. Director Yuan's admiration for this northeastern hell is insuppressible.[27]

As mentioned previously, the completed footage is far from the image of "hell" portrayed in the book; the red-light district in particular is

Photo 4.5: The Japanese Spy

Photo 4.6: The Japanese Spy

a fun, enjoyable scene of peace and tranquility. The shooting itself was reportedly enjoyable for the director, the actors, and even the news reporters.

The average citizens' curiosity about the exotic sex-oriented entertainment of the Japanese red-light districts was one of the reasons for the long scene about so-called "hell." Another reason was that depictions of enjoyment and pleasure were generally excluded under the strict film censorship during the war; therefore, the producers and audience were mentally "starved" for such delights. The main objective for films made during the war was to increase the people's fighting spirit; content involving pleasure-seeking was strongly discouraged.

Film censorship in Chongqing was strict without exception; in 1943, for example, the year that *The Japanese Spy* was released, 43 of the 143 Chinese films censored were required to remove some content, most of which were scenes depicting possibly "damaging customs" such as gambling, kissing, dance shows, and "obscene" scenes with women, as they did not match the spirit of the times.[28]

Films such as *The Japanese Spy*, though, set in Japan-occupied territories, could depict scenes of red-light districts or opium dens relatively freely under the pretext of realistically displaying the enemy's indecency and depravity. This pretext does not apply, though, to several long scenes which were not in the original work; for example, there is a scene in which a Frenchman, Mr. Caspe, who has been abducted by the Japanese, has an intimate conversation with his fiancé; they kiss and embrace. There is no mention of a fiancé in the book.

This scene was allowed ostensibly because it depicted a foreign couple. In China, only a small number of kissing scenes had been permitted in the films of the 1930s, and all other films released in Chongqing during the war had been required to cut all such scenes. It is notable that such a scene was allowed in a government-run national defense film made in China during the war.

Depiction of anti-Japanese civilian guerrillas

The kissing and red-light district scenes remained in the film,[29] but parts of *The Japanese Spy* had to be substantially re-shot to satisfy the government. The Nationalist Government president, Chiang Kai-shek, was dissatisfied with the depiction of the anti-Japanese guerrilla army in Manchuria wearing civilian clothes and ordered the reshooting of the relevant scenes. To highlight the national army's achievements against the Japanese, all anti-Japanese guerrilla forces were shown wearing Kuomintang army uniforms in the reshot scenes.[30]

Further, in the newly shot scenes, the guerrilla commanders repeatedly said things such as "a new China with the Three Principles of the People" and "our great leader, the military commander Chiang Kai-shek." Moreover, in the guerrilla headquarters in the mountain hideaway, the Nationalist Government's flag, the National Party's national flag, and Chiang Kai-shek's and Sun Yat-sen's pictures were hung in conspicuous places (Photo 4.8). In another shot, a picture of Chiang Kai-shek fills

Photo 4.7: The Japanese Spy

Photo 4.8: The Japanese Spy

much of the screen, and we can hear Vespa saying "China has such a great leader" in the background. All these reshot scenes tell the audience that it was the great Kuomintang army and its great leader Chiang Kai-shek fighting against Japanese.

Unfortunately, any viewer familiar with political situation of those days could see immediately this setting and these lines were completely inaccurate. Chiang Kai-shek had imposed a ban on patriotic guerrilla groups until the Xi'an Incident in December 1936, but Vespa had escaped from Manchuria in September 1936, so everything in his book happened before Chiang Kai-shek and his army joined the fight against the Japanese. In other words, it is not possible that an anti-Japanese government army received orders from Chiang Kai-shek in Manchuria when Vespa was there. Nevertheless, under orders from the leader of the country, the film makers had to "invent" such a scene to satisfy him.

Of course, none of the descriptions in Vespa's original work have any association with the images seen in Photo 4.8.

Vespa described the Chinese civilian guerrilla forces called "rebels" by the Japanese a "resistance movement and public protest movement that opposed and were rundown by the large and unjust military pressure."[31] However, the highest leader in the government ignored the historical facts as well as the intentions of the author and film producer, overriding them with a concrete directive for the film. *The Japanese Spy* might be the first example of this level of government interference in the history of Chinese film. Such interference, unfortunately, has been a constant in Chinese films since then, and such interference invariably serves to undermine a film's accuracy.

Conclusion

This paper explored the creation of the unique film, *The Japanese Spy*. The analysis of this work outlined some of the conditions faced by the film production studios run by the Chinese government during the Second World War.

Government-managed national defense films made during the war were produced for both a domestic and an international audience. Motivated by propaganda value rather than profits, the government was better placed to produce large-scale films than the private industry in Shanghai at the time; but freedom of expression was sacrificed to the state's ideological restrictions.

Notes

1 Han Yanli *A Reconsideration of National Defense Films*, 20th Century Chinese Society and Culture, Beijing: China Social Sciences Press, March 2013, pp. 105–124. Han Yanli *On the Production of Films in Chongqing During World War II- Focusing on 'Light of East Asia' A Historical Overview of the Yangtse River Basin,* Institute for Research in Humanities, Kyoto University, October, 2013, pp. 421–433.

2 Xie Rudi *Cultural History of the War Resistance of Chongqing*, United Publishing House, 2005, p. 156.
3 Shiyan "On 'Film Exporter'," *Xinhua Daily*, January 10, 1939.
4 "On 'The Japanese Spy': A Film that cannot be Ignored," *National Gazette*, December 3rd, 1939. "The Japanese Spy" Last night's main film, hailed as a successful work by viewers, *Cleanup Bulletin*, April 21st, 1943.
5 Vespa, Amleto; Translation by Yamamura, Ichiro. *Secret History of Chinese Aggression: The Notes of an Officer in the Special Agency*, Taigado, 1946, p. 13.
6 Ibid., p. 2.
7 Ohara Kaname, *Secret Military Agents, Vespa's escape from Manchuria*, edited by Hiratsuka, Masao "History of Showa told by the witnesses" Volume 3, the Manchurian Incident—From the assassination of Zhang Zuolin in 1928 until the creation of Manchukuo, Shinjinbutsuouraisha, 1989, pp. 201–202.
8 Vespa, op cit., p. 266.
9 Ibid.
10 Ibid., p. 4.
11 I am unable to determine precisely when it was first published in Great Britain and the U.S., but in 1941, it was republished in the U.S. by Garden City Pub. Co.
12 The Japanese initially experimented with the description of the "child of god," using the term in the title in parentheses, but from the second edition, the title was "The Japanese Spy" or "The Japanese Secret Agent."
13 Yuan Congmei "The Progress of the Production of The Japanese Spy" a special edition on "The Japanese Spy," China Film Studio, 1943. The citation is from Chongqing's Cultural Office Film studio "Films made in Chongqing during the war to resist the Japanese, 1937–1945" Chongqing Publishing Company, 1991, p. 580.
14 Wu Shuxun "The Making of The Japanese Spy," *Xinmin Evening News*, June 26, 1943.
15 Another government-run film studio, the Central Film Studio, was also hit by a bomb in an air raid. According to a newspaper article from May 1941 after the air raid, this was the fourth time that such a thing had happened. *Xinhua News Agency*, May 15, 1941.
16 *Cleanup Bulletin*, April 21, 1943.
17 A newspaper article requested people to provide clothing or winter garments at the time. "On 'The Japanese Spy'—A Film that cannot be Ignored". Ibid.
18 Wu Shuxun op cit. He also stated that 3 million products were manufactured.
19 "The Japanese Spy, last night's main film hailed as a successful work by viewers," *Cleanup Bulletin*, April 21, 1943.
20 *Xinmin Evening Edition*, May 17, 1943.
21 "On "The Japanese Spy'—A Film that cannot be Ignored," op cit.
22 "Summary of 'The Japanese Spy'—Chinese studio continues to seek actors," *The National Gazette*, December 31, 1939.
23 A newspaper article from February 1940, reported that "this week the third on-site meeting about the shooting of China Film Studio's 'The Japanese Spy' was held." "Inside and outside the filming site," *The National Gazette*, February 18, 1940.

24 Vespa, op cit., pp. 97–98.
25 *The Great Dictator* was release in Chongqing in 1942, and it became a huge topic of discussion.
26 Pan JieNong "Excellent filming techniques—The Japanese Spy's Cameraman Wu Weiyun," *Chongqing Xin Min News* April 30, 1943.
27 "Admiration from seeing the Northeastern hell," *The National Gazette*, February 25, 1939.
28 "Emergency Film Inspection Institute (1941–1944): Research on the Film History of the Second Capital," Communication University of China Publishing, 2009, pp. 157–164.
29 In fact, the "Emergency Film Inspection Institute" said that the depiction of the red-light district was "too much."
30 Yang Hansheng *A Battle in the Mud: Memoirs of Film and Television*, edited by Pan Guangwu, "Yang Hansheng's research materials," China's Theatrical Publishing, 1992, pp. 212–213. Furthermore, the dates in Yang Hansheng's diary indicate that the suspension of the film's screenings on April 28, 1943 was likely due to an order from this department.
31 Vespa, op cit, p. 159.

This chapter is a translation of an article originally published in Japanese: Yanli Han, "Senji-chuu no Jyuukei ni okeru Eiga Seisaku ni tsuite – 'Nihon-Kancho wo Tyuusin ni'," in Eks (ed.) *Essays on Language and Culture*, no. 9, Kwansei Gakuin University School of Economics, pp. 71–87, Mar, 2015.

5 Factors in the Establishment of the Animation Industry in Postwar Japan

Tomoya KIMURA

Introduction

Historical research into the Japanese animation industry tends to focus on trends among directors and the other artists involved. In this paper, I will instead examine the Japanese animation industry from an economic perspective.

This paper deals with full-length Japanese animated films that first appeared in the entertainment market in 1958 and the rapidly expanding number of animated television series on Japanese broadcast networks after 1963. By analyzing the commercial processes through which these products were developed from an industrial–historical perspective, I aim to locate the establishment of the Japanese animation industry within the framework of national economics in the postwar period.

Full-length animated feature films for cinema-release

Domestic production of animated feature films

According to Akiko Sano, *Princess Iron Fan* (1941) – the first full-length animated feature film made in Asia – was a stimulus[1] for the continuing production of animated feature films in Japan.[2] Its affects extended far beyond those creating animated films to many others in the entertainment industry. There was a rapid increase in the proportion of mid- to full-length animated films being produced against a backdrop of an overall decrease in the number of films released during the war. Some have suggested that this was, at least in part, due to the fact that the distribution of American animated films, which had dominated the Japanese market before the war, suddenly ceased due to wartime regulations.

The animated feature film *Momotaro, Sacred Sailors* began production in 1944.³ Mayumi Yukimura argues that this project in particular provided valuable experience for animated film-makers. In fact, it created the profession of "animator" as a specialized role distinct from the rest of the production process. This move would be foundational for postwar anime production.⁴

The film-making infrastructure established during World War II for the production of mid- to full-length animated films, however, did not directly contribute to the postwar industry. The animated programs produced during the war were primarily created in support of the Imperial Japanese Navy. So, they were well funded and guaranteed screening spots in the entertainment market. For example, *Momotaro's Sea Eagle* – a forerunner of the full-length animated films that would later become popular – was not only released in cinemas but was also the first film to be shown by the Japan Mobile Projection League, which was created by the Joho Kyoku (Bureau of Naval Intelligence) to travel around Japan and screen films in areas with no theaters.⁵

However, as these films were political propaganda in support of the war, there was no longer a place for them in the market after Japan's defeat. The Shochiku Moving Picture Laboratory, the production company behind *Momotaro, Sacred Sailors* considered producing a full-length animated film called *The Fire Fortress* in support of the Navy. But the plans never materialized.⁶

There was also a suggestion in the postwar film industry that as animated programs required more time production than live-action films, production should not be limited to mid- and full-length animated programs; short films should also be considered. During the war, the Toho Company produced short films for military training, employing many animators and technicians. After the war, however, most of these employees were fired.

A History of Japanese Animation reports that during a period of just over 10 years post-1945, only three works were produced: *Princess Baghdad, Buddha,* and *The King's Tail*. Of these, only *Princess Baghdad* was released commercially in cinemas. In other words, domestically-produced, full-length animated films had not yet become a commodity in the film entertainment market in the mid-1950s.

At the same time, the lifting of wartime restrictions on imports in the 1950s saw the release of many foreign, full-length animated films: *The Humpbacked Horse*, *Snow White and the Seven Dwarfs*, and *The Curious Adventures of Mr. Wonderbird*. Indeed, Walt Disney was releasing one or two films per year.

Continual production and release of domestically-produced, full-length animated films did not truly begin in Japan until the Toei Company released *White Snake Tale* in 1958 – the first full-length, color, animated film made in Japan. Previously, in 1956, Toei had purchased the Nichido Film Company, which had employed animators since before the war, and renamed it Toei Animation Co., Ltd. It took two years and five months to see *White Snake Tale* through from inception to completion. But it appears that most of this time was devoted to consideration and preparation, with the actual production time accounting for only about nine months.[7] When Toei Animation was established in July 1956, there were only 35 staff. By April 1959, it had nearly 300 workers.[8]

After *White Snake Tale*, Toei released one full-length animated film each year. Considering that Shochiku during the war had produced the work with the full support of the Navy, Toei's pursuit of full-length animated productions as a profit-making enterprise was unprecedented. What were Toei's intentions and expectations in creating a business that had no domestic precedent?

The people behind Toei Animation

Hiroshi Ohkawa, the president of Toei Company and, initially, of Toei Animation, described his motives in founding Toei Animation and starting to produce animated programs as follows:

First, compared with other countries, Japan's animation industry was unproductive, and foreign-produced work accounted for most of the films shown in Japanese cinemas. Second, there was a shortage of animated programs for educational purposes. Third, Ohkawa expected that Japan could advance into foreign markets, and fourth, animated works could also be considered for use in television, for example, in commercials.[9] In this paper, I focus on his third reason – advancing into foreign markets.

Here, Ohkawa stated, "the fact that Japanese is not an international language was an obstacle to the export of Japanese films," but a special characteristic of animation is that it "can communicate sufficiently through images and movement alone." Both the Toei Animation Company and researchers of Japanese animation have accepted this as sufficient explanation when seeking to understand Ohkawa's motives for entering the animation production business, without any deeper inquiry.

Hiroshi Ohkawa had worked at Japanese Government Railways before becoming an executive at the private rail company Tokyu, and president of Toei. He was, by all accounts, a manager and not an artist; it is unlikely that he held the kind of aesthetic views outlined above.

More recent research has noted the close involvement of Koichi Akagawa in founding Toei Animation.[10] Akagawa came to Toei from the Manchukuo Film Association, becoming head of the educational film department. One of his roles at Manchukuo had been to investigate animated film projects.

Further examination reveals someone with an even deeper connection to animation: Shin Uehara, who is credited as having written the original draft of *White Snake Tale*. Uehara, whose real name is Akihiro Yamane and whose initial stage name was Noubun (or Yoshibumi), was an artist who had worked in a puppet show troupe before becoming a member of the educational film department at Toei. Yamane's contribution to the document presenting Ohkawa's reasoning demonstrates a profound knowledge of animation, using the word *douga* ("moving image") to refer to an overseas animated feature film and discussing a broad spectrum of artists, including Lotte Reiniger, Norman McLaren, and Stephen Bosustow. Though he may not have had practical experience in creating animations, it is clear that Yamane had some understanding of its techniques and history.[11]

We might, therefore, assume that members of the educational film department such as Akagawa and Yamane, at the very least, supplemented Ohkawa's practical knowledge of animation. It might also be that Ohkawa had an interest in educational films as products, and exports – that is, as a prospect for corporate strategy – and this coincided with the educational film department members' aesthetic interests in animation.

However, we must be cautious when considering the extent to which animation could solve the problem of the Japanese language "not being international." In the present context, when Japanese animation is a highly successful commodity exported around the globe; it is difficult to comprehend the challenges in the 1950s of starting a company dependent on the export of animated films when the very future of animation was uncertain. Here, I would like to examine several documents to reconstruct the series of events that led to the establishment of Toei Animation, with the aim of understanding the surrounding context in more detail.

Animation and Toei's foreign marketing strategy

In 1953, Hiroshi Ohkawa spent two months visiting England, France, Italy, and the United States, beginning his trip on April 15th. In September 1954, Toei established the "Committee for Autonomous Production and Distribution of Educational Films," and in March 1955, the "Committee for Autonomous Production of Cartoons." The "Educational Film Department" was launched in June 1955, and the following November, Toei asked Nichido to produce a short animation, *The Merry Violin*. It was completed by the end of the year. In January 1956, the "Cartoon Production Research Committee" was established. In August 1956, Toei acquired Nichido and launched Toei Animation Co., Ltd.

Judging by this series of events, Toei had been considering the autonomous production of animated films before Nichido produced *The Merry Violin*. Hence, it is safe to say that the production of this film was not what sparked Toei's interest in animation, but was rather the materialization of a pre-existing interest by Toei, realized through Nichido.

What, then, drew Toei's attention to animation? In a report contributed by Ohkawa to an economics magazine after his return to Japan, he wrote about the technology and the scope of television, discussing his interest in the export of Japanese films. However, there was no mention of animation.[12] Ohkawa's interest seems to stem from the fact that Toei was seeking to capture a broader market share at that time.

The Toei Company had been created via a three-way merger between the production companies Toyoko Film Company and Oizumi Films and the distribution company Tokyo Film Distribution Company. According to Ohkawa, when Tokyo Film Distribution was formed in 1949, the three major domestic film companies were Shochiku, Toho, and Daiei, and market research suggested that "a fourth player was feasible."[13] However, in the following year, New-Toho Pictures Co., Ltd. broke off from Toho and began to handle its own distribution, raising the number of major companies to five. Ohkawa regarded this as a cause of deadlock for Tokyo film distribution. Further, Nikkatsu became the sixth main player when it began independent distribution in 1954.

When Daiei's *Rashomon* won the Gold Lion award at the Venice Film Festival in 1951, the companies realized that the market could be expanded by exporting films for a general audience rather than just for Japanese nationals living overseas.[14] This idea drew interest not only from within the film industry but also from the political, governmental, and business sectors as a way of earning the foreign capital necessary for Japan's postwar recovery.[15]

Masaichi Nagata, the president of Daiei Motion Picture Company, emphasized both producing work to present at Western film festivals and forming the Southeast Asian Film Producers Federation, which held its first film festival in Tokyo in 1954. To coincide with the festival's launch, Nagata released the film *Yukiwariso* in India. Ohkawa attended an international film industry conference in Switzerland as a representative of Japan in July 1954, and on the return journey, he visited India. He observed *Yukiwariso*'s success and quickly drafted a plan for collaboration with Indian companies.[16]

Collaborating with foreign companies was a profitable way to forge inroads into foreign markets. However, it was common for such plans to be canceled due to issues concerning the division of profits and international distribution rights. Indeed, Toei's plans for collaboration with Indian companies did not come to fruition.[17]

That was not his only attempt at collaboration, though. Toei Animation's first full-length film, *White Snake Tale*, was originally planned as a collaborative project with Hong Kong after Ohkawa attended the "Third Southeast Asian Film Festival" in 1956.[18] That same year, *The Legend of the White Serpent* was released – a live action film based on Chinese folklore and created via collaboration between Toho and Shaw Brothers Studio. Toei also considered working with Hong Kong-based companies on the projects "Journey to the West" and "Romance of the Three Kingdoms."[19] Subsequently, many works produced and released in China and the Philippines drew on *White Snake Tale*, conveying similar stories of a romance between a male human and a snake that assumes the form of a woman.[20]

Until then, Toei had focused on exporting films to Okinawa, which was still occupied by the U.S. army, and Hawaii. According to the Ministry of International Trade and Industry, around 1947, the American audience for Japanese films comprised "first and second generation Japanese people living in Hawaii, California, and two or three other areas."[21] Hence we can assume that exports to Okinawa and Hawaii were initially aimed at Japanese emigrants and their descendants.

However, in 1957, Toei exported *The Bride of Phoenix Castle*, which was released in a widescreen format in Japan and Thailand. Subsequently, Toei focused on exports to Southeast Asia countries. In 1960 alone, Toei completed export contracts for more than 15 films with Shaw Brothers Studio, which had a distribution network throughout Southeast Asia,[22] and there was potential for more films to be distributed.

Toei ranked second in the number of films exported per region for each of the six major companies in 1960, behind Toho. At that time, more than 70% of film exports were to America (including Hawaii and Okinawa). Exports within Asia, Japan's core cultural sphere, were only 10%.

These conditions are reflected in the films that Toei had produced until this time. In the 1950s, Toei earned vast sums from historical dramas featuring large and diverse casts. But this culturally specific approach did not produce films, such as *Rashomon*, which had potential for success at Western film festivals. In 1956, Toei considered submitting *47 Ronin* (a movie celebrating the fifth anniversary of Toei with an all-star line-up) to the Cannes Film Festival. The "Film Export Committee," though, comprising members from each of the domestic film companies, decided that "based on prior experience, submission of historical dramas is not advisable." They did not submit any film that year.[23] Unlike *Rashomon*, the epic historical dramas produced by these companies were deemed unsuited for Western consumption.

This was not Toei's only unsuccessful attempt to sell films to the West. At the New York–Japan Film Trade Fair in 1957, which Ohkawa attended as head of the Japanese delegation, Toei submitted a period drama called *The Idle Vassal,* which was poorly received and judged artistically substandard.[24] Presumably, Ohkawa found himself increasingly reluctant to attend international film festivals, conferences, and trade fairs as a representative of Japan – both for financial reasons and his personal honor.

Clearly, although historical dramas were appreciated in Asia, a different type of film was required for Western audiences. Toei therefore established the "Committee for Strengthening Contemporary Dramas," which paved the way for not only entertainment but also serious cinema about social problems.[25] For the purpose, Toei invited notable directors, for example Tadashi Imai and Tomu Uchida who is skillful at social cinema. This would lead to developments such as Imai's films *A Story of*

Pure Love and *The Rice People*, which won awards domestically and were even exported to South America. The fame and achievements by directors brought about the opportunity of award and export. It was under these circumstances that Toei produced the full-length animated film *White Snake Tale* to appeal simultaneously to both Asia and the West: The topic was familiar in the Asian market, and animated films were becoming more accepted in the Western market as an artform.[26]

Although early overtures toward collaboration were unsuccessful, exports of *White Snake Tale* earned Toei U.S.$95,000,[27] even more than the *The Rice People* which was the highest earner in Toei.[28] However, Toei's exports were not all so successful. Its next two full-length animated films earned only U.S.$100,000 combined. The company soon turned away from full-length animations toward low-budget, mid-length animated serializations of Manga stories.

Toei continued to export full-length animated films, but 92% of earnings, on average, were used to cover exporting costs. The average profit for Toei's exported film was about U.S.$200 per film. These were extremely meager earnings.

Thus, there was only a brief period during which there seemed to be an opportunity to develop an export-market for domestically-produced, full-length animated films. Soon, mid-length animated films and productions made for domestic television would form the central axis of Japanese animated film production.

Animation for television

On the eve of domestic production

This section will discuss domestic production of animated shows for television.

Currently, the most popular forms of animated television are programs that are broadcast weekly in a 30-minute time slot. However, before *Astro Boy* proved the success of this format, there were numerous forms of animated programs on Japanese television.

First were short animated films originally created with the aim of cinema release or to be sold in the educational film market. Both of these categories included both foreign and domestically-produced films. According to Hisateru Furuta, when television broadcasting commenced in 1953, short animated programs made in Japan before and after the war were broadcast on NHK. In 1956, foreign productions also began to appear, especially short-length animated films from the United States.[29]

There was substantial foreign content broadcast in the early days of Japanese television programs. Shortages of equipment, human resources, and capital made it difficult for Japanese companies to produce television programs. Furthermore, the "Five Company Pact" between the major film companies served to prevent popular actors and content from moving to television. Consequently, in the early days of Japanese television, the demand of cinema for air was filled with imported TV films and created by independent production houses that were not bound by the Five Company Pact.

Second, foreign animated products made for television were also imported and broadcast in Japan. Foreign productions were often the highlight of television programming in the 1950s; according to a 1959 survey, most imported programs were animated, and due to their high ratings, they were considered an extremely good prospect for the future of Japanese television.[30]

Third, Japanese programs were broadcast infrequently. Unlike the "30 minutes per week" format of animated programs today, these were either one-shot programs or very short serialized programs broadcast in the same time slot daily or almost daily.

There were also animated commercials, using both cell and puppet animation. Commercials provided most of the income for the animation production companies at that time. Even a company like Toei Animation, which produced one full-length, 80-minute animated film for theaters each year, benefitted greatly from the quick and lucrative profits that commercials provided.

In fact, the Television Corporation of Japan (TCJ), which would later establish a movie department and produce animated television series, began as a producer of commercials. In 1954, TCJ had already created the short anime *Maya the Bee*, directed by Iwao Ashida, who had also directed animated feature film *Princess Baghdad*. *Maya the Bee* won the special participation award in the non-drama category at the first Southeast Asian Film Festival.

TCJ and Toei Animation were the major forces in domestic production in the animation industry at that time, achieving a degree of success even before the era of animated television series.

The shift to producing animated series was not a supply-side initiative, though; it was demand-driven, a response to the needs of the television networks and advertising agencies. This stems from the economic conditions in Japan after the World War II.

The shift from foreign to domestic production

A 1959 survey found that 24% of all broadcasts on the five television channels in Tokyo were devoted to foreign programs,[31] while foreign-made films for television constituted 30% of prime-time television broadcasting.[32] This dependence on imports was largely due to the relaxation of the foreign exchange budget system that had regulated imports until then. This system was established under the "Foreign Currency and Trade Management Law" during Japan's postwar recovery in 1949 to compensate for the lack of foreign capital, which was a result of excessive imports from countries – mainly the United States – that used the U.S. dollar. This system is the government's centralized management of foreign currency, which was paid by companies. Payments for imports would then be allowed by the government based on a prepared budget, thus curbing expenses and ensuring that foreign currency was mostly utilized for importing essential goods.

This system of governmental approval of imports had two sections: the "Foreign Capital Allotment System," in which each type of currency and commodity was allocated a certain budget that had to be reviewed by the Ministry of International Trade and Industry, and the "Self Approval System," in which imports were freely permitted if they fell within the budget range for a given currency. The balance between these two sections gradually shifted toward the latter; in 1961, more than 50% of total imports were processed through the "Self Approval System." The budget also grew larger, which meant that each year, companies had more foreign currency available to use at their discretion.[33] This expansion of the "Self Approval System" was expected to boost the already-large domestic demand for foreign-produced movies for television. Simultaneously, there was also a fear that fierce competition for promising, but valuable programs could lead to increasing prices for imports.[34]

American movies made for television were also changing. In 1961, criticism from Newton Minow, the head of the Federal Communications Commission, of the excessive violence and commercialism of television programs prompted networks to change their plans.[35] The then Chief Editor of Fuji Television, Shichiro Murakami, traveled to the United States, where he spoke to the senior editors of the three major networks regarding their future plans. He had observed that the networks were beginning to produce fewer of the Western movies that were popular in Japan, and concluded that it would be necessary to reduce Fuji's reliance on imports.[36]

Thus, the television stations in Japan began to consider a major shift toward domestic programming. The initial reliance on imports, especially American movies made for television, was based on Japan's lack of production capabilities and the production costs – imports had been comparatively cheaper. However, with the cost of imports subject to increases due to deregulation and material shortages, broadcasters decided that changes in domestic demand might be easier addressed by working with the production companies within Japan. Their production capabilities were adequate. There was no need to increase imports from other countries.

With these structural changes, it was inevitable that television stations would also begin to consider producing animated programs, which comprised a major portion of imports. The television networks and advertising firms did not have internal production facilities for animation, though, and turned to independent companies that specialized in animation.

Toei Animation and TCJ were already well-established by this point. In 1961, manga artist Osamu Tezuka launched the Mushi Production Animation Department, which was incorporated the following year and renamed Mushi Production, Co., Ltd. In addition to the experimental animated film productions, Mushi Production began work on *Astro Boy*, an animated television series that would become the first program in Japan to be broadcast in weekly 30-minute installments.

From the beginning, *Astro Boy* rated well, with 20–30% of the viewing audience. It provided significant income for various companies through merchandizing and overseas sales. Its contract with NBC valued each episode at U.S.$10,000.[37] These earnings and the program's high ratings, motivated other networks and companies to action.

In 1963, there were four domestic animated programs broadcast in 30-minute installments each week. TCJ's *Eight Man* and *Gigantor* were aired on TBS, whereas Toei Animation's *Wolf Boy Ken* was broadcast on the television station NET (now TV Asahi), of which Toei was a main shareholder at the outset. Japanese animated series began to be exported to America, again drawing attention as "international commodities" that could generate foreign currency.[38]

Nevertheless, companies producing animated programs for television networks and advertising companies faced chronic budget pressures. When program sponsors compared animated programs with the alternatives, it was clear that animations require lengthy production periods and significantly larger budgets. Thus, sponsors had to consider whether the potential income would offset the larger costs; often, it seemed more prudent to invest in the alternatives.

Television networks attempted to seize the rights to the programs' associated merchandise and overseas sales. In some cases the production companies essentially became subcontracting manufacturers. For example, TCJ's merchandising licenses were seized by TBS. Under these circumstances, many production companies found it difficult to operate profitably.

Using exports to compensate for deficits was a practice limited to the very early days of animation. In 1972, ten years after debuting their first domestically-produced animated series, Toei Animation had to implement a major redundancy program in the administration department due to its accumulated deficit. The financial situation of the company was detailed at the time, including the full costings of exported animated television programs: production costs amounted to 88% of income; average profits from one episode were less than U.S.$10, less than 1% of the costs of producing a single episode in color at the time.

Mushi Production went bankrupt in 1973. In 1969, TCJ's television animation department separated from the advertising production department to form its own company, and in 1973, it became a fully independent entity. The income generated by animated television series was insufficient to ensure the success for production companies in Japan.

In the late 1970s, Toei Animation began to vigorously pursue overseas sales of animated television series. However, this venture was little more than a secondary avenue for selling content that had been created for the domestic market. Instead, Toei Animation, along with other companies, shifted its strategy toward obtaining copyright and merchandising rights for programs to earn profits domestically through rebroadcasting and merchandise sales.

Those animated programs made for domestic markets were sold at a reasonable price for western broadcasters because the primary purpose was not export. The unusual and long term programs were convenient for them, too. Ironically, it became a factor in Japanese animation expanding around the world.

Conclusion

Toei established an animated film production company in the context of a movement to export Japanese films, which was seen as a potential means of generating foreign capital during Japan's economic recovery after World War II.

The shift to domestic production of animated television series was stimulated by expectations of steep price increases for foreign films as the import restrictions imposed by postwar policies were lifted. The strength of demand for animated programs also influenced this shift.

Thus, in both film and television, the establishment of the Japanese animation industry was influenced by postwar economic policies.

Animated films and television shows during this period were basically created for children. However, they were produced in the industry as a commodity, and thus, they cannot be separated from political and economic factors. Further examination of the Japanese domestic and international developments would allow for a more comprehensive, empirical investigation of such matters.

Notes

1 *Princess Iron Fan* was an 85-minute animated film by Xinqon Cheung, a producer in Shanghai's movie industry. It is said that the project was inspired by Walt Disney's *Snow White and the Seven Dwarfs* (1937).
2 Sano, Akiko. "Manga eiga no jidai – talkie ikouki kara taisenki ni okeru nihon animation" (The era of manga movies: Japanese animation from the transitional period of talkies to wartime), *Eiga gakuteki souzouryoku – cinema studies no bouken* (Film and the Scholarly Imagination: Adventure in Cinema Studies), Jinbun Shoin, 2006.
3 Momotaro is the famous hero of a traditional Japanese tale. He was born from a peach (Momo) and conquered demons in Onigashima (Demons island) with

some animal helpers. In the wartime films, Momotaro fought against the American and British armies.
4 Yukimura, Mayumi. "Senso to animation – shokugyou toshiteno animator no tanjou process ni tsuiteno kousatsu kara" (Animation and war: Thoughts on the birth of animator as an occupation), *Sociology*, Volume 52, 1st Edition, 2007.
5 "Eiga Junpou" (Ten Day Report on Films), September 11, 1943, p. 212.
6 "Doumei Tsuushin Eiga Geinoh" (League News: Film and Public entertainment), issue number 3101, June 28, 1944.
7 "Toei Juunenshi" (Ten Years of Toei History), Toei Co., Ltd., 1962, p. 247.
8 See "Toei Juunenshi," p. 249.
9 Ohkawa, Hiroshi. "Toei douga kabushikigaisha no hossoku ni attate" (Regarding the launch of the Toei Animation), *Toei kyouiku eiga nyu-su* (Toei Educational Movie News), Issue 14, October 20, 1956, p. 1.
10 Akagami, Hiroyuki. *Post katsuji no koukogaku "katsuei" no media shi 1911–1958* (Post-type Archaeology: The media history of "Katsuei"), Kashiwashobo, 2013.
11 Yamane also had personal connections; he invited Kiyoshi Hashimoto to be art director for *White Snake Tale*. Hashimoto was an artist in the television sector, with a background in theater and performance art.
12 Ohkawa, Hiroshi. "Watashi no mita america no eiga kigyou" (The American film companies that I observed), *Keizai Tenbou* (Economic Outlook), October Edition, 1953, pp. 48–50.
13 "Toei wa big 3 ni hairu!" (Toei enters the Big 3!), *Kinema Junpo*, Late October Edition, 1952, p. 60.
14 Ministry of International Trade and Industry, Business Department, Commercial Affairs Division (Ed.). "Eiga sangyou hakusho" (White paper on the film industry), 1959, p. 38.
15 Federation of Economic Organizations. "Eiga no yushutsu shinkousaku nikansuru youbouiken" (Opinions in favor of policies to promote film exports), *Federation of Economics Organizations Monthly Report*, January Edition, 1954, pp. 30–31. Federation of Economic Organizations, Executive Office. "Eiga yushutsu shinkoujou no mondaiten" (Issues in Promoting Film Exports), *Federation of Economic Organizations Monthly Report*, February Edition, 1954, pp. 53–55.
16 Ohkawa, Hiroshi. "Naze watashi ga nichi'in gassaku eiga wo kikaku shitaka" (Why I planned a collaborative film project with India), *Scenario*, November Edition, 1954, pp. 8–9.
17 *Eiga Nenkan 1956 Nenban* (Film Almanac: 1956 Edition), Jiji Press, 1956, p. 146.
18 "Toei to Hong kong ga gassakueiga chouhen manga hakujaden" (The full-length cartoon *White Snake Tale*, a collaborative project between Toei and Hong Kong), *Yomiuri Shimbun*, June 27, 1956 (evening edition), p. 4.
19 See *"Film Almanac: 1956 Edition"*, 1956, pp. 146–147.
20 Ting, Qushung. "Hong kong nihon eiga kouryuushi – Asia eiga network no roots wo saguru" (History of exchange between Hong Kong and Japan: Searching for the roots of an Asian Film Network), University of Tokyo Press, 2007, p. 185.
21 See "White Paper on the Film Industry," p. 38.
22 See "Ten Years of Toei History," p. 268.

23 "On the Occasion of the 9th Cannes Film Festival" (official Ministry of Foreign Affairs document), March 27, 1956.
24 Koide, Takashi. "New York nihon eiga mihon'ichi yori" (From the New York Japanese Film Trade Fair), *Kinema Junpo*, Late February, 1957, p. 55. "New York nihon eiga shuukan no hankyou" (Reactions to the New York "Japanese Film Week"), *Kinema Junpo*, Early March Edition, 1957, pp. 73–75.
25 See "Ten Years of Toei History," p. 138.
26 As early as 1955, news of Cannes' "International Conference on Animation" had reached the Japanese film industry. "Cannes eigasai kokusai douga day ni kansuru ken" (Regarding the Cannes Film Festival "International Animation Film Day"), Official Ministry of Foreign Affairs document, January 30, 1956.
27 See "Ten Years of Toei History," p. 247.
28 Ministry of International Trade and Industry, Business Department, Commercial Affairs Division (Ed.). "Eiga sangyou hakusho" (White Paper on the Film Industry), 1963, p. 100.
29 Furuta, Hisateru. *Tetsuwan atom no jidai—eizou sangyou no koubou* (The *Astro Boy* era: The movie industry's offense and defense), Sekai Shisosha, 2009, pp. 69–75.
30 "TV eiga no wariate to gaikajoukyou" (Rationing and the state of foreign capital in tv movies), *Monthly Television Report*, December Edition, 1959, p. 16.
31 See "TV eiga no wariate to gaikajoukyou" (Rationing and the state of foreign capital in tv movies)
32 "Gaikoku TV eiga no shin'nendo yunyuu keikaku" (Plans for importation of foreign films in the new year), *Monthly Television Report*, December Edition, 1960, p. 14.
33 Satake, Tadayoshi. "Fukkouki no gaikayosanseido" (Foreign currency budget system for the recovery period), *The Ritsumeikan Journal of International Studies*, 2008.
34 "Dollar waku kanwa ni kyoku no eigahoushin" (Network movie plans in response to alleviation of the dollar framework), *Monthly Television Report*, January 1961, pp. 92–93.
35 Nagashima, Keiichi. "Bei terebi houdou to koukyou no rieki —darenotameno, nan'notameno housouka" (Report on American television and "public profit": Broadcasts for whom and for what purpose?), *Housou kenkyuu to chousa* (Research and surveys on broadcasting), May 2007, p. 65.
36 Murakami, Shichirou. *Long Run — masukomi hyouryuu 50 nen no kiseki* (Long run: The drifting focus of 50 years of mass communication), Fusosha, 2005, pp. 75–76.
37 "Kokusan manga eiga terebi e shinshutsu tetsuwan atom ga shigekini Toei douga nadomo seisakukaishi" (Domestic cartoons: Advancing to television, The Astro Boy effect, Toei Animation and others begin production), *Yomiuri Shimbun*, July 20, 1963 (evening edition), p. 10.
38 "Dollar nimo tsuyoi tetsuwan atom janguru taitei zenbei net e" (Strong even against the dollar: "Astro Boy" and "Kimba the White Lion," toward a network across the U.S.), *Yomiuri Shimbun*, October 17, 1965 (morning edition), p. 21.

6 Virtuous and Depraved: Portrayals of Women in North Korean Cinema

Benjamin JOINAU

Introduction

Recognized quite early by the regime as a unique ideological weapon, North Korean cinema used female figures as central characters in numbers far beyond what might be expected of a male-dominated socialist country. More than a quarter of all North Korean produced movies appears to have a woman as a major actant in the narratives, not only as major characters, but also as catalysts of the story. The central question of this research is "what kind of women" are being portrayed in the collective cinematographic text called "North Korean film"? A complex and contradictory imagery can be discerned over the period from 1949 to the present.

The hereditary regime governing DPRK (Democratic People's Republic of Korea) since the Liberation (1945) follows a patriarchal organization where the father-figure is dominant. The spouses of both Kim Il Sung and Kim Jong-il remained hidden from the public. Kim Jong-suk, the iconic mother of the latter, has been transformed quite late into a syncretistic figure: mother and resistance fighter. She was represented as the embodiment of the virtuous woman ("gentle mother and good wife") in the context of the growing dynastic cult of the Kims. A perfect Korean socialist mother is a family figure who inherited the traditional Confucian female virtues (fidelity, sacrifice, patience, reserve and modesty) and the qualities of motherhood. At the same time, she transcends mundane personal virtues through devotion to the country and to socialist ideals: she must be a mother of the nation… and a modern woman equal to man! Asked to participate actively in the creation of a new society as well as in the postwar reconstruction effort, women became key actors and symbols of the nation building process. They played a complex role of mother, wife, soldier, heroin, metonymic symbol for the nation, but also of the errant sinner and lost female. Is there an over-arching logic to these contradictory images?

The *instrumentalization* of women's representation through cinema intentionally to support the political regime's propaganda is the primary focus in this chapter. In a country like North Korea where the state controls every aspect of the society, mass media directly expresses official ideology, offering a rare insight into a political regime's imaginary. This is a study of the relationships between power, cinema and gender in a totalitarian state through a "mythanalysis" of a large corpus of movies.

Building a corpus, methodology at stake

Methodological bias

Critically defining the corpus
Literature about gender politics in the cinema of communist and/or totalitarian regimes is relatively scarce. It is not surprising then that academic studies of gender in North Korean films are even rarer. There are, though, some important publications that we will review before directly examining our subject, not only for the insights they provide, but also because they present typical methodological, if not epistemological, errors which must be addressed.

This is a classic and recurrent shortcoming in textual studies – whether film or literature – presenting a very limited number of works as "representative" of the period or the trend analyzed, often without even trying to establish their representativeness. Such papers depend upon a quasi-magical metonymy where few works of art supposedly represent an entire social trend or collective imaginary. These epistemological liberties, in the limited space of an article or book chapter, often provide a compelling illusion of a proof. If the quoted works are clearly presented as mere *illustrations* of an analyzed trend, they may be useful in communicating particular points, but they are not in themselves evidence that such a trend exists more broadly than in the text being presented. When they are the only real corpus on which the study is based, they suffer from the inductive fallacy: a puzzling pantheistic thought-process which assumes that a singular artistic creation fully represents every nuance and variation across an entire genre or society. This may be a useful way to draw a hypothesis of research and begin the introductory exploration, but it cannot serve as an objective demonstration. In fact, too often it serves to obstruct the analyst's view of the complexity of the reality observed, limiting the research to a gross sketch instead of fostering a more refined and nuanced picture. Many of the papers read during the course of this research contain a Manichean or simplifying dimension.

Several seminal articles published in Korean language in the early 1990s[1] have obvious qualities. But some of them display, and sometimes clearly assume, a teleological approach in which the scientific analysis is dependent upon the political objectives of the researchers in the context of the funding or publishing bodies (they all appear in publications about policy making institutions in the field of national reunification). The intentions are laudable (prepare reunification and/or woman's liberation), but that does not excuse the ways in which these articles appear to begin with a pre-existing conclusion that the data was made to fit.

Several articles related to our topic in Western languages suffer from similar problems,[2] displaying that "proxemic" contamination which transforms a fictional representation – which might provide a valid *comment* on or *insight* into a social phenomenon – into a direct representation mirroring a social fact. Reality is contaminated by analyzing social facts through a work of fiction when both domains are fused as one. This illustrates another unacknowledged epistemological shift when cinema studies aspire to be social studies.

Another bias concerns the "stereotypes." The stereotypes identified are informed as much by the researchers' preconceived categories and assumptions as they are by the representations of North Korean cinema. In other words, they found what they were looking for, and did not see things that did not fit into their preconceived categories. Unfortunately, the analytical frame in most of the above-mentioned articles is built around a "traditional/modern" dichotomy opposing two mutually-exclusive models of women. When employing this (and similar) frame(s), many female characters in North Korean cinema are overlooked or ignored, because they do not fit into the categories as defined by the analysts *before they begin* to analyze their data.

A two-steps analysis
It is useful to begin by locating these biases as an invitation to develop a more rigorous analytical methodology.

As argued above, the corpus and its justification are crucial to the validity of any study. The epistemological question pertains to the *representativeness* of fictional works and to their fidelity to the social realities that they purport to depict. As mentioned, an in-depth study seeking to exhume *socially significant* differences between movies must draw on more than a handful of works. This is a key difference between cinema studies, which approach movies as works of art, and social studies which examine films as sociological material. Hence, I have analyzed a corpus of almost 100 movies, chosen carefully according to criteria to be discussed below. This corpus represents around 12% of the entire North Korean cinema production, a large enough sample to reveal genuine trends.

A two-step analysis has been applied to these movies, either through direct viewing of those that were available (see below for the specific problem of sourcing and access to the materials), or through written synopsis of those that were not. The analysis has been tabulated in a pdf available online.[3] Of course, to have an empirically valid corpus, not only must we satisfy quantitative criteria, but also thematic criterion. Most of the authors mentioned above seem to have rather vague standards for selecting their movies: it is unclear whether their selection was made randomly, for practical reasons (availability, subtitles, etc.), or by some unspecified objective method. Rather than a mere "thematic" approach which revealed itself to be vague, I employed an *actantial* selection (see below) based on the agency of women in the movies.

The question of diachrony versus synchrony is another important issue. Yu China, for example, is the first to insist on the importance of a "redemarcation" of North Korean cinema, according to the evolution of political context and cinematographic functions, to remove it from the South Korean context of interpretation.[4] In the case of North Korea where films are produced by a state-operated apparatus expected to express the official ideology, regardless of market/ audience reactions, we have a tightly controlled context in which stability is favored over variation; in which story-lines are developed in accordance with the state's agenda, rather than the desires or demands of the viewing public. Therefore, reading cinematographic changes over time requires, to some extent, knowing the political agenda in the background. Yet, seeking understanding / knowledge of that political agenda is typically the driving motivation for research on North Korea, with researchers asking cultural productions like movies to provide clues which might help to ascertain what is going on at a deeper or broader level in North Korean society and politics. This is a vicious circle.

To escape this vicious circle, I strongly advocate an approach in two-steps: first a synchronic analysis, to draw the general topography, then a diachronic one, to determine a more refined landscape of the imaginary.[5] Focusing first on a synchronic approach over the entire sixty-year period can help us avoid the systematic political bias witnessed in other research. Trying to directly relate certain trends in representation to certain periods and political policies, in a context in which researchers are generally South Koreans or Westerners, invariably suffers from a political reading unduly influenced by preformed knowledge about North Korean society and its political regime in a (post-) Cold War context. Whether consciously or not, most such research seeks a key to analyzing larger political trends, an insight which could lead to a breakthrough in reunification or to geopolitical predictions: North Korean studies are rarely neutral. This slippage from film analysis to geostrategic policy is another epistemological quagmire to be wary of. A synchronic, then diachronic approach can help us to avoid that.

Durand's mythodology

My method is based on Gilbert Durand's approach called "mythodology."[6] For Durand, the collective imaginary consists of a set of "competing trends" (or *semantic basins*) that coexist with and sometimes oppose one another, with some disappearing while others become more prominent and struggle for dominance. At any given time, a society's collective imaginary consists in the cartography of these competing basins – a mapping Durand calls a "cultural topique," intentionally evoking Freud's "topography of the psyche." Indeed, for Durand – a Jungian – the individual imaginary works on the same symbols and structures as the collective one. In this scheme, the imaginary is a sort of interface between the subjective assimilating drives and the demands of the outside world, where contradictions and aporia seek resolution – especially regarding death or sex competition.

At play in this imaginary are two major regimes (groupings of similar structures): 1) the diurnal regime of images, which includes "heroic" or "schizomorphic" structures typically associated with male[7] images relating to the ascendant scheme and the standing, dominant posture; 2) the nocturnal regime of images, which itself subdivides into two categories: a) efforts to fuse opposites into a single entity, the "mystical" structures that convey feminine (or feminoid) images associated with the digestive reflex and the scheme of descent; and b) the "synthetic" structures (also associated with feminine images), which illustrate the copulative reflex and the cyclic movements that lead to the coupling of opposing pairs (*coincidentia oppositorum*). Although the nocturnal regime evokes images of comfort, serenity, and intimacy, it also evokes death. Feminoid images essentially present a potential for ambivalence.

By contrast, dominant symbols in the diurnal regime tend to fight *theriomorphic* (or monster-like) images, which spring from the dark side of the nocturnal regime. The diurnal regime is deemed schizomorphic because it is generated by an oppositional split between dark, menacing images and newly formed heroic images – a process which has a performative effect in the generation of images through a sexually valued opposition. Although all these structures and symbols are limited in number, they combine in an almost infinite variety of configurations with anthropological value.

North Korean cinema as a fragment

Researchers often approach North Korea as if trying to resolve archaeological or philological puzzles, as if they were examining a remote and extinct civilization fixed in time. Today we have many ways to access North Korean movies. Yet even the rich collection of the ICNK in Seoul's National Library is not complete. Recent English publications like *North Korean Cinema: A History*[8] are priceless for the information and anecdotes they provide, but they remain incomplete, as do the South Korean secondary sources like the excellent *North Korean Cinema History*.[9] Although it lists 653 film titles from 1949 to 2006, there are still many movies missing. My research indicates that that there have been around 750 or 800 feature films produced in DPRK to date. Even North Korea, though, has no comprehensive database on film production.

Where I could not access a movie (in whole or in part), I tried to fill-in the gaps with detailed synopses[10] that I found in primary and secondary sources (listed in the bibliography), but this is of course a stopgap measure. These practical limitations must be considered before drawing conclusions: in this field, one can only seek probabilities of likelihood, not certainty.

I have compiled a list of 90 movies that are pertinent to my subject, of which I have directly viewed 40 (44 %). My selection is based on neither "genre" (see below) nor "theme", both of which appear to be irrelevant in the special context of North Korean cinema. Instead, as mentioned, my selection is based on the actantial level[11] of the characters, that is: their agency in the narrative. *Actants* (agents) of the narrative had to be women, whatever the paradigm to which they belong: they could be subject or object, giver or recipient, helper or opponent; they could be alone, in pairs, or groups (one, two or several heroines); but at least one of the female characters had to be a structuring agent in the plot (a pivotal character, even if only a "minor character" or supporting role in overall screen presence). These broad parameters allowed me to select movies whose main character is male, where women are apparently minor characters, but where one of these women plays an essential role in the narrative (often helping the main character to become a hero).

Having selected movies, I categorized characters according to both their actantial level and moral archetypes associated to their functions (helper/opponent at the level of the action being in our case always doubled as positive or "good" / negative or "bad", with the exception of the character going through the plot and often thanks to the agency of the main agent, from opponent to helper, from bad to good). This produced the following categories: PMA (positive main agent, "hero" and "heroin"), A (helper, or assistant of the main actant), O (opponent), SO (minor or secondary opponent), PSA (positive secondary agent, "supporting role"), TS (transformational subject: character experiencing a transformation from opponent to helper, from negative to positive). These categories apply to both male and female characters.

Since there are no reported box-office results in DPRK, and since officially proclaimed "success" cannot be verified, it is difficult to assess – of the many movies I might have selected – which might be most representative.[12] I tried to locate movies which are mentioned in more than two primary sources in English, interpreting this as potentially indicative of their representativeness (having been officially "recommended" to international audiences). I complemented this list with recently released movies not mentioned in earlier publications, and with a selection of less known movies whose actantial structure was obviously related to this study. As I will develop below, I also took other criteria pertinent to time periods and genres into account. Despite all the limitations, this corpus represents around 12% of the total production of North Korean films and can be considered as an adequate base for observing pertinent structures.

Genres and structures of production

There appears to be an integrated, centralized cinema production system in Pyongyang. Various studios operate as the early Hollywood studios did, employing teams of technicians, script writers, actors and directors full time. They are, of course, state-funded public companies. Their hierarchical structures and mode of production seem to be highly controlled by the political apparatus. The division of labor and processes of production are not much different from other film-making industries, except that the governing regime provides the funding and controls the planning. The plot, narrative and representations in movies (the contents) are completely controlled by the Party's centralized censor.

From the 1960s to the 1990s, the North Korean leader Kim Jong-il was personally quite involved in movie production. Kim "wrote" books about the art of cinema which are considered to provide essential guidance for people involved in this industry. Cinema is officially recognized as a unique and effective method of political education (i.e., propaganda) and was a special interest of Kim's. Hence, North Korean movies do not seek to meet the market-audience demands as do commercially produced work in capitalist societies, and therefore they must be assessed according to a different paradigm. They may aim to entertain, but the aesthetic, entertainment and cultural dimensions of movies are both officially and theoretically secondary to their educational intentions. Films are regarded merely as tools or more precisely, ideological "weapons,"[13] rather than an art-form to be celebrated in its own right. As such, a diachronic analysis of a large sample of films might provide insight into the regime's socio-political agenda, a mirror of the regime's imaginary.

The primary materials we were able to access classify DPRK's fictional movies (*yesul yŏnghwa*) according to the following categories:
- Resistance against Japanese imperialism (aka "Revolutionary Traditions").
- Socialist reality: movies presenting a concrete social problem and its resolution.
- Korean War ("Fatherland Liberation War").
- Espionage ("Intelligence and Counterintelligence").
- Historic movies and tales: this category depicts a pre-colonial Korea with strong ideological features (anti-aristocratic or "anti-feudal"

criticism, while affirming nationalist values / sentiments through Korea's long history, etc.).
- "National Reunification": movies classified under this category typically also fall in to one of categories above, most commonly espionage or war.
- "Adapted from Immortal Classics": these also typically fall in to one of categories above, except these are North Korean "socialist" classics, such as *Sea of Blood* or *The Flower Girl*, which were originally literary works or operas (Kim Il Sung claims to have written *Sea of Blood* himself). These are the movies that the young Kim Jong-il worked personally in the 1960s and early '70s.

This typology can be simplified as follows, using ideological categories specific to the regime:
- history movies depicting class struggles,
- resistance movies as propaedeutic for the revolution,
- war movies portraying the way to national liberation,
- socialist reality as a tool for socialization.

This typology effectively summarizes the programmatic objectives of North Korean propaganda.

Socialist reality movies became an increasingly dominant part of the production output in the 1970s, with economic development and the changing social issues facing a post-revolution and postwar regime. It continues to be the most reproduced genre today. It follows the *sumŭn yŏngung ttara baeugi* principle (the path of everyday heroes, literally "let's learn in the steps of hidden heroes") recommended by Kim Jong-il. It brings the struggle from the resistance and war zones to the whole society seen as a battlefield on which citizens sacrifice themselves for the victory of the ideology and the Leaders who mastermind this victory ("Life is struggle and struggle is life").[14] There is no distinction between the public and military spheres, since, especially in the *sŏnkun shidae* (Army First Era), the entire people is seen as an army. Cinema in this context is merely a training device.

This categorization of cinematographic "genres" can help us to see the *performative* approach of cinema in North Korean system: North Korean cinema is primarily defined by its agency. In building my research corpus, I have attempted to select movies representing these different genres and periods. Note, however, that older movies – before the 1970s – are difficult to access, even in North Korea. Whether this is due to changes in ideological directions, because they are technically outdated, or simply because, as in the South, they were lost or destroyed is unclear. Whatever the case, it is very difficult to access films from the early years of the DPRK; and it seems that the only records of films made before Kim Jong-il directly involved himself in cinematographic production are mentions of film titles in various publications. In the following chart, one can see the proportion of movies produced in each decade from the 1940s to the 2000s.[15]

After selecting a first set of "representative movies," I attempted to complete the corpus by complementing the initial selection with other movies to closely match the chronological proportions of my corpus to those in the chart. It appears clearly that the core of the production occurred during the 1980s and '90s (52%), with 29% in the '80s alone. The final corpus of works gathered for this study are chronologically distributed in Figures 6.1 and 6.2.

The discrepancies between the two charts result from the absence of movies available for the 1940–60s period, which has been compensated for by including more recent movies. Although 1980–90 period is slightly over represented, the overall structure of the corpus closely emulates the distribution of total production, enhancing its representativeness.

Differential valorizations

Let us now begin our first-step synchronic analysis of the different valorizations of women in movies. The most obvious *topos* encountered in many movies is the positive value of female characters as "virtuous women" which assumes a very traditional set of archetypes. Other categories will develop on two negative valorizations of women actants: the woman gone astray and the deceitful female.

Virtuous women: a genealogy

The heroine of *Mother's Happiness* (2003) mourns the loss of her first son, who died as an officer in the army, but she doesn't view his loss as a misfortune. He served the country heroically while insuring the General's safety; as a mother, she couldn't wish for a better kind of happiness. She still has an unfulfilled desire, though: for her youngest

Virtuous and Depraved: Portrayals of Women in North Korean Cinema   125

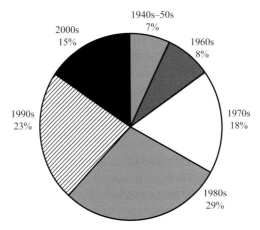

Figure 6.1: Total produced movies

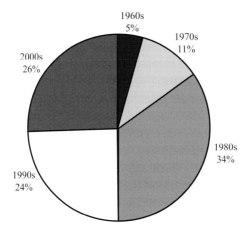

Figure 6.2: Corpus analyzed by periods

son, who is handicapped, to be cured so he, too, could join the army, and for her second son, a lazy lad, to "dress the uniform" like his brothers.

This mother is prepared for the ultimate sacrifice of a parent: to give up the life of her children for the sake of the *sŏnkun shidae* (the "Army First" era opened in the 1990s). This is far beyond what is usually expected from a mother, even by North Korean cinema standards. But precisely through these extremes, the basic virtue expected from women – sacrifice – is clearly depicted.

Motherhood is one of the most commonly recurring ways that woman is defined in the North Korean world-view. There are numerous movies portraying women as ideal mothers: *Mother's Mind* (1986), *Mother's Wish* (1987), *My Mother* (1990), *My Mother Was a Hunter* (1994), *Mother's Happiness* (2003) just to name a few of those with the word in the title. They all follow the seminal models of mothers set in "eternal classics" like *Sea of Blood* (1969) or *The Flower Girl* (1972). In *The Flower Girl*, in which the mother works herself to death in a rich family's house to earn a livelihood for her two daughters, we see a traditional figure: a mother who is willing to negate her own needs to provide subsistence for her children. We see the same theme in *My Mother Was a Hunter*, where the mother becomes a hunter living in the forest to feed her children: the perfect mother is a single mother (a widow) who finds self-realization through self-negation.[16] In these stories of self-sacrifice, a woman finds her identity not only in her role as a mother, but in her self-effacement for the sake of her offspring.

Luckily, not all the mother figures in DPRK films are so extreme. Many of the minor female characters depict softer images of motherhood, offering the image of a humble, discrete, dedicated lady covering her children with love. We find this imagery in the perfect grand-mother of *They Met on the Taedong River* (1993), a primary school director whose love permeates far beyond her own children; she is beloved by her pupils and an important protagonist in her niece's life. Here we find echoes of the qualities attributed to the Great and Dear Leaders, who have been compared to loving mothers. Their protection is evoked with the figure of the bosom (*p'um*). As Myers observed,[17] some paintings represent Kim Il Sung embosoming children-like citizens in his large white coat. In an example quite unique among socialist countries, this image is consistent with the shelter offered by the Party, which is often referred to as the mother of the people (*uri ŏmŏni tang*): the Leader is the Party, and the Party shares the guidance virtues (educational function of the parents) and protection of the supreme Guide.[18] This may be why local Party secretaries are played by women in their fifties or sixties, symbolizing a strong but warm control over the people who they oversee. Among many examples, the secretary of *Duty of a Generation* (2002) stands out, an older woman who provides support to and boosts the confidence of the male hero, an engineer who doubts himself and his decisions.

This indicates the possibility for women to be role models and assume a place in society beyond procreative and maternal functions. In *Sea of Blood* (1969), we see that women can have a political awakening. While fighting for their home and family, they may find the path to the socialist revolution. The mother in *Sea of Blood*, like the one in *My Mother Was a Hunter* (1994), transcends her own quest for survival, transforming it into a fight for the nation's freedom and communist ideals. Rather than exceptions, these female characters are quite common in our corpus. I have identified 63 movies – 70% of the corpus – in which the heroines are ideological models (PMA, or positive main agent). They may be Party representatives as in *Our Political Instructor* (2010), soldiers (*The Story of a Nurse*, 1980, *Harang and General Jin*, 1991, a historic movie, *Stretcher Platoon Leader*, 1995, *Daisy Girl*, 2011–12, etc.), or have less prominent positions, such as simple workers or farmers (*An Ambitious Girl*, 1984, *The Girl We Met on Our Trip*, 1983, *Ask Yourself*, 1988/89, *A Dutiful Daughter*, 1991, *Girls in My Hometown*, 1991, *Here We Live*, 1999, *A Faithful Servant*, 2005, etc.).

The role of ordinary women in the edification of a blooming socialist country is emphasized through the many characters fighting for the cause with their "natural endowment": motherhood, endurance, provision of food, cure and care. A paragon of this ideal is found in *Namgang Village Women* (1964), based on a true story of an event during the war. It tells the story of the women of a small village who dedicated themselves to help a platoon on the nearby frontline get their ammunitions across the river despite enemy bombing. Led by a charismatic woman, they challenge the dangers of the front to bring food to the soldiers, even dismantling their own houses for materials to build rafts. Their courage and dedication ensure the regiment receives the ammunitions needed to defeat the enemy. These women could have been portrayed as pure positive characters, but it is apparent that they only try to be as good as their men would have been in the same situation. More precisely, the movie repeatedly drives home the point that they are trying to be the best wives possible; their efforts to save the battle are almost secondary to their efforts to be exemplary spouses! One character clearly states: "I really wish we could be men." Here we find the obvious Confucian figures of the ideal wife transformed into the perfect communist spouse, who despite her achievements will never be more than support for the ideal (male) communist soldier.

Some have suggested that these perfect female socialist fighters are modelled after Kim Il Sung's mother, Kang Pan-sŏk, and his first wife, Kim Jong-suk who died in 1949. Narratives around these "perfect" women first appeared in the 1960s, but it was not until the 1980s that they became official ideology with an active "cult". For example, in 1984 Kim Jong-suk's bronze bust was placed in the center of the main row of heroes in the newly refurbished Revolutionary Martyrs Cemetery in Pyongyang. One of the first movies about her was released a few years later (*Wait*, 1987). Although they eventually came to represent the political and human values of the ideal socialist woman as a revolutionary soldier, a mother and a wife, they should be seen not as prototypes, but as post-facto reconstructions. Indeed, the peak period for main female characters as "ideological role models" in movies was in the 1970s, before the development of their cult.

Beside the movies set during the war, most of the female characters who have leading roles in the stories appear in the "socialist reality" genre. Reflecting the political, social and economic agenda of the time, these films portray a diverse array of professions: soy bean paste engineer (*A Dutiful Servant*, 2005), barber (*A Girl Barber*, 1970), wooden furniture worker (*A Letter from my Hometown*, 2002), fashion designer (*An Ambitious Girl*, 1984), shepherd (*Ask Yourself*, 1988/89), factory worker (*Flower in Snow*, n.d.), acrobat (*Flying Circus*, 1972), crossroad controller (*Guards on the Crossing*, 1986), nurse (*Song of Love*, 1986), truck driver (*The Girl We Met on Our Trip*, 1983), prosecutor (*The Prosecutor Accuses*, 1980), pig breeder (*To the End of the Earth*, 1977), botanic researcher (*The Fourteenth Winter*, 1980), etc. We can see that their professions are quite diverse; they are not confined to the education/housekeeping sectors usually reserved for women.

Some of these positive female characters are not protagonists, but rather secondary agents who help the main (male) characters ("helpers" in the actantial model), as in: *An Unattached Unit* (1993, army surgeon), *Japanese invasion of 1592* (1991–95, *kisaeng* or geisha), *Run and Run* (1985, researcher at the sport sciences institute), *The Story of the Kayagum* (1986, Song Mi heals the hero's eyes), *The Tale of Ondal* (1986, the hero gets help from perfect mother and wife figures), etc. But, at the narrative level, it is the category of female heroines (MPA) which is by far the most surprising in a regime and a culture which has been so often described as male chauvinist.[19] Around *one-quarter of the movies* that I could identify from 1949 to 2013 portray one or several female characters as main positive diegetic actants in the narrative. This suggests that the role of women is essential not only in North Korean cinema, but more generally in the regime's nation- and identity-building process.

Despite the apparent open-mindedness in the portrayal of women as positive leading agents, it is important to note that almost all these heroines are variations on a pre-modern pattern found in *Ch'un-hyang*. The tale and *p'ansori* (recitative solo singer vocal work) from the 18th century has been adapted to the screen many times in both South and North Korea. In DPRK, the first version was released in 1959, a second in 1980 and another in 1984/85 by Shin Sang-ok (*Love, Love, My Love*). Ch'un-hyang is the daughter of a *kisaeng* (a *geisha*, or "working girl") and a *yangban* (or aristocrat). Lee To-ryŏng, the son of the provincial governor, falls in love with her at first sight. Despite her humble origin, he decides to marry her. But he must go to the capital to take the national examination. A new governor arrives who is corrupt and unjust. He wants Ch'un-hyang, but she resists, remaining faithful to To-ryŏng, whom she has been waiting for without any news. She is tortured and sent to prison, but does not give-in. Meanwhile, To-ryŏng has become a royal officer responsible for conducting an inspection of local administrations. He arrives in disguise in the town of Namwon where Ch'un-hyang is due to be executed. He witnesses the corruption of the governor, his inequity and rough treatment of the people, as well as the incredible loyalty and virtue of Ch'un-hyang, who is prepared to sacrifice herself for love. To-ryŏng arrests the governor, assumes his position and is reunited with Ch'un-hyang.

This popular love story with its happy ending is well suited for the North Korean propaganda agenda with its embedded critique of social class and feudalism, which are of course emphasized in the DPRK's film versions. But although trying to mate two people from opposing social backgrounds while portraying the corruption of the system may seem somewhat edgy (if not revolutionary), the image it presents of the ideal wife is quite conservative. She embodies all the virtues asked by the neo-Confucian ideology of the Chosŏn dynasty: self-sacrifice, elegance, modesty, hard-working, housekeeping skills, entertainment ability (music, poetry, dance), faithfulness, righteousness, etc. Ch'un-hyang is willing to give all her goods to help To-ryŏng when she thinks he is ruined. Moreover, she is ready to die for her lover while resisting the injustice of her feudal master. All these virtues compensate the social imbalance between the couple, while the ordeals suffered by Ch'un-hyang lead to a redemption-purification that "qualifies" her to be To-ryŏng's wife, crossing that social-class divide. We might read her physical and moral suffering in prison as a process to wash away the stain of her birth as the daughter of an "entertainer". The Ch'un-hyang character as reinterpreted by the Northern regime is a mixture of the perfect mother/wife/female citizen not only according to Confucian values, but also, in many ways, to Christian values (note that the northern part of the Korean peninsula was the site of significant evangelical activity, and that prewar Pyongyang, where Kim Il Sung was raised, had sizeable Catholic and Protestant communities). She is also, as we have seen, the paragon of the virtuous women of the ideal socialist Juchean society: not only a good wife-mother, but a dutiful citizen, with high spirits, willing to sacrifice herself for the cause.[20] This Ch'un-hyang *topos* sheds light on the cultural roots of the representations of women in our movies.

Women gone astray

What is the diegetic role of all these positive female characters in the movies discussed above? Beside the heroine figure who saves the situation in war and resistance movies, there is a large troop of "unknown" everyday heroines in socialist reality movies. These characters have typically mastered a specialty, whether it be pig breeding or laboratory scientist. They generally must assert themselves in their new position: the girl with the truck drivers in *The Girl We Met on Our Trip*, the *toenchang* soy bean paste researcher in *A Dutiful Servant*, the traffic controller in *Guards on the Crossing*, and so on. They all face resistance from the people around them and require great perseverance and patience to make those people realize their mistakes.

The trope of enlightenment
Many of these stories, if not all, work on a neo-Buddhist trope of enlightenment, a narrative transformation corresponding to Greimas' "archetype of mediation."[21] Like the Buddha as a young ignorant prince leaving his palace-enclave, the characters must undergo a long awakening process. It rarely occurs through dialogue and persuasion alone: the enlightenment rarely results from a rational speech delivered by the hero/heroine (although the hero always delivers a monologue in which s/he

utters the expected politically correct message). An old man in *Girls of My Hometown* (1991) states that the girl gone astray cannot be taught by words, she must come to understand through her own experience. Understanding through personal experience is highly valued in Confucian education, but there, as in these films, it is often the experience of witnessing the practical example set by the hero/heroine – the role-modelling – that leads the other characters to understand their misguided ways. When they see the silent and noble suffering, the abnegation, the commitment, the passion, the faith, the loyalty embodied in the actions and attitude of the main character, the lost souls suddenly reach enlightenment. Similarly, in certain schools of Buddhism, the *sŏn* or zen school for example, satori cannot be achieved through reading scriptures. Sudden illumination of the spirit may be assisted, in more recent films, by evoking the Leader: he came to offer on-the-spot guidance, and sometimes a still image of his visit is shown on the screen (never a video – the Leader would lose his iconic status if shown in motion). His never-ending efforts on behalf of his people, his infinite love for them, his devotion to building a perfect socialist haven… The General or the Guide's verbal evocations, sometimes accompanied by a still photo of him (Kim Jong-il in *Flower in Snow*, *Wish*, *Duty of a Generation*, *Dutiful Servant*, *Mother's Happiness*, etc.), work as a *shifter* for the culprits. There is, for example, a very intense scene in *Mother's Happiness* where the heroine evokes, while gazing at snow-covered mountains in the distance, the General's endless care for his people, and his visits to all corners of the country. She asks herself, although in the midst of terrible ordeals: "We have at least in our homes a warm area on the heated floor to sit on, but where He is now, does He have such a warm place?" Then her suffering seems to lift in the face of so much compassion and devotion: his sacrifice becomes the ultimate model that women must emulate to be loving mothers and ideal citizens.

Before them, these virtuous women can find two kinds of culprits to save. Interestingly, there are many cases of men who have taken the wrong path: the manager of the soy paste factory in *A Dutiful Servant* (2005) who, rather than trying to improve the quality of his product, instead goes to a neighboring county to buy paste from another factory; the depressed tractor driver of *Here We Live* (1999) brought back to his research by the heroine; the men in *Outpost Line* or *Bellflower* (1987). But this is far from the most common case. Nor is it because a female character has become a role model that the males lose their positive status. In *Namgang Village*

Women, for example, women are leading characters, but the men are not portrayed as opponents; rather, the soldiers are heroic male figures being assisted by the village women. In this case, opposition comes from the radical other: the enemies from across the frontier.

The "righteous /wrongful woman" pair

It is more common for the heroine to be confronted by a female wrongful counterpart (SO, or secondary opponent) than a male. The two women work as a pair of antagonists providing a Manichean contrast easily recognizable by the viewers. Although the SO is on a reactionary path, the situation, in socialist reality movies, is never completely irreversible. The diegetic role of the heroine is to help her counterpart realize her mistake and correct herself. We see this in *Guards on the Crossing* (1986), when a former traffic controller, a friend of the main character – herself a traffic controller – comes to understand that she should not ask her friend to be lenient with her boyfriend, a recidivist traffic offender: her controller friend works hard for drivers' safety, and she should assist in that national interest task rather than pursuing her personal objectives. In *Duty of a Generation* (2002), the female researcher supports a lazy and old-fashion manager against a young engineer who came to reform their fabric factory. She comes to realize (with the help of the female Party secretary) that she was wrong – that the young man had a vision for the nation's economy. In *They Met on the Taedong River* (1993), the perfect grand-mother's sister is lost in reactionary thoughts. She wants the perfect man to marry her daughter, a water-ski champion crowned with many international medals. She scorns Tongch'an, who is in love with her daughter, because of his lowly status as captain of a sand dredger. Her wise sister, with the help of her "friend" the old Kang, leads the snob to understand that while heart and love are important, dedication to the country's future is above all: Tongch'an is a dedicated worker on an important construction project, a real socialist hero! Of course, she happily changes her mind to bring about a happy ending. Similarly, the fiancée of a wounded soldier in *Girl in My Hometown* (1991) allows her sister – who has been corrupted by foreign influences – to talk her into breaking the engagement, but has a moment of enlightenment when she sees the heroine marry a blinded soldier and devote her life to him.

This narrative structure (fault → awakened to the error by a virtuous helper → correction → happy end) is quite common, but not the most common in this genre. One alternative to the virtuous/wrongful female pair just discussed leads to a darker set of female characters portrayed in North Korean movies: the wrongful female/righteous male pair found in many socialist reality movies.

The "wrongful female/righteous male" pair
As mentioned, socialist reality movies were mostly produced from the late-'60s, when the need for conflict films which nourished the Cold War agenda was somewhat offset by the desire for the edification of socialist society. These movies have been the core of production for the last forty years (since 1965, comprising 80% of productions according to the available data, and more than 80% since 1997). The frequency of the appearance of the "wrongful female/righteous male couple" *topos* seems to be fairly steady over the four decades until the 2000s when it suddenly increased again, as it had in the 1960s. Whatever the reason for this change, this *topos* reveals an important diachronic structure of the North Korean imaginary.

Some women have gone astray because of a change in their approach to motherhood. Maternal feelings are positive as long as they focus on children' proper (i.e. socialist or *Juchean*) education. A mother should be a good mother, as we have seen, dedicated, caring, generous, and ready to sacrifice. But she should also teach her offspring the righteous values of Chosŏn while offering an example of love for the Nation and the Leaders. Her maternal feelings should also transcend her children to embrace the country, embodied by the Great and Dear Leaders. Every mother is a mother of the Nation and should devote her loving care to the Kims. The Leader, especially Kim Il Sung, is the Father *par excellence*.[22] He is both the Father and the Mother of the Nation. Under his infinite love, the whole population of Korea is one large family (made explicit in the title of the 1983 movie, *We are All One Family*). So the mothers represented in films are a sort of hypotyposis for the Guide as the Mother of the Nation. Hence, mothers' efforts on behalf of their family must rise above and beyond the personal, to advantage the entire society, or else they might fall into the selfish concerns of bourgeois motherhood.

A bourgeois reactionary mother cares only for the well-being of her own family. She is greedy, wanting to accumulate wealth for the sole benefit of her immediate kin. She raises her children in an individualistic fashion, merely for the vicarious satisfaction of her ego through their achievements. She is a victim of the illusion of small personal benefits and selfish desires. Such mothers are presented as quite snobbish women in movies. We have already seen this stereotype in the proud mother of *They Met on the Taedong River*. The young female in *Urban Girl Comes to Get Married* (1993) is another example, as a typical city girl who initially has only contempt for the country farmer she is to marry. In a series known as the *Problems* movies from the late 1970s to the 2000s (*Problem of Our Next-Door Neighbor*, *Problem of Our Uncle's Family*, *Problem of Our Younger Brother's Family*, etc.), there are several women who struggle for a nice apartment or a better position for their husband, concerned only with the social status they might achieve.

This model is clearly depicted by the snobbish future mother-in-law of *Our Fragrance* (2003). Wanting to impress her daughter's future in-laws, she prepares a "trendy" reception in her flat. She greets them with objects using English names, like "slippers", importing useless objects and foreign influences, even in the language itself! She has a "sofa" in her living-room instead of the "traditional" sitting on the floor. She has prepared a real treat: "salada" (a mixed salad with mayonnaise), spaghetti, cake with candles, coffee and even "champagne"! The grand-father who came to represent the groom's family reaches his breaking point and ejaculates his aversion to all these bourgeois affectations before his departure. She realizes quite late what a fool she has made of herself. It is, of course, characteristic of this *topos* that there is a wise man to awaken these women (a grand-father as in *Our Fragrance* or *They Met on the Taedong River*, an engineer as in *Urban Girl Comes to Get Married*, and sometimes a Party representative). The wrongful females invariably acknowledge their mistake and without much of a learning curve, correct their attitude and thinking, bringing them instantly back into the fold for a happy ending.

In this category of foolish bourgeois desires, we find a sub-category with a twist: corrupted by foreign influences (generally under the devil agency of either American or Japanese imperialists). This is clear in the teenage girl of *A Schoolgirl's Diary* (2006), a quite interesting film that attracted much attention abroad (distribution rights were bought by a French producer who screened it in Paris movie theatres). It depicts (like *A Mother's Happiness* 2003, or *Girls of My Hometown* 1991, for example), the problems of younger generations who are lazy, attracted to Western ways of life, not committed to the nation's glory, and even, sometimes, prone to juvenile delinquency. This movie may provide an interesting reflection of a growing social concern. The young girl is not a criminal *per se*, not even a bad person. But she is ideologically lost, she doubts, which leads her to erroneous views about her parents and her duty. This is a rare example of a wrongful female teenager, possibly indicating the need for an accent on ideological re-education on the younger generations.

The "corrupted motherhood" fallen in bourgeois faults category must be distinguished from those cases where we find a female professional, often dedicated to her job, who took a wrong turn because of ideological bias. This character is found in a textile dying researcher in *Duty of a Generation* previously mentioned, a gymnastic choreographer in *On the Green Carpet* (2000), a shellfish cooperative engineer in *The Sea of My Hometown* (2005), farmers in *When We Pick Apples* (1971), and so on. They all make bad technical decisions which block production or progress. Some are blinded by illusion of self-righteousness, others are just plain stubborn. The diegetic process confronts this wrongful female character with a symmetrically opposed male character. This positive male figure is in most cases another scientist who is a specialist in their field. He may not be recognized as such initially, but his role is to bring the errant female character to understand her wrongdoings through his achievements and example. This Manichean pairing wrong/right is correlated with the gendered pair male/female in a classical isomorphism where feminoid images are negatively valorized and male ones are heuristic.

A clear example of this is found in *Our Cook* (2000), in which the husband is a food scientist trying to develop different recipes using potatoes. He tries very hard to promote this tubercle in the "national" diet. His wife is a scientist very attached to the virtues of rice, which she studies specifically. But in these times of food shortages (the implicit subtext of the story), rice is a rare treat. It is considered to be reactionary to promote a cereal that is hard to grow and unavailable to a large proportion of the population. Of course, context matters. In other times she would have been seen as a guardian of Korean tradition (resisting the intrusion of foreign food, in this case), but in 2000, her motivations are misdirected. In contrast, her husband, committing what once would have been the heresy of promoting bread made with potato, is seen in this time of terrible harvests to be the real national hero. She finally understands how her stubborn opposition was wrong. Her husband is a nice, soft, hard-working character; she is strong and rigid. The fact that it is eventually "Doctor Potato" (*kamcha paksa*) who is the real hero is a surprising inversion of expected values (soft man/strong woman). Yet, this narrative structure is relatively common, since men typically embody the values of scientific progress and a shining future. It is also common in this trope that the male/female pair is a married couple, as we find in *The Sea of My Hometown* with the cooperative engineer Ok-hwa married to the researcher Il-mu. Where the engineer thinks that simply gathering shellfish for local consumption is sufficient, her husband seeks to improve the shellfish culture to foster sustainable aquaculture and a national supply.

We also find this trope in *A Couple of Managers* (2001) opposing a female manager running a soy bean paste (*toenchang*) factory – the leader in her industry by all output and efficiency measures, despite backward management methods – and her husband, the manager of an everyday household products factory who decides to modernize and rationalize his production processes. He starts with terrible results (32nd in his industry), but his efforts to join the 21st century "communication era" by installing computers, new management methods and new machinery eventually brings results: soon he is the industry leader, while his wife's factory has fallen to 32nd position! Not only was she wrong to maintain her outdated management policies, but also in her attitude in her relationship. She was bossy and exercised a man's prerogatives. This inversion of the couple's roles triggers the diegetic crisis. Only when she understands that her husband is right about everything can she work on correcting her factory's problem as well as her dysfunctional attitude in the household. In the process, her daughter, who was on her side, also realizes her mistakes.

In this movie, the gendered opposition male/female, and its isomorphic valorizations right/wrong, progressive/reactionary, is represented through an inversion of the male/female roles. This inversion is seen as the "original sin", a contradiction to be overcome in the semantics of the narrative, the catalyst of the plot. Only a couple with a proper demarcation of roles is a functioning couple. This is the traditional Confucian approach to married couples, based on the principle of separation of the sexes according to the five cardinal relations (*oryun*). Mixing roles leads to social (and economic) confusion.[23] The male positive characters in these movies complement these errant women, restoring the traditional balance to the situation: if we are one family, we cannot leave the "sinners" outside and lost.

These wrongful females are quite different to another, more radical figure of the woman gone astray: deceitful females.

Deceitful females

What happens when the woman image meets the figure of Otherness? And especially in the context of that special otherness that is the South Korean enemy? This otherness is based on a sameness, a paradox which complicates the situation, resulting in very negative characters. Females under the *remote* influence of Western or foreign societies (*Our Fragrance, A Schoolgirl Diary*, etc.) could still be corrected and saved. But there is no redemption for females who have completely crossed over.

Wilderness and Otherness
In North Korean movies, American and Japanese characters, and later the South Koreans who have been "corrupted" by them, are portrayed as cynical, cruel, depraved and bestial. Their wildness is portrayed through attributes they share with animals. The Americans – and their Korean impersonators in these movies – have long hair, even the army soldiers. They are also hairy on the body and face: usually wearing a beard (whereas Japanese have moustaches). Hairiness is a symbol of savagery for men, and of depravation for women. This *becoming-beast* aspect of Koreans who come into contact with Americans or Japanese is both the cause and the symbol of their otherness.

These films reveal the place and role of otherness in North Korean society, a society based on strong values of homogeneity, including obedience, order, commitment to the Party, unity, etc. In a Juche-led world, where autonomy is a central value, otherness is simply not acceptable; one's identity is to be constructed through the sameness of the same. But in this framework, South Koreans cannot be symbolically different, as radically other; rather, they must be treated as an impure and corrupted same, as seen in the famous movie *The Fate of Kumhui and Unhui* (1974). The characters in the title are identical twins, separated at birth. The sister who was bred in North Korea lives happily as a talented musician and dancer, while the sister who was raised in the South suffers a miserable life of poverty, prostitution, etc. They are twins, almost the same, but one was "spoiled" by the depraved environment of Americanized South

Korea, a kind of urban wilderness; a human jungle where people become savage beasts.

The island, symbol of metamorphosis

The symbol of the beast brings us to another set of images which have been developed in this cinema. The island is a place of *metamorphosis* where radical change occurs (see *Robinson Crusoe*, *Doctor Moreau*, *Lord of the Flies*, etc.). The island symbol is employed in *The Fate of Kumhui and Unhui*: the miserable sister, Unhui, is raised on a poor island where she meets her unfortunate fate: becoming a South Korean. But we also find soldiers transformed into heroes, as in *Wolmi Island*, or the courageous spy of *In the Den of Bats* (which draws an interesting comparison between U.S. soldiers and bats). That symbol returns again and again in more recent North Korean movies. Suffice to note for now that the island image is yet another feminoid symbol of the wild forces of nature.

A depraved feminine world

In *The Fate of Kumhui and Unhui*, the island is the place from where Unhui is introduced (forcibly) to the hell of South Korean society. South Korea as depicted in North Korean movies (as also in *True Color is Out*, 1970, or *Order n° 027*, 1986), is invariably a place of extreme poverty where the people live in slums. Disease, violence, and crime are everywhere. Streets are filled with U.S. soldiers and American jeeps, and lined with "cabarets" and bars where people fight with each other. In this depraved world, women have no choice but to work hard as factory-slaves or become prostitutes, another form of slavery (exploitation is a characteristic of imperialist systems). Corruption is everywhere, and women are sold like animals to work in brothels. Movies where South Korea and its "masters" (Japan and America) are implied usually belong to the espionage, war (Fatherland Liberation War) or national reunification genres. Contrary to expectations, this genre constitutes a minority of the movies, and were mainly produced during the first two decades after Liberation, until the early 1970s.

The True Color is Out (1970), a clear example of the espionage genre, depicts a positive female character, a researcher who is an exemplary citizen and scientist, dedicated to her country. When her friend Chŏnghŭi reappears after twenty years' absence, our lead is suddenly suspected of spying for the South. She is vindicated when attacked in her house, and the real criminal is finally found out: a horrible lady spy who underwent plastic surgery to assume Chŏnghŭi's appearance and thus was able to approach the researcher easily. The portrayal of the spy before her transformation once again is a stereotype of Western depravity: long hair on one side of the head, a seductress, wearing high heels and a strange body-hugging silk lined gown. The nurse attending her after her surgery might be an American caricature, as she has incredibly long and thick blond hair falling loose around her shoulders. These two characters symbolize corrupted women compelled to sell their souls in the imperialist world. The real Chŏnghŭi is, of course, a pure character, who wanted to return to her hometown in North Korea, where people live happily. This use of one character divided into two opposing figures, a pure innocent girl and a deceitful agent after plastic surgery, will reappear almost thirty years later in the South Korean blockbuster *Swiri* (1999), which launched the Sunshine Policy era of movies about the North.

Spies, especially double agents, are often female characters, as in *Order n° 027, True Color is Out*, but also *Black Rose* (1973), *Many Years Went By* (1982), *Unknown Heroes* (1979–81), *The Invisible Frontier* (1962), *Red Maple Leaves*, etc. This implies that women can be duplicitous, and they are especially vulnerable to temptation and "corruption," whereas men are more stable and righteous by nature (although, as we have seen, they are certainly not invulnerable to corruption and mistakes). We have seen that women can be easily defiled (a very old anthropological trope of the imaginary), at least ideologically, as noted in the socialist reality movies. In sum, women are depicted as easily "twisted", and it is the righteous man's duty to help them find the right way back. But for the depraved women who sold their souls to the imperialists, there is no coming back: most of the spies die or are arrested; even the miserable Unhui, a mere victim of her fate, does not make it.

These characters' ideological deviance goes beyond a temporary aberration that can be fixed. The influence of the imperialist enemy *alienates* them from their nature in irreparable ways. These female characters represent nocturnal images, showing deceitful women capable of metamorphosis, violence, and treachery; vamps using their powers of seduction to abuse men. In the dominant diurnal images of North Korean cinema, these characterizations of the dark side of the imaginary can only be perceived as purely negative. As suggested above, their alienation presents an intolerable otherness which must be eradicated to bring symbolic balance to the plot. Very few of these female sinners have a chance to reform and be reunited in the bosom of the Loving Leader. They no longer belong anymore to the Korean family – a terrible destiny for a woman in DPRK.

National division gendered

This correlation between the feminine, depravity, duplicity, otherness, as we have seen, extends to include the nation and its others. In North Korean cinema, South Korea is the corrupt and ambivalent feminine, an embodiment of the eternal female sinner, the universal prostitute. In contrast, of course, North Korea embodies all the positive male virtues. Thus, the national identity is expressed through a value-laden gender distinction producing the isomorphic North/South = male/female = pure/impure equation.[24] Reunification means, in this context: to re-educate impure South Korea, free from the negative influence of outside forces (America, Japan). But correcting a depraved soul requires a complex purification ritual. In many instances, one must pass through sacrifice and death. This is clearly a *schizomorphic* conception based on strong oppositions (outside vs. inside, South vs. North, bad vs. good, female duplicity and ambivalence vs. male rectitude and virtue, etc).

From this perspective, "salvation" can only be reached through male-virtues. A study of the North Korean imagination through representations of Kim Il Sung and Kim Jong-il would reveal an unambiguous solar,[25] heroic polarization, typical of a diurnal regime of images in which feminoid symbols are negatively valued when opposed to male ones. In "Kum-hui and Un-hui", for example, South Korea is always depicted at night or under gloomy conditions, people have dark complexions and wear dirty rags, but the North is always shown in bright sunlight, with people dressed in immaculate Korean cloths. Whereas North Korea is portrayed as the personalization of pure *Koreanness*, South Korea is, because of its openness, an impoverished version of it, perverted by foreign influences. North Korea portrayed itself in its cinema as the original or true Korea, and South Korea as a fake, decadent version. South Korea's otherness is partially denied, replaced by degradation, a decayed, inferior Same. South Korean portrayals are thus used in North Korean movies as devices to confirm and revalidate the national imagery and regime, while deprecating the "enemy" – the enemy as other, the Other as the enemy. In this logic, the negativity of otherness is strongly associated with feminoid images.

Note, however, that these negative portraits of South Korea almost completely disappeared from DPRK movies after the Sunshine Policy was adopted by South Korean president Kim Dae-jung from 1998. The Sunshine Policy sought to soften relations between North and South, and on this count, at least, it appears to have had some effect: South Korea no longer appeared as an explicit enemy in North Korean films, although it continued to be present occasionally as an implicit subtext. Perhaps the Sunshine Policy found an echo in the solar imaginary of the North? Regardless, what we find is that *other others* – Americans, Westerners or Japanese – were brought in to replace South Koreans and continue to be portrayed as the agents of depravity and defilement in the most recent movies.

Reading the regime's imaginary

How should we interpret these basic *topoi* in the context of ancient and recent North Korean history? Can we find statistical trends in our corpus that might help to define a "semantic basin,"[26] or a diachronic imaginary of the regime over the period under consideration?

A diurnal regime of images between tradition and modernity

The Chosŏn dynasty (1392–1910) adopted neo-Confucianism as official ideology. During this period, women slowly lost whatever status they had previously enjoyed. After the 16th century especially, confucianization rendered upper class women totally dependent on their father, husband and sons (the *samchongjiŭi* or triple guardianship position). The *Kyŏngkuktaejŏn* or General Code of the Kingdom made the principle of *namchonyŏbi* or "respect for men, disdain for women" law. Roles were strictly separated along the model of the basic father-son relation. Women and men were supposed to respect strict physical and functional separation, materially manifest in the structure of traditional homes with distinct male and female quarters. In that strict patriarchal structure of opposition and separation (typical of schizomorphic diurnal imaginaries), women had only one avenue towards integration: to try to approach male perfection. There was a place for iconic virtuous women, like Shin Saimdang, whose portrait is on the South Korean 50,000 won note. These *hyŏnmoyangch'ŏ* (gentle mother and good wife) could even be granted a *hongsalmun* or red gate recognizing their honor by the neighborhood. *Hyobu* (dutiful daughter-in-laws) and *hyonyŏ* (dutiful daughters) were female expressions of *hyo*, or filial piety, the highest of Confucian virtues. Virtuous Confucian women are celebrated for their sacrifice, like the only woman in Korea to be honored with a national shrine: Nongye. This *kisaeng* (geisha) threw herself in a river to kill a Japanese general during the Imjin War (1592–1598). It is noteworthy that the only Chosŏn woman deemed to be deserving of a shrine was a prostitute who had to die to be honorable. Other qualities expected of women were silence, patience, devotion, loyalty, fidelity (one could be executed for adultery), and modesty. These are also the qualities we find in virtuous socialist women in North Korean movies.

Thus, the pre-modern Chosŏn regime's official ideology displayed a clear *differential valorization*[27] of women and men (low versus high) even while luring women into an illusory possibility of equality and recognition through the promotion of standards like the *hyŏnmoyangch'ŏ*. Women were controlled and exploited by the regime through such *ideologemes* to secure the patrilineal and patriarchal order of society. These ideals of devoted wife and mother and of self-sacrifice, were quickly internalized by women themselves, especially by those from the upper classes. There was of course resistance to that order; we find instances of them in popular culture, like *p'ansori*, mask dance, literature, folk tales, songs, shaman rituals, etc. But the counter-culture was mostly confined to the lower classes; with an increasingly influential bourgeois class willing to adhere to *yangban* elite values, the counter-culture was increasingly marginalized, and the Confucian ideals of woman were eventually popularized and adopted among the lower classes as well.

By the end of the 19th century, the Confucian virtuous woman was increasingly being augmented by a Christian vision of female virtue which was gaining ground. In many respects these two sets of values are perfectly compatible. Christianity was associated with Western science and progress, though, and the new ideal woman was soon to become a "modern woman" by Western standards,[28] while continuing to aspire to be a *hyŏnmoyangch'ŏ* or paragon of virtue according to traditional Korean morality. We can see here a very specific complex of somewhat contradictory drives between modernity and tradition, which produces an ideal woman who must be both privately an obedient wife and mother, and publicly a perfect citizen who can, if necessary, sacrifice herself for the nation, like Nongye (or, like Mary, give her only son for the greater good).

To sum up, the ideal woman was a good wife and mother, who at best could achieve a simulacrum of the ideal man. Her main quality was *effacement*: humility, sacrifice, and even *defeminization*.[29] Notably, this woman image was used from the beginning of the 20th century as a symbol of the nation itself, with the invasion and colonization by imperial Japan being portrayed as *rape* by foreign powers.[30] This laid the foundations for a long isomorphic association woman = nation, which is found at the core of contemporary Korean collective psyche. As we have seen, North Korean cinema explicitly reflects these schemes.

There is a continuum from traditional to modern evident in the representations of ideal women in the Northern socialist regime, which can even be seen in the decision to retain the traditional term "Chosŏn" in the official name of the modern nation. This continuum, encompassing reactivated Buddhist and Confucian tropes and newly imported Christian ones, may have helped define the *topoi* developed by the new regime. As we have seen, this syncretism has generated some interesting twists to the traditional tropes. Typical mother characters continue to be defined by their self-negation, their nurturing and caring for others. But the virtuous mother caring for her personal family is no longer enough under socialism: she must transcend her personal and private motherhood to attain the zenith of the models, the loving care of the Leader. His bosom is the paragon of protection and sacrifice for the nation. In this comparison, it is not that the Great Leader is being feminized but that the perfect mother is being redefined. For mothers and spouses to be good socialist *hyŏnmoyangch'ŏ*, they must follow the example of the (male) soldier fighting for national independence and prosperity. In this diurnal, heroic regime, polemic and belligerence becomes the ultimate reference. So virtuous women are those who have learned from the example of the Guide's motherly attitude, and through a neo-Buddhist enlightenment trope, transcended their femininity. In that (political and imaginary) regime, women must be good wives and mothers, but also dutiful citizens (*hyomin*); but here "dutiful citizens" also means "soldiers" fighting for the good of the nation, which in turn means a radical masculinization; which brings us again to the trope of effacement. Herein lies the possibility for many women characters in the movies to become heroines (74% of female characters of our movies are positive actants). But diurnal regimes are characterized by oppositional schemes of rise and fall, as well as purity and defilement. In that context, woman as a simulacrum of man always remains inferior to man itself. Hence North Korean films portray female characters who attempt "no more" than to negate their femininity and achieve the absolute perfection of the (male) Leader; an impossible task and therefore a frustrating ambition.

This inversion of female attributes can lead to unusual figures: female soldiers and hunters who do not threaten males (unlike Diana, for example, in Greek mythology). When masculinized, these virtuous women become more wholesome, cleansed of their impurity and inferiority. This process is represented in the Ch'un-hyang tale, in which the heroine must suffer ordeals to be purified and accepted into the masculine order. At the same time, in an inverse yet complementary move, the figure of the Father (Kim Il Sung/Jong-il) is completed with the addition of the maternal qualities of the protective bosom. This gives him a cyclic dimension – belonging to nocturnal feminoid imagery and unavailable to most male heroes – thus opening the path to eternity (infinite repetition). His androgyny evokes the Christian dialectic of the Trinity (Father-Son-Holy Spirit/Party), transforming a sterile and morbid homomorphic regime into an endless dynastic fantasy.

We have seen that women who don't follow the virtuous path, those who go astray, can be "saved" by another character – whether female or male – in an antagonistic pair through which they are re-educated and returned to the righteous way. Once the intolerable inversion weak man/ strong woman has been corrected and proper roles restored, these errant women can be re-embraced into the bosom of the nation. In these cases, as we have seen, the men are often scientists. The trope of science and progress is strongly represented in DPRK cinema. This is no surprise: Marxism developed in the 19th century Promethean imaginary,[31] portraying itself as a science of progress and universal well-being.[32] All communist regimes were influenced by that imaginary to some extent. North Korea remains deeply indebted to that late romantic semantic basin with its strong Faustian temptation (including the "sorcerer's apprentice," as can be seen in recent years with its nuclear bargaining stratagem). As Durand remarks, the late romantic imaginary is quite misogynist, portraying numerous ambiguous and depraved temptresses. We have seen this, too, with deceitful females defiled and alienated by a malign foreign influence. In these cases, once she has "crossed-over", there is no return. In espionage and war movies, prostitutes and spies represent the corrupted South, a metonymy of the corrupting Others. Along with the male-female opposition in these movies, the divided nation itself is gendered and located within that schizomorphic, oppositional diurnal regime of imagery. Solar images of the hero, explicitly and symbolically represented by the Kims' portrayals as Suns of the nation, are extended to encompass the entirety of North Korea and opposed to the theriomorphic others of the nocturnal, dark Southern side of the frontier.

We have also seen a strong isomorphism: perfect mother of perfect citizens // Mother of the Nation, which leads to another isomorphism: country, nation // hometown (*kohyang*) // family // founding fathers (national heroes and Kim Il Sung). Many movies are set in the *kohyang* and deal with issues of local identity opposed to the dangers of globalization and corrupting contact with the outside world (*Girls of My Hometown, Here We Live, Mother's Happiness, Our Fragrance,* etc.). That patriarchal family-oriented imaginary, clearly centripetal, in total accord with Juche theory, portrays the family/nation as a cell. Protected from outside influences, it is characterized by its singularity and purity.[33] This is strongly opposed to otherness and its consequences. The potential appeal of imaginary structures of fusion (i.e. reunification in political terms), is counter-balanced by the fierce diurnal polarization, preferring opposition to union: union here is realized through the opposition to others. The temptation of the nocturnal imaginary is only expressed through a morbid and regressive fascination with images of unity, sacrifice, abnegation – death. This is why the genuine otherness of others, whether women or foreigners, is simply denied. This is a clear example of the "autistic" radicalization of this kind of imaginary when not balanced by other regimes of images.

Diachronic reading of the imaginary

Let us try now to place this analysis in time. Table 6.1 summarizes the trends found in our corpus to help us decipher a timeline.[34]

It is very difficult to characterize films made before the 1960s since very few are available. As mentioned, it is unclear whether they have simply

Table 6.1: Diachronic trends in our corpus

	Male characters	Female characters	General trends
1960s	Peak of males as main characters 100% of main male characters are positive 30% secondary characters are negative	70% of all female characters are negative or to be reeducated Peak of secondary and negative female characters	
1970s	Peak of negative male characters (> 40% main characters) 23% of male characters have to be reeducated	Peak positive female main characters Peak of secondary and negative female characters	Peak of negative characters in general (30%) Opposition main positive female character ↔ male main character and/or secondary characters (fem or male)
1980s	Peak of negative male characters (> 70% male characters)	Main female character has tendency to be the lead role Peak of positive female main characters	
1990s	Absence of main male role > 30% of movies Absence of secondary male role > 50% of movies More positive male characters (40%) but still peak of male characters to be reeducated (24%)	Main female character has tendency to be the lead role	Peak of positive characters in general (93%) Shifting of paradigm: from negative to positive criticism, and slow revalorization of male characters
2000s	Fewer negative male characters (less than 10% of secondary roles) More than 50% of male main characters are positive	60% of main female characters are to be reeducated! // 1960s	Peak of positive characters in general (93%) Inversion of tendency: strong remasculinization of cinema – opposition positive man to negative female to reeducate

disappeared or were purposely withdrawn for ideological reasons. We can only infer some trends by comparing with the films of the 1960s and with other cultural productions of that time, like theater plays.[35]

"Pre-revolution" (prior to 1945) traditions were harshly criticized and banned as "reactionary," yet they were quickly reenacted in various fields[36] to serve the regime's political and economic agendas. After a period of revolutionary measures promoting the gender equality officially enshrined in the 1946 Constitution, the regime seems to have quickly returned, once the war was over, to traditional values to promote an image of woman that was useful to the nation's development.[37] At first, the regime needed women "soldiers of ideology and production,"[38] to help build the new nation. This image was resurrected every time the country entered a new era of mobilization (war, reconstruction, etc.), which required *participative* gender politics.[39] While officially retaining the Marxist-Leninist doctrine of sexual parity, another model appears to have emerged in the 1950s–60s with Kim Il Sung's consolidation of power and the country's economic development, returning women to the private sphere.[40] The country needed mothers to re-establish the centralizing control of the family cell, therefore the regime revalorized motherhood in a newly divisive politics which once again separated the roles of the sexes. But it was impossible to completely turn back the wheels they had set in motion, so the "new socialist woman" became a mixed model of tradition and modernity. As we have seen, based on the traditional Confucian *hyŏnmoyangch'ŏ*, the new woman had to be an ideal mother and wife, as well as an ideal socialist citizen, both a heroine of production and a soldier of the ideological struggle. This led to a new type of film character embodying the conflicting ideals expected of women in modern North Korea: they must be perfect, and to achieve that goal, they must be more than women – so to speak, *superwomen*.[41] Lee U-yeong refers to this model as a "double exploitation" of women, at home and in the work place.[42] We can trace a similar trajectory in the ideal of the "new woman" in Stalinist USSR, with same impulse toward equality, followed by the "great retreat" of the 1930s–40s, which has been described as the "Stalinist step backward in the legislation and social practices as a stabilization of society."[43] Women were in great demand for the industrial workforce, but they were also required as reproductive labor to meet the birth-rate objectives – their bodies were instrumentalized by a typical patriarchal biopower. North Korea followed closely in those steps.

But this very general analysis provides only a glimpse of the cleavage of the 1940s–50s, when the "new new woman" emerged in the official North Korean imaginary. Returning to the analysis from our corpus provides a richer picture. The 1960s were clearly captured by a masculinist imaginary, in which all the main male characters are positive, and 70% of female characters, generally minor or secondary characters, are negative actants. This may be indicative of an effort to reassert control over the roles of women in society by re-instating traditional values through a divisive policy. The 1970s indicate an inversion of that trend, with more negative male characters, many of whom (23%) need "reeducation". Simultaneously, there was a peak in positive female main characters, as well as minor secondary characters, often placed in opposition to those negative males. A clear oppositional scheme remains, but there has been a transvaluation that now favors the main female characters. Is this due to Kim Jong-il's interventions in cinema at that time? Does this development mirror an economic situation which requires women to be valorized both at home and in the office/factory? Whatever the reason, female imagery in the DPRK cinema continues to evolve toward more positive and leading roles. In the 1980s, 70% of male characters in our corpus have negative agency. As the film production itself reaches its peak, movies with plots centered around women also peak, while the unambiguously negative female character disappears with the decline of spy and war films.

The 1990s see a clear shift in pattern. The death of Kim Il Sung in 1994 which brings his son Kim Jong-il to power, followed by the terrible famine of the late 1990s, opens the "army-first era" (*sŏnkun shidae*). There are more leading female characters in movies, with male characters correspondingly decreasing in our corpus. At the same time, male characters are increasingly in positive roles (40%), although there are still a lot of men needing reeducation. Moreover, the overall tendency is towards more positive than negative characters in movies (93%, if characters transforming from negative to positive are included), a trend that continues into the following decade. This reflects the new paradigm of "positive criticism"[44] in these years, and a slow revalorization of male characters. The emphasis on female characters in this period can be explained by the importance of women in times of hardship, when men are requisitioned for hard labor in the fields and construction sites.[45] The death of his father may also have encouraged Kim Jong-il, who until then was kept in the shadow of Kim Il Sung – the Father of the nation – to foster female characters and feminine characteristics. As noted, it was during this period that the cult of his mother, Kim Jong-suk, was actively promoted. The tendency grows stronger in the 2000s, with a concerted "remasculinization" of North Korean cinema. More than 50% of male main characters of our corpus are positive agents, whereas suddenly 60% of main female characters must be reeducated, a situation reminiscent of the '60s. We have again a gendered opposition, as in the '70s, but this time between a positive man and a negative woman needing reeducation. War movies (a war against an invisible, untold enemy) as well as spy films (mostly against Japan) also returned to the screens. None of these trends are surprising in the "army first era", especially after the end of South Korea's "Sunshine Policy" (2009). The challenges of political survival in times of international isolation, with its constant acts of nuclear and ballistic defiance, may explain this shift back towards a more radical diurnal imaginary. But the industrial efforts needed to pursue economic reforms may also explain the re-emphasis put on the political education of women, who perform vital roles as both workers and executives in many factories. It also reflects their increasing role since the 1970s in Korean society and economy, and the possible threat that their growing importance may cause to this "enormous national patriarchal society."[46] We also know they play important roles in the underground economy, especially the food black market.[47] The "deviant" female type may be the target of reeducation through this cinema. Does this indicate that the "superwoman" injunction was too heavy to wear? Perhaps. But we should not forget that in the "positive criticism" era, most of the female characters are, in the end, brought back to normal, becoming once again good mothers, faithful wives, ideal citizens in the bosom of the *taegajŏng*, the "great socialist family."

Conclusion

We have insisted on the importance of the methodology in this study. We worked on a carefully defined corpus, first in a synchronic approach to determine the range and diversity of *topoi* in the narratives; then a diachronic analysis of the same corpus was applied to try to understand the evolution of these *topoi* during specific periods. A mixed model emerged, as in Stalinist USSR, merging tradition (neo-Confucian values) with modernity (ideals of the "new woman" or socialist heroine equal to men). But this model changed its polarities depending on the specific socio-political context. Whatever these evolutions may be, the synchronic analysis proved that there is a specific valorization of female and male characters in North-Korean official imaginary. This imaginary of the regime spreads along what should be called a Juchean *bassin sémantique*,[48] that is a specific set of images, symbols, myths and ideologems which must be read in itself, and not continuously understood through Chinese, Soviet, Japanese or even South-Korean models.

The *topoi* found in the movies, structured in three different categories, are rooted in Confucian, Buddhist and even Christian tropes. From the perfect woman offered as an iconic model to the deceitful female who must be re-educated, and to the sinful woman to be sacrificed in a "purification" ritual, we meet three different figures, but all of them can be considered as under the same diurnal regime of images. They draw an interesting topography of the feminoid symbols in DPRK, which may help us to locate and confirm the structures of the imaginary of this unique totalitarian system. The perfect heroines are viragos with the same qualities as the ideal male hero. They are placed under a strong solar regime, like the Father figures of the Great and Dear Leaders. We find here women warriors, women fighting against the "beasts", whether the actual animals of the forest as hunters, or the imperialist monsters of the human world. They are just transpositions of male figures, transgendered to fit the propaganda of the regime. Because, in this schizomorphic imaginary, females cannot be as such positive complements of males, but must be opposed to and separated from them. If they cannot achieve through the socialist virtues their masculinization and emulate the models (the Great Leader as the Mother of the nation), they become sinful women to be corrected or eliminated – which is typical of the heroic structures of the imaginary. As we have seen, the erosion of the public civil sphere to the profit of a martial structuration of both the society and the imaginary leads to women who have no other choices than to be soldiers fighting for a three-folded cause: the production, the ideology and the defense of the country/ family. In this, they meet the terrible injunction also imposed on North Korean men: to sacrifice themselves for the country as perfect soldiers, or as it was expressed in USSR, as "martyrs of communism."[49] But for women, there is a double sacrifice: it is not only their life that they must devote to become socialist heroines, they must also give up their symbolic femininity which is completely denied by the leading diurnal regime of images.

In terms of narrative structures, as far as films are considered as texts, the cleavage between personal aspirations and patriotism can be seen as the narrative core of most of the analyzed movies. Women characters are used as a *narrative trigger*, working through their opposition to men or their inner contradictions. Female characters as *plot agents* are also used to symbolize the class struggle in feudal relationships (like in Ch'unhyang's tale): they are symbolic victims sacrificed for the sake of the narrative.[50] But they can also be *catalysts*: women can purify other characters when they are agents of correction. This illustrates the way the *gender function* is used in cinematographic narratives and how woman as a structuring image is central to North Korean cinema, and as a whole to DPRK's political imaginary.

This female image is more complex than one might expect. Between tradition and modernity, between individual and collective happiness, hereditary oligarchy and communism, woman, as a guardian of the family, is a symbol of the nation itself seen as a *taegajŏng* or "big family". We find here an isomorphism woman = nation, where woman, even if lost on an errant path, symbolizes the people-as-a-child who finds his way under the loving guidance of the Leader (father) and the Party (mother), parents of the nation. Exploited, North Korean woman is under the double contradiction of her antagonist desires (personal vs. collective happiness) as an agent of the narrative, as well as the double-bind "Confucian tradition vs. socialist modernity" as an instrument of the politics and propaganda of the regime. Her alienation has never been so great, despite a legal and social context which could suggest that she has an advantage compared to her South-Korean counterpart. The hybridization of the socialist "new woman" figure obliges her to be a superwoman ready to make all the sacrifices.

Yet, we must acknowledge evolutions in time and in the general historical context. There were constant comings and goings between divisive and participative politics. In our movies, women have a central role as agents, and moreover, statistically speaking, a positive role (74%). Completely negative characters are rare, with many of the opposers finding at the end of the story the way to reeducation. We have noticed a recent "remasculinization" of North Korean cinema, but it works mainly as a revalorization of male characters rather than as a devaluation of women. What is new, is the fact that women became in the 1970s an interface between the public and private spheres, which, in a long-term context can be seen as revolutionary. But the price to pay for that new role is high, since it costs the very femininity of the woman: this is what it takes to be that interface, in a society where man is still the ideal standard and the leading regime of images are schizoid structures.

In that imaginary, the sanctum of motherhood is transcended into the martial image of the soldier sacrificing her/himself to the nation. Femininity is simply denied in such a (political) regime (of imaginary) – as is any kind of otherness. We have seen that foreigners and South Koreans are accepted only if they become North Koreans in the bosom of the Party and embrace Jucheism. This particular attitude towards otherness is not surprising in a political regime so radical in its totalitarian effort to control every aspect of social realities, moreover a regime built on the myth of sameness/oneness. We could be tempted to see here another confirmation of the intuition developed by Durand in his *Introduction to Mythodology* (1996), that totalitarian regimes in the 20th century suffered from a strongly unilateral diurnal imaginary insufficiently balanced by other regimes of images. But what we have seen in these movies is just an expression of the propaganda of the state. We know almost nothing about the real reception of these films. It would be fascinating to be able to study the actual penetration of this "official imaginary" in the people's collective psyche, and to know to what extent there has been resistance to it… Is the image of women that we see in movies so different from the representation of women in the actual collective imaginary? Does it differ from real social practices? Until reunification happens, at this point, the investigation must give way to the speculation…

Annexes (chart and graphs) available online:

1 Table of movies-actantial levels. Available online at: http://www.benjaminjoinau.com/uploads/4/1/5/9/4159632/table_of_movies-actantial_levels.pdf
2 .Graphs displaying actantial structures and predicates. Available online at: http://www.benjaminjoinau.com/male-female-characters-in-north-korean-cinema.html
3 Diachronic chart of roles by genders. Available online at: http://www.benjaminjoinau.com/uploads/4/1/5/9/4159632/diachronic_chart_of_roles_by_genders.pdf

Notes

1 Lee, Woo-young, 1993. *Pukhan chŏngch'isahoehwaesŏ chŏnt'ongmunhwaŭi yŏkhal: pukhanyŏnghwapunsŏkŭl chungshimŭro* (Function of traditional culture in political socialization of North Korea: centering on an analysis of North Korean cinema). Seoul: Institute for Reunification; Yu, China, 1999. "Pukhanyŏnghwaŭi t'alshinhwahwawa chaeguhoekhwa uihae 80nyŏndae hubankwa 90nyŏndae chŏnpan yesulyŏnghwa naerŏt'ibŭ chŏllyakkwa chendŏginŭng" (For a demystification and re-demarcation of North Korean movies: Gender function and narrative strategy in the late 80s and early 90s). In *Proceedings of the 37th seminar T'ongilmunjehaksul.* Seoul: Sookmyung University T'ongilmunje Research Institute; Lim, Hye-gyŏng and Sin Hŭi-sŏn, 2000. "T'ongil munhwa hyŏngsŏngŭl uihan nam.bukhan yŏnghwa sokŭi yŏsŏngsang pigyo yŏngu" (Comparative Study of Feminine Images in North and South Korean Movies for the Formation of a Culture of Reunification). *Aseayŏsŏngyŏngu* 39: 251–336.
2 For example, Coppola, Antoine, 2012. "Stéréotypes des femmes dans les films sud-coréens et nord-coréens" (Female stereotypes in North and South Korean movies). *Sociétés* n°115 (1) (juin 25): 41–50.
3 Table of movies-actantial levels. Available online at: http://www.benjaminjoinau.com/uploads/4/1/5/9/4159632/table_of_movies-actantial_levels.pdf
4 Though she intentionally chooses movies which supposedly break with the usual stereotypes of DPRK movies, her corpus of four movies from 1985 to 1993 seems to lack any diachronic perspective. Yu China, 1999; see also Lim and Sin, 2000: 253.
5 This "landscape of the imaginary" is what Durand calls a *bassin sémantique*, a concept which encompasses the evolution of imaginary structures over time. Durand, Gilbert. 1996. *Introduction à la mythodologie*. Paris: Albin Michel.
6 Durand, Gilbert. 1992. *Les Structures anthropologiques de l'imaginaire*. Paris: Dunod. See also Durand 1996.
7 "Male" and "female" in this perspective refer to a gendered polarization, not to the actual sex or gender. This is why, when possible, we prefer the use of "feminoid" instead of female or feminine; and "viriloid" instead of male or masculine, to stress the difference.
8 Schönherr, Johannes, 2012. *North Korean Cinema: A History*. Jefferson, N.C: McFarland & Company, Inc., Publishers.
9 Lee, Myŏng-ja, 2007. *Pukhanyŏnghwasa* (North Korean Cinema History). Seoul: Communication Books.
10 There is also a series of printed storylines published in Pyonyang by Munye Ch'ulp'ansa.
11 See Barthes, Roland, 1966. "Introduction à L'analyse Structurale Des Récits." *Communications* 8 (1): 1–27; Greimas, Algirdas-Julien, 1984. *Structural Semantics: An Attempt at a Method*. Lincoln: University of Nebraska Press.
12 Here, representativeness does not relate to the truth of social representations in movies, but to the possible penetration of a movie in audience's imaginary (the "success" of a movie generally denotes a larger impact on public's *representations*).

13 Kim, Jong-il, 1989. *On the Art of the Cinema*. Pyongyang: Foreign Languages Publishing House, p. 2.
14 Kim Jong-il, 1989: 41.
15 Based on Lee, Myŏng-ja, 2007. Most attempts (e.g., Schönherr's 2012) to construct a timeline for North Korean cinema seem rather arbitrary, perhaps a reflection of the analysts' preconceptions of North Korean policies. I therefore prefer, at least in the initial stage, a neutral, although conventional, timeline based on decades.
16 In *My Mother Was a Hunter*, the mother wears the signifiers of Diana, the Huntress, an archetypal symbol of the imaginary: later we will see this figure again.
17 Myers, B. R., 2011. *The Cleanest Race*. Brooklyn, N.C: Melville House Publishing.
18 It is to be noted that the complex relation between the three figures (Kim Il Sung, his son – or now his grand-son – and the Party) has many similarities to that between the Christian God, his Son and the Holy Spirit. These triads work functionally as a single entity. In the former-USSR, the Party was seen as both the mother and the family of the people, and Stalin, although rarely explicitly represented as such, was the father of the nation: their roles were well separated along this gendered distinction. Bernier, François, 2011. "Dictature et littérature : l'homme nouveau et la femme nouvelle sous Stalin" (Dictature and literature: New man and New wife under Stalin). *Le Manuscrit*. http://www.revuelemanuscrit.com/index.php/le-manuscrit-edition-thematique/hiver-2011/91-dictature-et-litterature-lhomme-nouveau-et-la-femme-nouvelle-sous-Stalin. Accessed 2013/08/08.
19 And this category is also by far the most represented: only 12 out of 90 movies show female characters as helpers to a main male character for a total of 35 female helpers and 63 positive main female characters.
20 For complements to Ch'unhyang, see Jager, Sheila Miyoshi. 2003. *Narratives of Nation Building in Korea: A Genealogy of Patriotism*. Armonk, N.Y: Sharpe: 65–68.
21 Greimas, 1984.
22 See for example Sŏ, Chŏng-nam, 2002. *Pukhan yŏnghwa t'amsa* (An Inquiry into North Korean Cinema). Seoul: Saenggakŭi namu: 371, and Myers, 2011.
23 See Jager, 2003, for South Korean context.
24 On this question, concerning South Korean nationalist historiography and "division as rape", see Jager, 2003: 69, and about the prostitute and miscegenation themes see p. 72.
25 References to the sun in relation to Kim Il Sung, Kim Jong-il and now Kim Jong-un, known as the "Sun of the 21st century", are structuring the regime's mythology. See Joinau, Benjamin. 2014. 'The Arrow and the Sun: A topo-mythanalysis of Pyongyang." 14(1): 65–92.
26 Durand, 1996.
27 Héritier, Françoise. 1996. *Masculin/féminin*. Paris: O. Jacob; and Héritier, Françoise. 2002. *Masculin/féminin 2, Dissoudre la hiérarchie*. Paris: O. Jacob.
28 See for example Jager, 2003: 43.
29 Defeminization as a neutralization of "dangerous" feminine attributes.

30 See Jager, 2003: 79: "The appeal to the feminine in the language of the resistance in contemporary Korea, much like in colonial times, carried with it values of purity against filth, and of chastity against contamination, evoking the explicit sexual implication of the division as rape."
31 Durand, 1996.
32 Boia, Lucian. 2000. *La mythologie scientifique du communisme* (The scientific mythology of communism).
33 See Myers, 2011.
34 Detailed results of the corpus statistical analysis can be consulted online at http://www.benjaminjoinau.com/male-female-characters-in-north-korean-cinema.html.
35 Lee, Sang-woo, 2005. "Pukhan hŭigoke nat'anan isangjŏk yŏsŏng-kukmin ch'angch'ulŭi yangsang (The aspects of idealized female-nation building in North Korean plays)." *Hangukgŭkyesulyŏngu* 21.
36 Lee, Woo-young, 1993; Lee, Sang-woo, 2005.
37 Kim, Suzy, 2013. *Everyday Life in the North Korean Revolution (1945–1950)*. Ithaca, N.Y.: Cornell University Press: 174–203.
38 Lee, Sang-woo, 2005: 288.
39 Ueno, Chizuko, and Yamamoto, Beverley, 2004. *Nationalism and Gender*. Melbourne, Vic.; Portland, OR: Trans Pacific Press.
40 Yun, Miryang, 1991. *Pukhanŭi yŏsŏngchŏngch'aek* (Woman Policy of North Korea). Seoul: Hanul.
41 Chŏng, Yŏng-sŏn, 2017. *Pukhan'esŏ yŏjaro sandanŭn kŏt* (To Live in North Korea as a Woman). Seoul: Kyŏngchin Publishing; Lee, Sang-woo, 2005: 286; Yu, China, 1999: note 11)
42 Yu China (1993) shows that the double exploitation of women by industrial society began to be addressed in South Korean cinema in the 1970s and 1980s: we find similar images of women portrayed in that cinema too (the reproductive mother, the self-sacrificing woman, etc.), but here they are intended to provide a critique of the tradition, and are often depicted in opposition to the rebellious and energetic woman who tries to resist her exploitation (see also Lim and Sin, 2000: 285–88). In North Korea, this bi-polar valorization is represented by a single character: the perfect socialist woman is both a traditional Confucian female *and* a revolutionary heroine. As Lee Woo-young (1993) notes, there is an internal contradiction in that North Korean superwoman character. But as Yu China observes (1993: 125), there is also a "superwoman complex" in South Korean cinema: the happy endings depict modern women who are independent, *but still* respectful of traditional family values. One must wait until the 2000s to see female characters emerging in South Korean cinema who try to free themselves from this "double bind" imposed by the society (Coppola, 2012).
43 Bernier, 2011: 3.
44 Schönherr, 2012: 109–110.
45 Kim Won-hong sums up the evolution of the roles prescribed by the Democratic Women's Union, quoting for the *sŏnkun shidae* era: "Realization of 'gunstock families' and 'motherhood heroes' proposed as goals – Women's traditional role, i.e. their responsibility for child care and education, is emphasized and the role of a revolutionary mother is defined as 'bearing as many children as possible

who can later join the military' and supporting their children to their fullest after they have joined the People's Army." Kim, Won-hong. 2014. *Women of North Korea: A Closer Look at Everyday Life*. Seoul: Institute for Unification Education, Ministry of Unification: 64–65.

46 Lee, Sang-woo, 2005: 310. Movies like *We are All One Family* (1983), with a very performative title, show that there were issues to be addressed concerning the changing roles in couples: the heroine cannot take care alone of her household because she works, the husband is also too lazy to help, responsibilities for the crisis are on both sides, and it is eventually the role of the community (society) to help them find a balance.

47 Haggard, Stephan, & Noland, Marcus, 2011. *Gender in Transition: The Case of North Korea*. East-West Center Working Papers n. 124. Honolulu, Hawai'i: East-West Center; Kim, Won-hong, 2014; Lee, Mi-kyung, 2005. "The Issue of North Korean Women by Examining Gender Awareness of Female Defectors". *The Korean Journal of International Studies* 45 (5); Park, Kyung-ae, 2011. "Economic crisis, Women's changing economic roles, and their implications for women's status in North Korea." *The Pacific Review* XXIV (2): 159–77.

48 Durand, 1996.
49 Bernier, 2011.
50 Yu China, 1993.

7 Dual Language, Dubbed Cinema: An Enlightened Colonial Subject in *Homeless Angels*

Youngjae Yi

Two censorship systems in 1941: Japan and colonial Korea

The period of "unification of Japan and colonial Korea" (*naisenittai*)[1] which followed Japanese colonization raised existential questions about the place and role of Korean cinema. Was it possible for Koreans to make film under the colonial regime without being seen as collaborating with the oppressors? This chapter examines the case of Ch'oe In-gyu,[2] a Korean filmmaker who received a great deal of attention and praise from both Japanese and colonial Korean audiences and critics, and who perhaps epitomizes the model colonial filmmaker during the unification of Japan and colonial Korea.

Ch'oe In-gyu's film *Tuition Fee* (1940) tells the story of a group of Korean schoolboys who become full citizens of the Japanese Empire through the enlightening tutelage of their Japanese teacher. His subsequent work *Homeless Angels* (1941) was immediately recommended by the Korean divisions of the Japanese Imperial Army Press Section and was praised by both colonial Korean and Japanese film critics, one of whom said that "*Tuition Fee* and *Homeless Angels* come first when speaking of Korean films."[3]

After the recommendation by the Imperial Army Press Section, *Homeless Angels* passed censorship screening by the Secret Service and was designated a Recommended Film by Japan's Ministry of Education, Science, Sports and Culture.[4] *Homeless Angels* tells the story of a group of Korean street children who are enlightened[5] by a local pastor who dreams of Japanese Imperialism. After its initial praise, the film-makers were surprised when it was released for Japanese audiences; not only

Photo 7.1: Tuition Fee *(left),* Homeless Angels *(right)*

were nearly 200 meters removed in 35 cuts from the original film after re-inspection by the censors, but only the Japanese-dubbed version was allowed to be shown to the public.[6] The Korean-language version with Japanese subtitles was never released to the general public, but in the dubbed version, the national identity of the pastor – the enlightening leader – is vague. In the end, no clear reason was given for the censorship. What are we to make of the severe censoring of this highly acclaimed film?

This chapter examines the process of the film's censorship and the reasons behind it, as well as how the case has been remembered in history. The latter, of course, is inseparable from issues of continuity and discontinuity between the colonial and post-colonial periods.

The question posed in this study is two-fold: to what extent could a colonized man become a full citizen of the empire? and what was the effect of *naisenittai* and the colonized male elites' attempts at re-masculinization[7] in the post-colonial period? The *Genkai Sea*, the impassable space separating Japan and Korea, will be defined as the limit of re-masculinization, and thus the limit of the control of colonized men. Put differently, the object of this study is to identify the spatial and hierarchical frames which determine the possibilities and obstacles for national subjects in colonial Korea.

New but disturbed system of colonial Korean cinema

Immediately after the screening of a dubbed version of *Homeless Angels* in Japan, the film was the main topic of discussion at a symposium on colonial Korean film held by the Japanese film magazine *Eiga Junpo*.

History reveals that the censorship of *Homeless Angels* had a significant impact on the future direction of colonial Korean films. This film was the result of collective efforts by many prominent figures in the Korean film industry at the time. Ch'oe In-gyu, the director, had come into the spotlight for his creativity and profitability, in both Korea and Japan, with the films *Tuition Fee* and *Homeless Angels*, and the films' producer, Yi Chang-yong, was a leader in the colonial Korean film industry. Yi Chang-yong had developed an understanding of the *naisenittai* film-making context much more quickly than others. Nishikame Motosada, who wrote the screenplay for this film, was an employee of the Publication Division of the Governor-General of Korea. Nishikame was also the executive producer for *Tuition Fee*.[8] Another important figure in this group was Im Hwa, one of the greatest literary critics of the time, who wrote the Korean dialogue for the film. Im Hwa was a leading theorist at KAPF (the *Korea Artista Proleta Federacio* in esperanto) and was deeply engaged in KAPF's cinema-related activities as an actor and dramatist. At the same time, he was writing *Korean Cinema*, the first general history of colonial Korean cinema. After serious deliberations about what could be shown in the Japanese (mainland) market, this team of luminaries produced *Homeless Angels*, thus setting the direction for colonial Korean film during *naisenittai*. *Homeless Angels* was the result of the Korean film makers' dedicated efforts to hit the Japanese market. Therefore, Yi Chang-yong asked for a clear explanation for the censorship.

> We must consider a policy for future productions, so we would like you to state clearly the opinion of the Ministry about the issue of *Homeless Angels*, from various points of view. That will be very helpful for us to decide our future policies.[9]

This was not only Yi Chang-yong's view. In his review of *Homeless Angels,* which appeared in the same issue, Japanese film critic Suzuki Yukichi also mentioned the unfairness of not giving any reason for the censorship.

> This case will cast a dark shadow over the future of Korean film, which is now about to make a new start in a novel and sound direction, I request a clear explanation not only for the sake of Korean film but also for the sake of "our film world," which includes Korean film.[10]

The censorship authority's handling of the film was inconsistent and clearly unfair. Why did this issue arise? Why would the censorship authority not provide a clear explanation?

This course of events unfolded while colonial Korean cinema was being completely re-organized to assimilate with Japanese cinema. That re-organization was not, however, entirely coerced. The colonial Korean film industry had already been faced with the challenges of expanding its market to cover the rapidly increasing costs of production following the introduction of talkies in the mid-1930s. Under these circumstances, *naisenittai* seemed to offer promising opportunities to meet the demand for entry into new markets[11] through an intimate connection between colonial Korean and Japanese film. As such, these opportunities were the source for some optimism in the Korean film industry; they did not see the situation simply in terms of collaboration with the colonial government. On a pragmatic level, integration into Japanese cinema was seen as an opportunity to secure advanced technology and capital, as well as a larger market on the Japanese mainland and in the Greater East Asia Co-Prosperity Sphere, including Manchuria.[12]

It soon became apparent, however, that such optimism was misplaced. From the 1940s, the colonial Korean film industry had been reduced to a production house for Japanese film, under the direct control of the Japanese government, and had to face the prospect that "Korean film" might disappear altogether. Korean film makers nevertheless clung to their hopes with one hand, while with the other hand, they tried to negotiate with the Governor-General of Korea to find a way to resolve their difficulties. Yi Chang-yong, the producer of *Homeless Angels*, was a typical figure in those negotiations. A former cinematographer for Na Woon-gyu Productions in the early 1930s, he moved into film production and planning before founding a film distribution agency in the mid-1930s. Even under the Japanese government, his Koryeo Film Company developed rapidly toward his plan to establish a large-scale integrated film production company in 1940, aided by his close relationship with the Japanese Governor-General.[13]

Yi Chang-yong's path clearly reveals the dilemma of the colonial Korean film industry. Integration with the Japanese film industry offered a possibility for colonial Korean cinema to rapidly expand, but at the expense of creative and cultural freedoms, raising questions about the value of its existence. If Korean cinema became wholly a sub-division of Japanese cinema, would the distinctiveness of Korean cinema survive? Yi Chang-yong stated that the Korean film industry was eager to invite Japanese technicians, but were opposed to inviting directors and screenwriters, citing the "peculiarity of Korean films."

The term "peculiarity" is troublesome here. Although it is being used as a synonym for distinctive or unique, the word also connotes deviance from the norm, which in this case serves to acknowledge a material hierarchy of dominant and subordinate, and thus to accept the ideology of assimilation. It then becomes a base for further assimilating the colonized into that ideology and, in turn, further eroding the distinctiveness / peculiarity of *Korean*. The following quotation elaborates on the term's ambiguity. Suzuki Shozo, of the Movie Censorship Office of the Governor-General of Korea, told a symposium on the "Peculiarity of Korean Films":

> I think the Korean Film Company was founded by the peculiar circumstance of Korea. Even though saying the peculiarity can be thought as a contradiction, on the ground where *naisenittai* is being insisted upon, such a path is very natural indeed when reviewing the situation.[14]

Once this peculiarity is recognized, another issue arises. That is, while the peculiarity in question refers to the distinctive flavor and style of Korean film-making, with its different culture and life, the broader implications of the term rapidly reach into other matters, such as the peculiarity of a subjugated colonial having the resources and power to produce films telling stories of the colony. The peculiar censorship of *Homeless Angels* no doubt arises from this line of thought. The issue was not about a single film, but is a manifestation of the psychological warfare between the government and colonized male elites.

Until a film copy of *Homeless Angels* was discovered in 2004, its reputation as his greatest work was based on written commentaries which praised its literary realism, unique to this director.[15] This is merely an affirmative echo of the evaluation in the colonial period: for example, the collection, *The Film Critics: Homeless Angels,* cites the following commentary:

> Watching *Homeless Angels*, I am made to think about the issue of realism from several points of view... [E]ven now the light of an electric car on the Jongno of Keijō [Seoul] seems to be blazing before my eyes. Such a rare experience is made possible by the excellence of this movie.
>
> I have long heard that *Homeless Angels* is one of the masterpieces of Peninsula film, better than *Tuition Fee*. But, now I understand that this is a correct evaluation, watching this film. It is an excellent work, and at least the finest among 10 Peninsula films I have watched.[16]

The Dictionary of Korean Filmmakers, published in 2004, says Ch'oe In-gyu "is a scenarist who understands cinema from a technical aspect much more than any other. At the beginning, he showed a tendency toward critical realism reflecting society, but later this was converted into a lyrical realism accepting nature broadly."[17]

It is noteworthy that the evaluations of *Homeless Angels* from the colonial and post-colonial periods are so similar, considering how much has changed for the viewers over that 60-year period. Recall that even before the Ministry recommendation, the Japanese Imperial Army Press Section had already recommended the movie. This suggests that there was no problem with the movie's contents or message, and the consistency of the post-colonial critical evaluation is confusing.[18]

Ch'oe In-gyu made a clear statement regarding his intention in producing *Homeless Angels* in *10-years: My Movies and My Writing*, which appeared in *Samcheolli* in 1948.

> Why are only colonial Korea's streets full of beggars? It was my true intention to protest this to Japanese politicians through the movie. The film won an award from the Governor-General of Korea and the Minister in Tokyo, but by strange Japanese intrigue, the Minister's award was unprecedentedly withdrawn and at the same time, approximately two hundred meters were removed from the original in the re-inspection.[19]

Of course, this can be viewed as an excuse – a *post-facto* self-justification – which was quite common around 1948. If that is the case, such statements simply become errors of recognition, that is, lies, told for self-protection immediately after the war. I, however, do not think that this particular statement, which has been repeatedly quoted in histories

Photo 7.2: Homeless Angels

of Korean film, falls into this category of self-justifying lies. It is possible that Ch'oe In-gyu's intention was to describe the desperate situation of street children as a protest to Japanese politicians, and he might have viewed the award from the Japanese government as recognition of his efforts (he was very angry when the "Minister's award" was withdrawn). But we must ask whether he sincerely believed this, for the answer may hold a key to understanding two quite distinct things: the unusual things that happened to *Homeless Angels* in 1941; and the selective kind of memories that permeate the history of Korean film. Was the fundamental conflict between the governing body and the colonized male elites already depicted in the movie? The movie was made, the story told, by the colonized male elite; a subjugated colonial subject is telling a story about imperial enlightenment; the film is both a story of re-masculinization and an act of re-masculinization by the story tellers. As such, it presents a symbol of men which will dominate the world described by post-colonial Korean film.

Was Korean a real problem? Mechanisms of separation

Homeless Angels opens with a scene in Jongno, the center of Keijō (Seoul). As night falls in Jongno under a tangle of electric wires, we see it is already a grand, neon-lit city. Myeong-ja and Yong-gil, sister and brother, must make money selling flowers for their vicious foster father, the gangster Gwon. That night, after a beating from Gwon, Yong-gil runs away, and spends the night on the street. The next day he is found by a pastor, Bang Seong-min, who takes the boy into his home. The house is already crowded with other children rescued from the streets. Maria, the pastor's wife and mother of his two children, is frustrated with her husband for filling her house with strangers. Pastor Bang wants to provide accommodation for all the street children and asks In-gyu, Maria's brother, to lend his country house. The house is a place of fond memories, where In-gyu, a doctor, had lived for a period with a German woman after returning from studying in Germany. With In-gyu's consent, and despite his wife's objections, Pastor Bang takes the children and his family to the country house in *Hyanglinwon*. There he teaches the boys diligence, sincerity, and the value of labor and regulations.

In the meantime, Myeong-ja is saved by In-gyu and has been given a job as a probationary nurse in the hospital. One day, Yong-gil falls into a river while stopping two boys from running away. In-gyu comes to save Yong-gil, and Myeong-ja and Yong-gil are re-united. Their story is reported in a newspaper, and donations begin pouring in to support the home. When the donations are also reported in the media, Yong-il's foster father Gwon and his gang decide to steal the donations. At the critical moment when Gwon's gang attacks the house, the bridge collapses and the gang fall into the river. The fallen villains are surprised to find themselves not only rescued, but also given medical treatment. In gratitude, they gather under a flag raised by Pastor Bang, and recite the Oath of Imperial Subjects.

The narrative in *Homeless Angels* appears to be a well-considered and well-crafted response to the Korean situation in 1941. The movie theater was "a place of education approved by the nation,"[20] and children were seen as both the "general" audience for films and the specific audience a movie should address (1941 was also the year that the term elementary school was changed from "shogakko" – school for small children – to "kokuminngakko"– national school). In this context, a Korean movie that describes the redemption of street children – children beyond the control of homes and schools – into "loyal Imperial subjects" should not have posed much of a problem for the colonial authorities.[21]

The film critic Hazumi Tsuneo says the fundamental reason for withdrawing the Monbusho recommendation was that it was a "Korean film." Hazumi speculates that:

It means a film with spoken Korean is not welcome. A film spoken in Japanese is allowed even if it is a Korean film. There can be various reasons for this and that, but it is the fundamental reason. Don't use Korean, and speak in Japanese. It is thought that if that policy is set out, it can be observed by us.[22]

But that policy was not set out – not explicitly – which perhaps explains the uneven treatment of the film: the first censors confirmed that it conformed to the explicit censorship regulations, but then higher authorities decided that it did not conform to the implicit intention of the censorship regime. If the principle that only Japanese should be spoken had been clearly stated, the situation would not have arisen.

This argument appears to be persuasive when considering the ideological burden on Korean language and culture at that time. From 1938, when the third Korean Education Ordinance was introduced, specifying the exclusive use of Japanese for education in common schools, Korean was no longer an official language. Colonial Korean society was wrought with a sense of crisis for its culture. *Kokuminbungaku* (Imperial Literature), the only surviving Korean culture magazine after an earlier flurry of mergers and closures of magazines, was published only in Japanese from the May/June 1942 issue. By 1943, all films produced in colonial Korea were in Japanese (at least officially).

In the cinema, however, the language spoken has an enormous impact on a film's appeal to audiences. With only a little more than 20% of the population of colonial Korea literate in Japanese,[23] the Japanese-only policy for films had a devastating effect on the local market. This dilemma between government policy and market demand was ever-present from 1943, resulting in movies being produced in Japanese according to the rules, but also in a Korean version to suit the market.[24]

However, *Homeless Angels* was released in 1941, before the policy for the complete abolition of Korean was made explicit. Yi Chang-yong said, contrary to Hazumi, that the Governor-General of Korea did not provide any guidelines or rules regarding the use of Japanese. He insisted that Japanese was used "along with" Korean in *Homeless Angels* "so as not to go too far" in the context of the film. In fact, *Homeless Angels* was intended to "naturally" depict the dual use of languages in Keijō at the time. In the process, it reveals the hierarchy of a world ranked by language use. People are divided into Japanese language and Korean language regardless of gender, age and class.

Pastor Bang and Maria's brother, In-gyu, are the most fluent Japanese-speakers in this movie. Japanese and Korean are used naturally between them. For example, "I'm the kind of people sometimes drinking and sometimes making a living by small things" (in Korean, In-gyu) "Maria always worries about that" (in Korean, pastor Bang) "Ha, ha, ha, is this my turn? (in Japanese) It is you who Maria worries about, not me (in Korean)" (In-gyu). Pastor Bang speaks to the children using both Japanese and Korean, and the children reply in Korean. In a scene of children only, they use Korean and very simple Japanese words. The people who are furthest from Pastor Bang's world of fluent Japanese are Gwon and his gang. Those illiterate, dirty and cruel people live a depraved life in which they cannot speak or understand Japanese. None of the women in the film use Japanese, regardless of social class, although class differences between the female characters are abundantly clear. For instance, Maria is treated as though she speaks Japanese even though she does not say anything in that language, while Myeong-ja can speak and understand only Korean. There is only one exception: the waitresses in a bar in the opening scene depicting the nightlife of a modern but decadent Keijō speak and understand Japanese.

These representations of the distinctions between Japanese and Korean seem quite realistic, as Yi Chang-yong claimed. It unsurprising that Gwon's gang, and Myeong-ja – people of the lowest class, who received no education – cannot understand or speak Japanese. And one might expect the waitresses to use Japanese language and Japanese names, as their main customers are middle class Korean men, who share fantasies typical of colonial Korean men about Japanese women.

Nevertheless, we must recognize that this realism is intentionally contrived, and a closer look reveals inconsistencies in this contrivance. For example, how is it that Myeong-ja cannot understand Japanese, but Young-gil can (he even speaks a short sentence)? And what about the other street children? Excluded from the education system, they are unlikely to speak Japanese well. If the suggestion is that they learned Japanese on the street to make a living, then Gwon's gang and Myeong-ja should have as much capacity. In another example, one wonders why the educated woman, Maria, doesn't speak any words in Japanese? and why Pastor Bang and Maria's brother intersperse Japanese and Korean sentences? If it is intended to establish their fluency in Japanese, why are the only words in the film Pastor Bang speaks to Maria, who does not understand his great duty, "Can you go with me not only as my wife but also a mother to the children?" in Japanese?

Japanese occupies a privileged position in these depictions, overriding even divisions by gender and class.[25] The world is divided and ordered according to the ability to speak Japanese. At the lowest level is Gwon and his wicked gang. At a slightly higher level are boys with the potential to become imperial subjects. And at a higher level again are male elites who are fluent in the "imperial language." In this final case, one is a pastor who heals social disorder and the other is a doctor who treats physical disease. Who could be more suitable characters as purveyors of enlightenment? (even though their Japanese is sometimes mixed with Korean, and is thus not "pure" Japanese – i.e., the highest form). Meanwhile, women who "do not speak" Japanese are wholly marginalized within this hierarchal structure: there is no possibility that they might achieve the status of the male elites (in contrast male children with low-level Japanese have the potential to grow-up to speak fluent Japanese). This does not, however, mean that women are excluded from the hierarchical order. They are expected to be able to follow instructions and obey orders given in Japanese, a language of regulation, order, duty and loyalty. Women should be able to understand what is said even though they cannot speak; what is expected of them is to be an "ear", not a "mouth". Similarly, the enlightened subject, the one who speaks Japanese, holds a privileged position, especially for Japanese men in relation to Korea. The Japanese fluency of the colonized is not about *creating* order, but about *reproducing* the imposed order; hence it only requires an ear to hear. This applies especially to the subordinate gender. Declaring the "Japanese of the empire" as the sole medium for laws and orders, strictly positions subjects according to their ability to comply with the order and their role in its performance. Within this hierarchical order, although Korean films were produced in Japanese, the basic subordinate position of the colonized cannot be transcended. The imposition of Japanese was not merely a matter of language; it was fundamental to the hierarchy of the empire.

Ideals of integration: Colonized subjects in seclusion

Pastor Bang's home for street children, Hyanglinwon, represents a small sanctuary created by the men of colonized Korea. Isolated by the river that surrounds it, it functions as a metaphor for the Korean peninsula throughout the film.

Presenting Hyanglinwon as an ideal space isolated from the Japanese world – a closed and self-sufficient world populated only by Koreans – may lie at the base of the film's trouble with censorship.

Next to the Hyanglinwon, a refurbished warehouse, is a western style mansion in which Pastor Bang's family live. Maria, Pastor Bang's wife, is an ideal type of woman for the colonized male elites: she sometimes plays the piano in the living room yet always wears traditional Korean clothes, with her hair up in a chignon; she understands Japanese yet does not speak it; she is never seen outside the home. She is a sincere mother and wife.[26] In short, Maria and the mansion provide the ideal setting for performing the role of the enlightened man. Meanwhile, next door, Hyanglinwon satisfies the desire of the subjugated man for a place where he is in control, autonomous, free to do as he sees fit. Here, Pastor Bang has absolute power; no one else in Hyanglinwon can override him. He is the only male adult in the space; the oldest, wisest and most virtuous. He lives as a passionate humanitarian, with no self-interest or selfish desire. He expresses no anger, haste or frustration. Morally faultless, he is the absolute and sole "goodness" in this world. Within this enclave, he seeks consent through endless persuasion and understanding, and finally creates a world of order and rules.

Every morning at Hyanglinwon, the day begins with a trumpet call by Pastor Bang's young son. The children get up in the common house. On the wall is a bulletin board indicating their position. The children are assigned to different working crews, each assigned tasks to support self-sufficiency; achieving their assigned tasks is the daily goal. Cleanliness is the top priority. It is not an accident the place itself looks like a small barracks. It is an ideal setting for a story about implementing the "national policy" of *naisenittai*, while at the same time depicting a world autonomously created by the colonized male elites; a world characterized as ordered, well-ruled and clean.

Of course, such an achievement does not come effortlessly, or without resistance. The children of the street have little resistance to temptation, and despite their seclusion, temptations arise from the outside, typically represented by sensuous things like taffies. Il-nam, for example, goes out to fetch water but on the way is tempted by a taffy seller. Temptations are stronger in idle times, too; for example, during the monsoon season when their labor is disrupted, two children plan to run away from the home. Their plan to cross a fast-flowing flooded river in a worn-out boat is thwarted by Yong-gil, who nearly sacrifices his own life to save theirs. The film returns the children to the world of order and rules through love and sacrifice, rather than, say, discipline and retribution. After Yong-gil prevents them from getting on the boat, Pastor Bang sends one of them, Young-pal, to fetch In-gyu, the doctor, without scolding or recrimination. Young-pal fulfills his duty and Il-nam, who is still on the run, eventually returns of his own accord. Thus, the would-be rebels return to the fold. Even Gwon's gang are re-born as "imperial subjects" through the efforts of the doctor and pastor. They are all "redeemed," an activity affecting the heart. The result of redemption should be expressed by "behaviors" coming from the bottom of the heart. The last scene of this film, in which the cast is gathered under the Japanese flag and recite the "Oath of Imperial Subjects,"[27] is the very completion of redemption.

This final scene arrives rather suddenly in a narrative describing a humanistic passion providing guidance to street children. Guidance means leading others in the right direction. In 1941, it is unsurprising that "the right direction" is depicted in a scene with the gathered cast reciting the "Oath of Imperial Subjects." The cast of diverse characters gathered together regardless of gender, class, and age under the flag symbolize the twenty million people of the Korean peninsula. It was Pastor Bang's solo achievement to lead them sincerely into imperial subjecthood. But, this representation of unification secluded from the outside world risks being interpreted as a metaphor for a nation-state or a sovereign nation – especially if the "Oath of Imperial Subjects" is left aside. From another perspective, the completed point of enlightenment is familiar, although it is arrived at by different ideals or mottos. Reciting the Oath of Imperial Subjects is an achievement in itself; and, at the same time, it declares a bond to something beyond the enclave – to the world outside. It serves as a medium connecting Hyanglinwon to the outside, connecting the Korean peninsula to Japan.

From the perspective of empire, there was a risk that this film's use of Korean might highlight intrinsic structures of discrimination in the empire. That risk is observed in a more fundamental sense also. In the film, colonial Korean subjects approach directly, unmediated, the principle of imperial subjectivity itself, and they rush for the core of *ikkunbanmin* – equality as the people of the Emperor – with no agent or mediator.

Photo 7.3: Homeless Angels

The Empire demands Japanization throughout the colonies, but also holds it out as a means by which the colonized man can achieve both enlightenment and re-masculinization. However, achieving this ideal violates the imperial hierarchy, in which Great East Asian subjects are intrinsically subordinate (socially inferior, feminine) to the dominant (masculine) Japanese. From that perspective, Ch'oe In-gyu's depiction of the "idealized" imperial subject's space as one in which the colonized

Photo 7.4: Homeless Angels

people are separated from the governing body, self-sufficient and capable of achieving enlightenment independently of their social superiors, threatens the dominant:subordinate structure if, when juxtaposed to the viewers' lived-experience, it reveals that the promise of Japanization is empty. That is, Pastor Bang's "excessive achievement" exceeds the possibilities "really" available to the colonized man in the imperial hierarchy.

In *Homeless Angels*, the enlightenment is made possible by the social seclusion of Hyanglinwon, a space separated from the "outside" world, isolated both physically and symbolically by the river surrounding it. It is a place full of memories, where In-gyu lived with a German woman. The German woman signifies that a man of the yellow race in the colony can fall in love with, and be loved by, an impossible object of another race. This pre-history continues to infuse the villa even as it is transformed into Hyanglinwon. The river seems a specific metaphor that separates the colonized men from the reality of colonial Korea in 1941, where they are inevitably limited as men of the colony.

This river, understood as a metaphor of the *Genkai Sea* – the liminal zone between Japanese and Korean – is important as a device of isolation and closure. Although loyalty and commitment to Japan are affirmed through the "Oath of Imperial Subjects," the primary political agent on this peninsula throughout this story is a male intellectual colonial Korean. The colonized man, who is responsible for the enlightenment of Koreans using both Korean and Japanese language, is in the privileged position of connecting the *naichi* to the *gaichi*. It might even suggest that they "know Korean better than others," that *only* the Japanese-enlightened Korean has the wisdom and insight to build a bridge connecting the two. And furthermore, this colonized man who "knows" intends to spread the knowledge; Pastor Bang is a proselytizer. The threat posed by the film's use of both Korean and Japanese is apparent in other places. As long as Korea exists, there is a potential for "male elites in the colony" to attempt to assume a privileged position in the Japanization and enlightenment of the peninsula. In effect, every person who takes the Oath "to become a soldier" makes a very specific request for the "expansion of the *naichi*" – absolute unification – effectively abolishing the distinction between *naichi* and *gaichi*.

Ch'oe In-gyu had already told a story of the complete enlightenment of Korean (children) by Japanese, in the "Japanese" film, *Tuition Fee*. *Homeless Angels* can be seen as a sequel to *Tuition Fee*. The male subjects, both Japanese and Korean, must walk shoulder to shoulder with others toward imperial subjectivity. The government authority unexpectedly discovered that permitting the film's use of "Korean language" and "space" posed a threat to the imperial order; an "indecency" in the censors' terms. Despite the final, explicit endorsement of unification, the structure of the narrative is premised on a specific separation. There are very few films which so explicitly present this "indecent" possibility of the colonized subject acting outside of the governing structures.

Limits to the search for a new father

> Now Korea is only thankful and sacrificing ourselves for you. All is given to the Emperor and entrusted to the Emperor, pledging loyalty – that is everything. And to the homeland (Japan) people, as our superiors, respect

will be shown. It will not be forgotten how much their forefathers suffered and spilled blood. It will be the right attitude for Koreans to respect, believe, love and follow them as a superior and as an elder brother.[28]

Yi Gwang-su, a pioneer of modern Korean literature, which developed along with the colony, suffered all his life from the trauma of being orphaned in childhood. His orphan-complex entailed a strong awareness of lack, or absence – a sense that something important is missing. A similar sensation affected colonized Korean intellectuals more generally in various ways.[29] The absence of a father, in particular, is made present to them from the beginning. Yi Gwang-su looked continuously for a new father. At various times he attached himself to prominent figures, such as Hukuzawa Yukichi, Abe Mitsuie and Tokutomi Soho. Eventually this led him to an absolute father, the Emperor: "Your majesty is a father and the imperial house is a head family house," he said.[30]

Japanese people are represented as "elder brothers or seniors" by Yi who describes himself as a subject of the head family of the Japanese Empire. In place of the conservative and incompetent Korean fathers, like the one who deserted him, the new father is perfect for Yi Gwang-su, a person pursuing social evolution and enlightenment, who produces literature to express the enlightenment. That is his vision of a modern nation: a world made by the subject's loyalty to the sovereign and the father's affection for the son. These emotional bonds of loyalty and affection give the nation its strength.[31] Once he has embraced the new father, he can stand with his head held high, having overcome the limitations of the colonized. "In developing the Greater East Asia Co-Prosperity Sphere, Korea becomes a head and a leader. In other words, we will be a master of all East Asia."[32]

Homeless Angels appears to be a story about the quest – and its culmination – which Yi Gwang-su had pursued throughout the colonial period: to become a father. The male elite, portrayed as an active and positive subject, who is physically and mentally competent, plays the role of the father in this film. Assuming, as Yi Gwang-su does, that to become a father he must first find himself a father – the film appears to satisfactorily address that with the final oath, which Pastor Bang has been working towards all along. The political difficulty arises in *Homeless Angels* because Pastor Bang was the only "father" portrayed, because he acts independently and unsupported by *his* "father." In Imperial Japan, the nation is composed of the *tenno* (emperor), as the great head of the family, and his subjects[33] perceived as *akago* (infant), in an expanded concept of *ie* (family). Anyone with the status "father" other than the absolute father is merely a medium for guiding the infant to the emperor. From this perspective, Yi Gwang-su said, it is natural to "respect, believe, love and follow the Japanese as superior and as an elder brother."

But *Homeless Angels* excludes the Japanese almost completely. It expressly signals this exclusion through the physical isolation of its setting: Hyanglinwon. The producers, of course, may not have intended to send such a strong message, and did not anticipate such a strong response from the empire. No doubt, persons tasked with governing a colonial situation, with its inevitable levels of anxiety, must be ever vigilant for slights to their authority. In a sense, the increasingly severe censorship imposed on this film might be explained by the slow realization of how it expresses the subtle, unconscious desires of the men of the colony. It is inevitable that the governor's perception of danger differs significantly from that of the colonized, who is himself a "danger." In which case, self-censorship which completely conforms to the official censors' criteria might be impossible.

Nevertheless, this problem was averted in two other *naisenittai* films from Korea, produced by Japanese directors, *Young Looks* (Toyoda Shiro, 1943) and *Suicide Squad of the Watchtower* (Imai Tadashi, 1941), as well as Ch'oe In-gyu's *Love and Fealty,* made with Imai Tadashi, and completed in July 1945, immediately before the end of the war. A brief comparison with these films can help to tease out the precise details of this problematic in *Homeless Angels*. The only father-figures in these three movies are Japanese. They are strict but affectionate, looking after and protecting their "subjects" with consistent justice. They have absolute authority. They are guardians both in name and in practice.

Returning to the main issue: recall that the controversy over *Homeless Angels* arises at the point when the film is sent to Japan for release. The producers had only intended the movie for screening in Korea. The movie tells the story of a colonized man successfully realizing the enlightenment that the colonizing authority has assigned to him. Maintaining order in the endless chains of colonial hierarchy requires the cooperation of colonized male elites who aspire to improve their status in the imperial order. *Homeless Angels* portrays this story quite well. And yet, as a representation of the peninsula at that time, it could not transcend that extreme place, the *Genkai Sea*, because

Photo 7.5: Homeless Angels

spreading enlightenment must be the sole preserve of the colonizers – both physically and symbolically – as mediators / representatives of the empire.

Although the characteristics and obligations of re-masculinized male subjects were conceived in that limited history and space of colonialism, the trope grows in importance in the post-colonial era. After 1945 – when the outside authority disappears – they come to have much more impact, and it is the re-masculinized elite subject who performs the work of constructing the post-colonial state in real life.

Once the empire has collapsed, and Korea becomes the Republic of Korea, elites finally find themselves with a leading role in enlightenment. This, in turn, was decisive in the post-colonial re-appraisal of *Homeless Angels* as an auteurial achievement of "realism." Although a judgement after the fact, the censorship controversy surrounding *Homeless Angels* may have resulted from its portrayal of the possibility of the colonized male's self-transformation into enlightened subjects in a future post-colonial state.

Grammar of the Korean film history: Method or value of realism

Let us now consider Ch'oe In-gyu in the context of Korean film history. The thing to note is that "realism" is a privileged term in discussions of Korean film. "Achieving realism" is one of the highest accolades for auteur

Korean movies, assessed along a spectrum between popular movies such as "Chungmuro films," belittled by the critics, and European modernist films, adored as paragons of auteur theory. But this realism must always be consistent with a Korean value system, which includes a "resistant nationalism."[34]

In *General History of Korean Films*, the foundational work of Korean film history, Yi Young-il wrote,

> Ch'oe In-gyu presented neo-realist movies, one of the streams of the world film history, through *Homeless Angels*, even before the theory had come to colonial Korea. As will be indicated ... realism in its cinematic form should be remembered to be the last line of resistance for authors in the days of cruel militarism... Ch'oe In-gyu took the pulse of bright realism in Korean films despite the complete darkness of the film industry during the period of Japanese Imperialism and the disordered post-liberation.[35]

Yi Young-il, who has extensively studied Korean film history from its beginning, considers the final stages of the colonial period to have been a "dark period" for Korean film. At that time, Ch'oe In-gyu was the only director who could be considered an auteur in terms of the consistency of the topic he explored (poor children) and the style he employed (location, long-take), despite the limitations of those times. Considered from another point, it might be Ch'oe In-gyu, as a typical model of male subjects and substance in film history, who connects the colonial and post-colonial state on a plane beyond ideologies.

But, what does realism mean when it is referred to as the "last line of resistance" in the days of cruel militarism? Yi Young-il does not limit his use of the term realism to formal issues. And considering that he wrote this book in 1969, when Park Chung-hee, a spiritual son of Japanese Imperialism, led the military dictatorship, the "cruel militarism" he invokes is not confined to the past, either.

Although Yi Young-il categorizes the history of Korean cinema according to the degree of realism in a film, he sees realism as a minimum negative moral concept. This negative moral awareness penetrating the 20th century, a response to "cruel militarism" – absolute evil – is the basis of the cultural ideology of realism.[36]

I'm not a realist, but a critic. My concern is to overcome realism. But, if I who study and teach Korean film history, break out of the frame of realism in Korean cinema – which is dissatisfying and doubtful – then Korean cinema loses its foundation and future. Not because of the fact that realism is the only object to be adored, but because of the fact that the blood, sweat, grief, affection and physical pain and joy of Korean film people are all combined in realism, it should be invariably supported.[37]

The realism that Yi Young-il invokes in this passage is an attitude and a fortress for a minimalist ethics, beyond style and trend. It is, thus, something to be protected in the history of contemporary Korea and at the same time, it must be changed into something more suitable for the day when Korean society has other "social experiences." In that context, he says, the concern is "how to overcome realism" as a social attitude. How can Korean society transcend this realism defined by the encounter with evil to realize a different social experience? When put that way, we see the stirrings of social revolution. And to that end, social realism movies serve an important purpose. When the other party cloaks its evil intentions behind claims of divine authority and empty promises of liberation, the way to overcome that evil is to expose it. From that perspective, Yi Young-il cannot help but evaluate Ch'oe In-gyu's movies as achievements of realism. Furthermore, the structure of Ch'oe In-gyu's stories in which street children become enlightened subjects by clearly identifying and overcoming their weaknesses, remains central to the Park Chung-hee government's modernization agenda, in which a new nation is anticipated by "sweeping away the old customs." The idea that the social good can only be pursued by cleaning up the residual evils in society is the very consciousness that keeps a (post) colonized people tied to the colonizing power.[38]

Thus, realism has become a dogma for describing the history of Korean cinema, following Yi Young-il. Within this framework, *Homeless Angels* depicts "the painful lives suffered by the colonial Korean public, through a method of images, in which the sensitive and rhythmical tempos of Ch'oe In-gyu are well balanced".[39] This rhetoric about the suffering and ethics represented by realism is a grammar for summarizing the history of Korean film. The word "realism" immediately evokes values and ethics.

So, is the high praise of the post-colonial critics for this sample of realism from a colonized film maker simply misunderstanding of context, or deeper currents? No – similar themes and devices continue to be found in post-colonial Korean films. Yu Hyôn-mok, for example, a typical director of Korean cinema who regards *Homeless Angels* to be an "educational film", completed *Study Tour* (1969), a children's movie, in the same year that Yi Young-il was writing his book. In this film, poor boys, girls, and their uneducated parents are enlightened by a devoted teacher who comes from Seoul. On a school tour to Seoul, to see the rapid economic development being achieved, the children promise to be "good children of the novel country". This movie was produced in the year when the results of the first Economic Development Plan (adopted in 1962) were being reported and celebrated. In this movie, the role of leading people toward the enlightenment of imperial subjectivity shifts seamlessly to national enlightenment. Film historians keep up with developments in Korean film theory and style, but consistently overlook the "purpose" and "context" (of the empire or the national state) in which such stories are told, foregrounding subject and method instead. By reflecting on nation and realism, movies from the dark period of Japanese Imperialism continue to be relevant in the Republic of Korea because the two different subjects pursuing imperial subjection and modernization are actually one and the same, the elite male seeking to assert his masculinity / re-masculinization by creating order in the world around him.

Notes

1 *Naisenittai* is the policy of forced assimilation in Korea. Michael Robinson describes it as "the ultimate eradication of all differences between the citizens of the Japanese homeland and population of colonial Korea… It would be achieved only when Koreans had been completely stripped of their Korean cultural identity and had become Japanese both in name and in reality, in body and soul." Michael Robinson, "Forced Assimilation, Mobilization, and War", Carter J. Eckert, Ki-bail Lee, Young Ick Rew, Michael Robinson, Edward W. Wagner, *Korea Old and New: A History*, Harvard University Press, 1990, pp. 315–16.

Dual Language, Dubbed Cinema 179

2 Ch'oe In-gyu 1911–?, was born in Yeongbyeon, Pyeongan Buk-do, North Korea. He left the Pyeongyang high primary school in mid-course in 1924, and made his directorial debut with *Frontier* (1939). Ch'oe gained attention with his second feature film *Tuition Fee* (1940). After Korea's liberation from Japan in 1945, he made the well-known *Hurrah for Liberty* from a screenplay by Jeon Chang-geun in 1946, the first of the films about independence, and became a typical filmmaker of the liberation period (1945–1950) with *An Innocent Criminal* (1948) and *Seasonal Fish Market* (1949). During the Korean War, he was abducted and taken to North Korea.
3 Kuroda Shozo, "Miscellaneous Thoughts on Korean film: *Tuition Fee* and *Homeless Angels*', *Eiga Hyoron,* July 1941, pp. 47–48. Iida Shinbi, "*Homeless Angels*", *Eiga Hyoron,* March 1941, pp. 86–87. The criticism and articles published in Japan about *Homeless Angels* at the time included: Suzuki Yukichi, "*Homeless Angels*," *Eiga Junpo,* 11 November 1941, Nakaoka Kousei, "*Homeless Angels*," *Nihon Geijyutsu,* December 1941.
4 *Japanese Film 1942,* Japanese Film Magazine Association, p. 7–1.
5 Throughout this chapter, the term 'enlightenment' and its cognates refers specifically to one's attitude to the Emperor / Empire, seeing the light of the Emperor, awakening to the true superiority of the Empire. The quasi-religious connotations are appropriate in a context in which the Emperor is regarded as Divine.
6 *Homeless Angels,* which is the first colonial Korean film recommended by Japan's Ministry of Education, Science, Culture and Sports, was inspected three times in Japan (the Korean version twice, and the Japanese version once). It was unprecedented for a film to be re-examined in Japan. After passing the first censorship on July 17, the importer, Dowa Co. gave a preview on September 20 and promoted it as the first colonial Korean film recommended by the Ministry. At the same time, the Secret Service applied for it to be re-inspected. Following re-inspection on September 22, a total 218 meters of the film, including the last scene, were removed. The original edition was judged as "unsuitable for the public" and prohibited from screening. The revised edition, dubbed in Japanese, was screened from 2 to 6 October, after passing re-inspection. Neither the Secret Service nor Ministry commented on the censorship or final version.
7 Re-masculinization here refers to a process that was common across the territories that Japan colonized. During the fifteen years of Japanese imperialist expansion, including the Manchurian Incident, the Sino-Japanese War and the Pacific War, the colonized subjects were emasculated through their subjugation to 'Japan,' but were provided with mechanisms for re-masculinization: through 'collaboration' (being an imperial soldier) and adopting the associated modern rationality in the interests of national defense.
8 It seems that Nishikame Motosada, who had worked with Naruse Mikio in the early 1950s, entered film circles through his time as an official screen writer for the Governor-General of Korea. *Homeless Angels* is the first film written under his own name.
9 Yi Chang-yong, "To Establish New System of Chōsen Film (symposium)", *Eiga Junpo,* November 1, 1941, p. 16.

10 Suzuki Yukichi, *Eiga Junpo*, 11 November 1941, p. 30.
11 "How to Promote the Enhancement of Our Movies," *Dong-A Daily Newspaper*, January 1939
12 On demands in the Korean film industry and the Japanese policy response in the talkie era, see Yi Jun-sik, "Film Policy during the Japanese fascist period and trend of film industry," *History of National Movement Study Society*, 2003.
13 The December 1940 issue of *Samcheolli* contained an article about the formation of a film company with two million Korean won capitalization by Yi Chang-yong, along with councilor Han Sang-ryong, Kawakita Nagamasa of Tokyo Towa, Negishi Minoru of Manchurian Film Co., broadcasting networks, financial cooperative associations and others. The enterprise fell apart completely in 1942 with the formation of 'Korean Film Co., Ltd.', an integrated film production company under the direct control of the Japanese Governor-General.
14 Suzuki Shozo "Peculiarity of Korean Films (symposium)" *Eiga Junpo*, July 11, 1943, p. 10.
15 See, for example, Yi Young-il, *General History of Korean Films*, Sodo Publication, 2004 (First Edition 1969), p. 202 and Yu Hyôn-mok, *History of Korean Film Development*, Hanjin Publication, 1980, p. 213.
16 Oda Sakunosuke, "Depiction of Homeless Angels," Murakami Tadahisa, "See *Homeless Angels*," 1941.
17 *The Dictionary of Korean Filmmakers*, which was compiled by Guild of Korean Filmmakers and published by Kookhak Community Corporation, includes enormous amounts of information, including personal profiles and lists of works of all the directors from 1919 to 2000. Yi Chang-dong, who was Minister of Culture and Tourism at the time, said when launching the publication that it was a 'revolutionary event which opens a new phase in the history of Korean films.' The book is an important basic source for reviewing the history of Korean film, especially, movies prior to the 1950s, which are rarely databased. According to this publication, my appraisal of Ch'oe In-gyu can be considered as the accepted view of the Korean film industry.
18 The root of those evaluations is, of course, related to several factors regarding the personal life of Ch'oe In-gyu. Even though he was a typical cooperative film director, such as *Love and Fealty,* which describes a Korean boy applying to become a kamikaze pilot, and which was made as a joint production with the Japanese filmmaker Imai Tadashi, he was also the director of *Hurrah for Liberty* (1946), which was the first post-liberty film, which offered him a chance to make a direct comment in cooperation with the United States Information Service in Korea. Also, the leaders of Korean films in the 1950s and 1960s, Hong Seong-gi, Sin Sang-ok, and Jeong Chang-hwa, were all disciples of his and learned dramaturgy from him during the liberation period.
19 Kim Jong-won, et al., *The Dictionary of Korean Filmmakers*, Kookhak Community Corporation, 2004, p. 626. It is quite interesting to see the quotation in this book, which is a typical assessment for Ch'oe In-gyu in the Korean film history, from the perspective expressed by Ch'oe In-gyu at the time of 1948. In the same space, he said that the production of *Sons of Sun* and *Love and Fealty*, which were for encouraging Korean boys to volunteer for the air force service, inevitable due to the 'forced requisition' of the Japanese Army and that it was

necessary for cultivating the future of our film persons. This excuse may appear impudent, but expresses his sensitivity to the technique of movies. He directed the "Independence trilogy" – *Hurrah for Liberty* (1946), *An Innocent Criminal* (1948), and *The Night Before Independence Day* (1948) – after Korea became independent. The comment is rather honest in revealing the unconsciousness of the colonial Korean film industry obsessed with advanced technology.

20 Kabayama Aisuke, "Fundamental problem of Propaganda", *Bungeishunshu*, January 1938.
21 After the film was re-discovered, it was first screened in the "Excavation Film Festival" of Korean Federation of Film Archives (2005) and again in the 2006 Busan Film Festival. In Japan, it was screened in the Yamagata Film Festival (2005) in a special Korean residents in Japan section of movies with the title 'What living in Japan means'. Kawasaki Kenko clearly describes the confusion over the discrepancy between the movie that was screened and the one described in the written film history. She argues that the controversy in Japan over *Homeless Angels* is indicative of the Empire's film policies' closed-attitude toward other cultures. "Movie Network on Gaichi-Korea, Manchuria, China 1930~1940", ed. Yamamoto Taketoshi, *Academic Knowledge of Empire Japan 4*, Iwanami Shoten, 2006, p. 252.
22 "To Establish New System of Chōsen Film (symposium)" pp. 15–16.
23 Japanese literacy rates are shown below. According to the statistics, after 1938, people with 'national language' literacy increased by almost double. Even then, if these statistics are correct, almost 80% of Koreans were illiterate in Japanese in 1943.

Korean literacy rates in Japanese

Literacy	Population	Rate
1923	712,267	4.08
1928	1,290,241	6.91
1938	2,717,807	12.38
1940	3,573,338	15.57
1943	5,722,448	22.15

Kondo Kenichi, *Government of Korea in the late Pacific War*, Korean Historical Records Publication, 1961, pp. 199–200.
24 According to *Eiga Junpo*, July 1943, Ikeda Kunio of the Governor-General's Film Censorship Office spoke bluntly to the symposium on Korean Films about the broader implications of this dilemma, saying: "A special case such as a military draft should be enforced completely and swiftly... For example, we cannot help using Korean to make those people without [Japanese] understand the military draft and how to apply and so on. Considering the efficiency of Korean language for that reason, films of the Japanese language version are produced, along with a Korean language version for actual use." *Eiga Junpo*, July 1943. p. 13.
25 It is also a language of order and rule, for example, the back of the fried noodle machine which is brought to Hyanglinwon says, 'one: To learn how to make noodle. Two: To clean' in Japanese.

26 In the colonial period, the male elites' expressed hatred of modern girls is quite complex. The modern girl portrayed by male writers threatens public morals, is ungrateful, shameless, and above all, is lacking in maternal instincts. Arguably, this vehemence can be seen as masking mixed feelings: love, admiration, desire, and fear expressed as hatred for educated women. Most intellectuals (i.e., the writers) married 'traditional women' in early life, and had flings or more serious affairs with modern women, before abandoning their 'traditional wives' for a second marriage with a modern woman. Thus, expressions of severe hatred for the modern girl can be seen as attempts to salve a guilty conscience in some ways.
27 The 'Oath of Imperial Subjects' was reportedly written by a Korean officer in the employ of the Governor-General of Korea in 1937. Ishida Takeshi sees this as indicative of a process through which 'Japan' was re-made – both materially and conceptually – through the reimportation to Japan of the Japanization which was imposed on the colonies. Ishida Takeshi, *Politics of Memory and Oblivion: Assimilation Policy, War Responsibility, Collective Memory*, Meiseki Shoten, 2000, p. 156.
28 Kayama Mitsuro (Yi Gwang-su), "Third anniversary of Sino-Japanese War," *Samcheolli*, July 1940.
29 Yi Gwang-su lost his parents during the Donghak peasant war. For an exploration of orphan awareness as a motivating experience of modern Korean literary men including Yi Gwang-su, see Kim Yoon-sik, *Yi Gwang-su and His Days*, Sol Publication (Seoul), 1999 and others.
30 Yi Gwang-su, "Japanese Culture and Korea", *Maeil Newspaper*, April 23, 1941
31 For the meaning of affection (情) and its connection to one's relationship with the Japanese emperor, refer to Yi Gyeong-hun's *A Study on Pro-Japanese Literature by Yi Gwang-su*, Taehak Publication, 1998, p. 48, which analyzes Yi Gwang-su's conversion to Japan, indicating that for Yi Gwang-su, affection is a modern thing, different from the feudalistic relationship, and affection mixes conservative affection and father-and-son affection with the emperor. He wanted to believe that Korea could overcome the heartlessness of imperialism through a relationship of 'affection' with the emperor.
32 Yi Gwang-su, "Ethics of Modern Times", *Modern Times*, January 1941.
33 According to Inoue Tetsujiro's commentary on Japan's Imperial Rescript on Education, the position of subjects relative to the ruler of the nation is the same as the children relative to their parents. In this view, the nation is a magnification of the family, and a ruler giving an order to his subjects is no different from a parent giving orders to their children – out of love and responsibility. Thus, when the emperor speaks to the nation as his people, the subjects are to listen carefully with the love that children have for their strict father and their affectionate mother. Inoue Tetsujiro, Commentary on the Imperial Rescript on Education, 1899, p. 59. For the theory of the emperor system as a magnification of family, refer to Fujita Shozo, *Principle of the rule of the emperor state (The Collection of Works of Fujita Shozo 1)*, Misuzu shobo, 1998.
34 Ju Chang-gyu reads the dominant cultural discussion in Korea as a male nationalist marxism, summarizing the views which have governed discussions of Korean films in terms of the nation, realism and auteurship. Ju Chang-gyu, *A Study on the Cultural Modernity of Chungmuro Films*, doctoral thesis,

Chung Ang University, 2004. Kim So-young's work in the 1990s managed to escape from the dominant realism framework. Her efforts to escape the conventional canons of Korean films and to re-organize the sub-genres, such as soap-operas, horrors and action, provides an anti-thesis to the male-oriented realism discussions and suggests a new reading of the history of film. Kim So-young, *Cinema, Blue Flow of Techno-Culture*, Yeolhwadang, 1995. Kim So-young, *Ghosts of Modernity*, People to Sow Seed, 2000.
35 Yi Young-il, *General History of Korean Films*, p. 202
36 Alain Badiou argues that the moral matters of our days are constructed by evil. He sees the construction of ethics based on that 'evil' as providing the moral basis for World War II and the postwar period. He contends that at their roots, the moral consciousness of Nazis and anti-Nazis is identical, both depending on the reproduction of evil. Alain Badiou, *Ethics: An Essay on the Understanding of Evil (Wo Es War)*, translated by Peter Hallward, Verso Books, 2002. The issue of the foundation of goodness through the reproduction of evil can be understood by the ethics of reproduction, that is, the ethical foundation of realism.
37 Yi Young-il, *Lecture for Korean Film History*, Sodo Publication, 2002, pp. 177–178.
38 We are, of course, unable to advance these observations to a more fundamental level. Paradoxically, the kind of realism that seeks the 'minimum line of resistance' by disclosing evil, remains influential in the general ideology of modern Korean history, which continues to be based on 'the minimal ethical response to evil' and can only express its political platforms in negative terms.
39 Kim Su-nam, *A Study on Korean Scenario Writers*, Yeni, 1995, p. 155. Yu Hyôn-mok, a leading director in the 1960s, makes this evaluation. His 1961 film, *Accidental Firing*, is considered one of the greatest Korean movies in the style of realism since *Arirang*. His works can be summarized by their themes of nationalism, enlightenment, anticommunism and Christianity. Yu Hyôn-mok, *History of Korean Film Development*, Hanjin Publication, 1980, p. 213.

8 Double-edged National Imagery: From *The Daughter of the Samurai* to *My Japan*

Takeshi TANIKAWA

Introduction

For the past ten years or so, Japanese creative industries have been seeking to increase exports under the "Cool Japan" banner. This banner is flown by private sector animation studios, TV broadcasting companies, and major film companies, as well as by government agencies such as the Ministry of Economy, Trade and Industry, and the Agency of Cultural Affairs. All are eager to increase exports of creative 'content'.

One of the effects of this export focus appears to be an increasing tendency for such products to be carefully designed to appeal to overseas audiences, often at the expense of domestic sensibilities. Yet the domestic market appears to be easily appeased, *provided that* the product actually is well-received by overseas audiences. This may reflect a Japanese cultural tendency to more value things that have been proven overseas, often described as "worshipping imported goods."

This chapter examines a film produced specifically for overseas markets more than 80 years ago, long before the current "Cool Japan" campaign. Careful analysis of this early example of creating content specifically for overseas markets – including the critical and market responses – helps to elucidate the cultural tendency to "worship imported goods" and may provide insights for thinking about "Cool Japan".

The case in question begins in 1937 with the production of *Atarashiki Tsuchi* (*Der Tochter des Samurai; The Daughter of the Samurai*), the first co-production between Nazi Germany and Empire of Japan. Two versions of the film were made. One of them, directed by Dr. Arnold Fanck (German Version), would be both financially successful and critically acclaimed both in Germany and Japan. The other, directed by Mansaku Itami (International Version) was ignored, both at the box-office and by the critics. Comparing the two versions reveals how these two filmmakers – who disagreed vehemently – sought to convey certain messages in the film(s), and how these efforts were received or rejected by the audience.

The main reason that the International Version received no mention, although produced specifically for English speaking audiences, was that no distributor in either the U.S. or U.K. would handle this film co-produced by Nazi Germany and the Empire of Japan. English speaking audiences did, however, see several sequences from *Atarashiki Tsuchi* in one of the most disturbing anti-Japanese propaganda documentary films, *My Japan* (1945), produced by the War Finance Division of the Office of War Information, U.S. Treasury Department.

The original concept of both versions of *Atarashiki Tsuchi* was to foster cooperation and goodwill, and to explain merits and benefits of developing Manchuria as a nation to foreign audiences. In contrast, *My Japan* quite intentionally portrays the Japanese as a cruel and fanatical race who are brutally colonizing north-eastern China. And it uses footage from *Atarashiki Tsuchi* to do so, reversing the meanings intended by the original film makers. As we will see, even a simple scene of a family in a field has double-edged meanings.

Atarashiki Tsuchi (The Daughter of the Samurai)

On 8 February 1936, Dr. Arnold Fanck arrived at Kobe harbor to direct the first Japanese-German co-production, *Atarashiki Tsuchi*. Fanck was known as the maestro of the mountain film genre for work such as *Der Heilige Berg* (*The Holy Mountain*, 1926), and *Stürme über dem Montblanc* (1930) starring a young Leni Riefenstahl. Neither the story nor the film's title had been decided when Fanck agreed to direct it. He reportedly read Pearl S. Buck's bestselling novel *East Wind: West Wind* while on route, which strongly influenced the story he created after arriving in Japan. As well as bringing expensive zoom lenses which no-one in Japan possessed, Fanck was accompanied by an actress, Ruth Eweler, who would play the German girlfriend of the leading character.[1]

This entire enterprise is a direct product of the political situation of the time. The Empire of Japan and Nazi Germany had signed the Anti-Comintern Pact in November 1936, and Japan was eager to be a member of the Tripartite Pact – the so-called Axis alignment. Goebbels, the Nazi Minister of Propaganda (Leitung von Propagandaminister) wanted to introduce Germany's new partner to Europe through cinematic-cooperation. Yuji Segawa's recent study of *Atarashiki Tsuchi* argues that the widely repeated suggestion that *Atarashiki Tsuchi* was planned to promote the Anti-Comintern Pact, is based on false information and is incorrect.[2] But I share Ebisaka's (2002) view that it was probably Nagamasa Kawakita, the film's producer, who initiated this first co-production.[3] Kawakita, who established Towa Shoji & Co., Ltd. in 1926 – one of the most successful film distributors in Japan – and would establish China Film Co., Ltd. in Shanghai in 1939, is remembered for his pioneering efforts to introduce Japan to Europe through Japanese films in the early 1920s, and his lifelong devotion to pursuing "unity of the Eastern and Western worlds"[4] by importing hundreds of great films from European countries and the U.S., and by international co-production of films. Regardless of who conceived it, it is clear that this film was intended for export from its inception.

Fanck was given full responsibility for the German contribution to this project. Both artistically and politically, his mission was to introduce Japan to German and other European audiences in a favorable light; portraying Japan as a friendly nation and suitable ally for Germany, in accordance with Goebbels' film propaganda policy. In contrast, Kawakita was just a private citizen who willingly supported Japanese national policy of justifying the colonization and development of Manchuria, and developing a friendly relationship with Germany. Notably, *Atarashiki Tsuchi*, a film of nationalist propaganda, was a private production, with very limited support from the Japanese government.

Details of the initial production budget are unclear, but reportedly, the original cost-estimate of 450,000 Japanese yen and six months production, blew out to 750,000 yen and twelve months production. Reports also state that Terra Films, which contracted Fanck, paid 300,000 Japanese yen, with Towa Shoji and JO Studio sharing more than 400,000 yen, and risking bankruptcy if it failed at the box-office. There is no evidence of Nazi German government funding for the production, although it received strong distribution and publicity support from Goebbels for its European screenings. The Japanese Ministry of Foreign Affairs' Division of Cultural Affairs granted a production subsidy of 15,000 yen.[5]

Double-edged National Imagery   187

Photo 8.1:   Advertisement of Towa Shoji & Co., Ltd. (Year Book of the
              Japanese Motion Pictures 1936)

The original structure of this co-production was that, Kawakita, Yoshio Osawa (the founder of JO Studio) and Fanck would be the producers. Fanck would write the script and direct the film, and Richard Angst, who was known for his collaborations with Fanck, would be the cinematographer (Angst was summoned from Germany, arriving March 24).[6] The story was set and filmed entirely in Japan. All the principle actors were chosen by Fanck after auditioning Japanese actors and actresses in Tokyo. Fanck reportedly wrote the first draft of the script on board the ship on route, and then started location hunting while polishing the script and selecting actors immediately upon his arrival in Japan. Yet it seems likely that Fanck had decided the basic narrative device, a love-triangle between the Japanese male lead, his German girlfriend, and his Japanese fiancée, before he started writing, since he had brought a German actress with him. The title of the film was not yet decided, though, as is evident from Towa Shoji & Co's advertising in *Year Book of the Japanese Motion*

Pictures 1936, which was printed just five weeks after Fanck arrived; this co-production gets the top billing, but is described as "Fanck Japanese Film (Title Undecided)."[7]

Perhaps recognizing the need for a local to coordinate the production in a foreign country with different language and custom, Fanck invited Mansaku Itami, one of the leading Japanese directors of the time, to co-direct the film.[8] What happened next is a well-rehearsed story, with countless film historians described the detail in as many books and articles. I will therefore confine myself to a brief summary. These two prominent directors clashed immediately after shooting began, and it was soon apparent that there was no hope of any sort of reconciliation between them. Faced with the potential collapse of the project, Kawakita offered a surprising proposal: that each director would direct his own version of the film. Most accounts agree that the primary source of the conflict was radical differences in the two directors' perspectives and visions. Itami could not bear Fanck's approach, which inaccurately portrayed Japanese geography and customs, as if shooting his personal fantasy world through the orientalist gaze. From Fanck's perspective, though, the objective was just to make a film that would appeal to German and other European markets, even it meant taking liberties with his depictions.

At one level, the irresolvable conflict between the two directors, and the ensuing two versions of the film, suggests a failure of the project, insofar as the German-Japanese co-production was intended to foster cooperation and goodwill. But at a much more fundamental level – arguably, the one that matters – the completed film *Atarashiki Tsuchi*, or, at least its German-Japanese version *Der Tochter des Samurai* was a resounding box-office success both in Germany and Japan, and was therefore deemed to have accomplished its purpose, despite the abject-failure of the Japanese-English version *The Daughter of the Samurai*. Before exploring the audience and critical reactions to the two films, let me briefly outline the story, beginning with Fanck's version.

It begins with the scene of an earthquake in a rural area near Mt. Fuji, where the poor peasant Kanda family lives, an elderly couple and their young daughter. Kanda's son, Teruo (Isamu Kosugi) was adopted into the wealthy Yamato family and then allowed to study in Germany for eight years. When he returns to Japan, he is accompanied by his German girlfriend, despite the fact that he would become Iwao Yamoto's (Sesshu Hayakawa) heir by marrying his daughter, Mitsuko (Setsuko Hara), with whom he is engaged. Teruo is distressed when he finds he cannot easily break the rules of adoption; but gradually his western attachment to individual freedom (*Individuelle Freiheit*) begins to recede with help from his sister, and he re-discovers the beauty and virtues of Japan. Although Gelda, the German, decides to leave Teruo to preserve their friendship, Mitsuko attempts to commit suicide by jumping into Mt. Aso. Teruo rescues her, and then marries her. The young happy couple decides to move to Manchuria, which they believe to be the "New Earth (*Atarashiki Tsuchi*)" and take up modern farming.

In the closing sequence, in Manchuria, the couple have an infant child; Teruo stops hoeing, and places his baby on the ground, saying "You also should be a child of soil", while a Japanese soldier of the Kanto Army overlooks and protects them. The soldier glances at the young family and briefly smiles, then resumes his serious duty.

Itami's English-Japanese (international) version is substantially different. Itami erased all traces of Nazi Germany, such as a ship-board scene with flags of the Swastika and Rising Sun. Itami's Teruo studied abroad in England, and returned with an English girlfriend, Aveler. Itami also erased Teruo's monologue about Manchuria as the future land of the Japanese race, and did his best to correct geographical and cultural inaccuracies. This version also ends with the scene in Manchuria, but the soldier remains in the distance, unengaged.[9]

Photo 8.2: The last sequence at Manchuria of Der Tochter des Samurai

Thus, *Atarashiki Tsuchi*, the first co-production between Nazi Germany and Empire of Japan, was produced in two significantly different versions. It opened in Japan on February 4, 1937. It was launched at large-premier screening at Teikoku-Gekijou in Tokyo on February 3, attended by more than one hundred diplomats from Germany, England, the U.S. and Italy, as well as members of the royal family. Although Fanck gave a speech at this premier, Itami's English-Japanese (international) version was shown, with diplomatic consideration for the attending nations. Interestingly, the film opened in Manchuria, which the film described as the "New Earth," on February 1, before the Tokyo premier.[10]

For the domestic market, Itami's English-Japanese version was shown in fifteen theaters for one week, and then was replaced by Fanck's German-Japanese version, which ran for the next two weeks.[11] These three weeks were a tremendous success for both the distributor and the exhibitors; many theaters reported achieving new box-office records. The reviews, though, were mixed. Many critics reviewed both versions and argued over their respective merits. Many judged Fanck's version superior, implicitly casting Itami's version a failure and then treating it with silent contempt. Note, however, that after carefully analyzing many of these reviews, Irie (1996) demonstrated that many reviewers had simply mixed-up the two versions, criticizing Itami's English-Japanese version for shortcomings they observed in Fanck's version.[12]

Geographical inaccuracies in Fanck's version would be obvious to every Japanese viewer; no specific knowledge required. For example, the Yamato family house is near Mt. Aso, but when Mitsuko passes through the garden of the house, she arrives at the Itsukushima Shrine. Likewise, Teruo and Gelda are seen arriving in the port of Yokohama, and stay at a local hotel (which seems to be near the Great Buddha at Kamakura), but the night lights in the streets which Gelda says are no different to European cities were apparently shot in the Kansai area, while the hotel scenes seem to have been shot in the Koshien Hotel, in Hyogo Prefecture. Japanese audiences reportedly "could not stop laughing" at these scenes.[13] Nevertheless, reviewers and audiences stood by the Fanck version and rejected Itami version.

Why the Fanck version is considered superior to Itami's despite these flaws is not entirely clear. One contributing factor, though, was the sense of pride derived from the fact that a first-rate, world-famous German film director came to Japan specifically to shoot a film about Japan. This could be understood as external affirmation of Japan's successful efforts towards becoming a leading modern nation since the Meiji Restoration, which is in turn reinforced by a tendency to have more faith in things that are endorsed; "worshipping imported goods."

In this context, *Atarashiki Tsuchi* – or, more precisely, the German-Japanese version – was a critical and commercial success. The two faces of Japan that Gelda observed through astonished eyes – an ancient nation which inherited the tradition of the Samurai and whose people worship the Emperor as patriarch of a nation imagined as family, and a new modern nation on a par with western countries in its developments in heavy industry and shipbuilding – was exactly how the Japanese wanted to be seen. The Fanck version simply painted this picture without hesitation and regardless of contradictions. In other words, Fanck produced a visual landscape that stoked the pride of the Japanese in ways which Itami's more realist portrayal failed to do.

Another factor in Fanck's success was the young actress, Setsuko Hara, who played Mitsuko. Hara was just sixteen years old, and a new face in cinema. Giving her the role was something of a gamble, but Fanck predicted that her prettiness combined with the faltering accent with which she spoke German would be well-received in Germany,[14] and he was right. The Japanese name Mitsuko was already familiar in Europe through the marketing of a perfume by that name.[15] Apparently everything about this project was geared to success.

Various reviews from the time point out differences between the two versions. For example, the film critic Chiyota Shimizu declared the Itami version a failure, but observed that it still had its good points. For example, he notes, Itami

> emphasized Mt. Fuji and temple bells in the sequence of Teruo Yamato's awakening to Japanese spiritualism ... For foreigners' eyes, Mt. Fuji is seen just as a 'beautiful mountain,' but it is one of the characteristics of Japan for us, Japanese. I quite agree with the director showing Mt. Fuji over and over again while Teruo is standing at the foot of Mt. Fuji. However, that scene is not effective enough as 'Film for Export' to compare with Fanck's ... Two approach that depicting Mt. Fuji as personification and showing Teruo ringing the bell seems more truthful depiction for the Japanese which making us spring out our Japanese spiritualism, to compare with showing Miyako Odori (dancing) or Noh Play or Sumo Wrestling. I wish if only I

wanted Teruo make a deep bow to Ise Shrine ... Of course, I know it is not understandable for foreign audiences and the way which is not effective at all for exporting.[16]

One thing that stands out from this review is that at least some film critics understood that Itami had not been striving to appeal to a foreign audience, but instead aimed to be true to his sense of being Japanese. But the project that produced *Atarashiki Tsuchi* had intended it to be a 'film for export' from the beginning, and in that sense, the Fanck version was the one which achieved the original objectives.

Fanck and his staff left Japan on February 12, 1937, once it was clear that his version of *Atarashiki Tsuchi* was a box-office success. Shortly thereafter, Setsuko Hara, who had been invited to Germany set sail with her brother-in-law, the film director Hisatora Kumagai, and the producer, Nagamasa Kawakita, who travelled with his wife. Then they landed in Dalian and moved overland to Fengtian (Shenyang), where they boarded the Trans-Siberian railway to Moscow, and finally arrived in Berlin early on March 26, the day scheduled for the premier of *Der Tochter des Samurai*. But the premier had been moved forward to March 23, attended by Hitler, Goebbels, and Hermann Göring at the Kapitol Theater. The change of date was for the convenience of these important guests.

Despite missing the premier, though, Setsuko Hara had an opportunity to greet a German audience on stage of the Kapitol Theater. They were immediately fascinated. A two months' promotional tour to all the major German cities helped *Der Tochter des Samurai* achieve unprecedented box-office success. Distribution to other nations began with Denmark from October 6, Finland from November 21, and the Netherlands, France, Greece and Sweden followed. For the Japanese film industry, *Atarashiki Tsuchi* demonstrated that they could produce a film that would be well-received in Europe and win international acclaim.

JO Studio's pride and boost in confidence over the success of *Der Tochter des Samurai* can be seen in an advertisement in *Cinema Year Book of Japan 1936–1937*, which features two still photos from the film. And it was not only the people of Towa Shoji and JO Studio; the entire Japanese film industry seemed to be spiritually uplifted by this international success. For example, *Cinema Year Book of Japan 1936–1937*, which was edited by international Cinema Association of Japan, was published by Sanseido Co., Ltd. in May 1937. It was the first English publication on the

Double-edged National Imagery 193

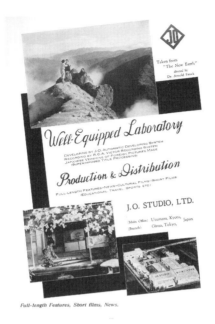

Photo 8.3: *Advertisement of JO Studio, Ltd.* (Cinema Year Book of Japan 1936–1937)

Japanese film industry, and was a viable project because of the success of *Der Tochter des Samurai* in Europe. The book includes an essay by Fanck, 'On the Exportation of Japanese Motion Picture Films,' a transcript of his lecture at the Imperial Hotel, Tokyo on October 31, 1936 to The Japan Motion Picture Foundation (Dai Nippon Eiga Kyokai).

The contrast between the German-Japanese version's box-office success in both Germany and Japan, and what happened to the English-Japanese version which was supposed to be distributed in the English-speaking world is telling. It is generally accepted in Japanese film history that "The Itami version was ignored, both in Japan and in Germany."[17] But it would be a mistake to conclude from this that the Itami version was poorly crafted or just plain bad.

After Kawakita went to Europe with Setsuko Hara and Hisatora Kumagai, he moved onto England, and then flew to New York in June, for negotiations about distributing the International version of *Atarashiki Tsuchi*. Finally he went to Hollywood, and from there returned to Japan.

He reported that "England is not favorable for cooperation with Japan and Germany," and in the United States, they just entrusted distribution to "Mr. B of company M."[18]

Regardless of the identity of Mr. B or company M, they do not appear to have made any efforts to distribute *Atarashiki Tsuchi* in the U.S. Neither *Atarashiki Tsuchi*, *The Daughter of the Samurai*, or *The New Earth* appear in the list of feature films imported during 1937 in *The 1938 Film Daily Year Book of Motion Pictures*, and there is no other trace that the film was distributed in the U.S.[19]

No doubt the trouble for this film in the U.S. stems to some extent from increasing hostility in the U.S. towards Nazi Germany, and thus a German-Japanese co-production. This antipathy became quite apparent a year later, when Leni Riefenstahl visited the U.S. to promote her film *Olympia* (1938), which won first prize at the Venice International Film Festival and was a major box-office success across Europe. Despite this success, though, her film was boycotted for being 'a tool of Nazi Germany' soon after she arrived in New York in November, 1938. The boycott followed her to Hollywood, and eventually she returned to Germany, without even getting to meet any important Hollywood figures (except Walt Disney).[20] It is easy to imagine that Hollywood's antipathy to any films associated with Nazi Germany was already strong when Kawakita visited in 1937. Thus, Kawakita's original ambition to produce a film that would appeal to global audiences, ended with two films whose reception were diametrically opposed; great success for Fanck's German-Japanese version in Europe and bitter failure and sealing of Itami's English-Japanese version.

My Japan

In 2006, Clint Eastwood produced and directed two film versions of the WWII battle of Iwo Jima: *Flags of Our Fathers* and *Letters from Iwo Jima*. The two films stand beside one another as mirror images: the same story told from the quite different perspectives of the U.S. and Japan. Both films had good reviews, both in the U.S. and Japan, but *Letters from Iwo Jima* earned three-times as much as *Flags of Our Fathers* in the Japanese box-office, mainly because it tells the story from the Japanese perspective, and because its lead actor was Ken Watanabe, the most successful Japanese Hollywood actor since Sesshu Hayakawa.

In an important scene; Baron Nishi speaks to a captured U.S. soldier who is frightened that he will be killed. Nishi speaks often to the soldier, in English, and at one stage asks if he knows who Douglas Fairbanks and Mary Pickford are. The answer is "Yes", of course, these Hollywood stars are commonly known among U.S. citizens. Nishi then shared that he had once been invited into their home and met them because he too was a kind of celebrity: an equestrian gold medalist (show jumping) at the 1932 Los Angeles Olympics. The soldier is amazed because he had been taught that the Japanese are a cruel and fanatical race – inhuman monsters, even. The soldier's amazement at encountering a Japanese intellectual deserving of respect, was no doubt replicated across the U.S. as audiences for perhaps the first time were presented with images of their WWII enemy as human beings. It is perhaps surprising that it took more than six decades to depict Japanese soldiers as equal to U.S. servicemen.

So, let us consider the kind of image that was commonly constructed for depicting the Japanese enemy. A typical example can be seen in a 16 minute-long documentary-style propaganda film, *My Japan* (1945), produced by the War Finance Division of the Office of War Information, U.S. Treasury Department. *My Japan* is one of the most disturbing anti-Japanese propaganda films produced during WWII, pitched towards enticing the public to invest heavily in war bonds.

The film's structure is twisted around some reverse psychology. The narrator is presented as a Japanese man who speaks English with a strong accent, but was in fact a pseudo-Japanese, played by a Caucasian actor with make-up. He resembles Peter Lorre as Mr. Moto. His make-up is equal to that used for Paul Muni to play Wang in Pearl S. Buck's *The Good Earth* (1937) and Katharine Hepburn to play Jade Tan in Buck's *Dragon Seed* (1944), but not as caricatured as Mickey Rooney as the strange Japanese neighbor in *Breakfast at Tiffany's* (1961). He explicitly addresses stereotypical images of the Japanese, such as protruding teeth and thick eye-glasses, explaining that they are incorrect. He offers, instead, "the truth" about the Japanese, using "captured war footage" to make the viewer feel that they are privy to Japanese secrets and motivations to continue the war against the U.S. Throughout this government propaganda film, the narrator taunts and insults the viewers. For example, he says;

> So, you are the enemy? The methods you propose amuse us. You say you can destroy us by starving us out. You forget that we are not like you. We have no soft bellies crying for beefsteaks and butter and candy. You say you can destroy us by making sacrifices. How we suffer when you do not have a full tank of gasoline... How we tremble when you have to wait to get into movies, restaurants, nightclubs. Sacrifices? What a delightful and foolish sense of humor you have.
>
> They [Japanese] work longer hours than you do, twice as long, quite often. Why not? They're not working for the clock. They're working to win the war! They do not make as much money as you do. Well, they are not working to make money. They are working to win war! They work every day of every week. Is this so strange? They are not working to get days off, they are working to win the war!

He also explains the Japanese sense of beauty and virtue, showing images of cherry trees in full blossom, Mt. Fuji, a volcano, a beautiful young Japanese woman in a Kimono, ordinary Japanese peasants working hard in rice paddies and diligent workers in an iron factory. All these images are presented as "captured war footage", it is, in fact, all footage from *Atarashiki Tsuchi*. How the U.S. military came to possess a print of *Atarashiki Tsuchi* is unknown; it might have been from anywhere that the Japanese had occupied before the tides of war turned.

He warns the viewers that not only the Japanese army, but its ordinary people will never give up the fight against the U.S., and says there is no use in the U.S. army continuing to fight because the Japanese willingly die for the Emperor. He continues;

> Guadalcanal, Tarawa, Saipan, Iwo Jima – you boast of them as major victories; to you they are. To us they are minor defeats – the loss of island outposts. You Americans are fond of saying 'look at the score.' Very well, look at it. You sent your finest troops against these outposts. They died by the thousands. Here they are massacred, slaughtered. But you took the islands, you say. Yes, we expected you to. That is why we garrisoned them with second-rate troops. The best of your lives for the worst of ours. We too, know a thing or two about bargains. You have not yet faced the best of our armies. You have faced only ten percent of our worst!

Photo 8.4: Scenes from My Japan, *which ends with a close-up of Kanto Army soldier, taken from* Der Tochter des Samurai

This film also used footage from newsreels – both the American and Japanese – as well as archival footage shot by U.S. troops. Some of this footage was perhaps sickening, showing dead babies and children, a decapitated human head, a brutal shooting of hostages, etc. The narrator emphasizes the Japanese cruelty and inhumanity with the statement that the lives of both friend (Japanese) and foe (U.S. soldier) are less valued in Japan than in the U.S.

It is clear that the Fanck version of *Atarashiki Tsuchi* was the main source of this film; it borrows a shot from the final scene, the close-up of a Kanto Army soldier protecting Teruo, Mitsuko and their son. As discussed, in the original, the soldier glances at the young happy family and briefly smiles, before resuming the serious countenance of his duty. In *My Japan*, there is no evidence of the young family; the audience sees just the soldier grinning at the audience and then turning serious. The change of context totally changes the impression of this smile, from caring and kind to cruel and inhumane.

By juxtaposing scenes of Japanese beauty and virtue, taken from *Atarashiki Tsuchi*, with newsreel footage of Japanese soldiers' savage cruelty, and then finishing with the shot of the grinning Japanese soldier turning expressionless, this film conveyed an image of the Japanese as an inscrutable enemy; one who is fanatical, yet cool-headed; who loves both cherry blossoms and merciless killing.

Conclusion

My Japan is not the only propaganda film produced by Allied Powers during WWII that depicted Japan with images borrowed from *Atarashiki Tsuchi*. The most famous one is *Know Your Enemy: Japan* (1945), produced and directed by Frank Capra for the War Department as part of a series of documentary films. It was narrated by Hollywood stars, Walter Huston and Dana Andrews. The film was conceived after the success of the *Why We Fight* series which was encouraged to release for general audience by President Franklin D. Roosevelt,[21] which were originally planned to explain why U.S. soldiers have to fight against Germany, Italy and Japan. The production of *Know Your Enemy: Japan* began in 1942, but was not completed until August 1945. It was released to cinemas on August 9, 1945, three days after the atomic-bomb devastated Hiroshima.

Like *My Japan*, *Know Your Enemy: Japan* juxtaposed archival footage shot by U.S. troops with imagery from Japanese feature films which had been captured in areas formerly occupied by Japan. Much of the footage inserted to depict the beauty of Japan and the virtue of the Japanese were taken from *Atarashiki Tsuchi*. These scenes were intended to help foreign audiences understand Japan, but the editing focused on the cruelty and inhumanity of the Japanese soldier, as did *My Japan*.

Another propaganda film – *This Was Japan* (1945), from the U.K. – also used footage from *Atarashiki Tsuchi*. This film was directed by Basil Wright, a leading documentary film maker in the U.K., who produced and directed the classic *Night Mail* (1938). It was narrated by Esmond Knight, an actor who appeared in some of the most famous British post-war films like *The Red Shoes* (1948) and *Hamlet* (1948). *This Was Japan* was released in the U.K. in September 1945, after the war was over.[22]

How should we evaluate these developments? One possibility is that the visual images of Japan in *Atarashiki Tsuchi* were simply good enough, at least as images that Westerners expected of Japan. The important point, though, is that these images are taken from the version of *Atarashiki Tsuchi* produced by a Western film director, Arnold Fanck, rather than from Itami's more realist Japanese version, which was at least in part intended to counter Fanck's orientalism.

In 1938, the producer of *Atarashiki Tsuchi* reflected on the differences of direction in the two versions of the film, pondering which approach is more effective in an essay titled 'Eiga Yushutsu no Shomondai (Various problems of Exporting Films)' in the film magazine *Nihoneiga*. Kawakita explains that his opinion is based upon his own experiences as a producer of co-produced films such as *Atarashiki Tsuchi* or *Touyou Heiwa no Michi* (The way for Peace in the East) with foreign countries. He provides the following categorization of films for export:

> Regarding exporting Japanese films, I divide them into two categories. First is the case of films originally produced for the domestic market and then selected for export due to their quality. *Gonin-no Sekkouhei* (Five Scouting Soldier) is a good example.
>
> The second is films produced specifically for export. These must be further categorized as:
>
> a. Pure Japanese films produced with special care to be easily understood by foreigners. For example, we can adapt the story of *Chushingura* in a way to be understood by foreigners.
>
> b. Co-production with foreign capital. *Atarashiki Tsuchi* is a good example.
>
> c. Films produced by foreign directors, actors or other crew. *Kokumin no Chikai* (A Pledge of people) is a good example.
>
> d. A production which is shot entirely or in part in foreign places. For example, the French film *Takaranova* was shot in Italy.
>
> The first is the ideal method, used commonly in the U.S. and France where film production is highly developed. I say few Japanese productions should be exported with this method, although its use should be increased little by little as the standard of film production in Japan develops.
>
> The second is adopted by second-rate film producing countries, including Germany, Italy, and Britain, as well as smaller countries like Czech, Hungary and Sweden ... I doubt the punctilious Japanese will agree with this method, but the Japanese standard of film production requires it. We would be better to mix the first and the second, and then try to increase the first method gradually.[23]

The following quote sympathizes with Kawakita's views on exporting films:

> Is it really possible in Japan to make a picture which can be understood in Europe and America? Until a few months ago, I thought it may probably be impossible to make one, as I was then trying to make an export film myself, but now I have completed my first production of a picture, I would like to answer "Yes." Yes, it is possible to make a splendid export film in Japan, which can be understood in foreign countries. Furthermore, it is possible to make Japanese export motion picture film reach the height of technics such as rightly claimed in foreign countries by technical method that can be used in Japan at present. The way is not easy, of course, but as long as I have an experience the way will become easy.[24]

This is, of course, Arnold Fanck's reflections, from his previously mentioned essay.

Though Fanck's reflection was shared before he knew of the financial success of his version in Europe, he may have foretold its success. Kawakita, however, spoke with the confidence and authority derived from the financial success of *Atarashiki Tsuchi* in Germany and other European countries. Their views of the best way to produce Japanese films for export are firmly based in their personal experiences. Despite their obvious authority, though, their views are not widely repeated in Japan today, for the fact that they once co-produced films with Nazi Germany is today a blemish on their history.

The only thing that can be said with certainty about the Fanck version of *Atarashiki Tsuchi* is that it was produced with a clear intention of appealing to a foreign audience – unambiguously and created as "contents which are calculated to win" – and was successful in generating positive sentiments toward Japan among European audiences. Furthermore, it is clear that its box-office success in the Japanese domestic market was significantly boosted by having been well received in foreign markets. And yet, some of its most striking footage was used in Allied propaganda films to generate antipathy and hostility toward Japanese among the general public in the U.S. and U.K.

This is the double-edged potential of motion pictures. The question now is how we make use of this priceless insight in our continuing efforts to make Japan a major content exporter.

Notes

1. Takashi Ebisaka, *Atarashiki Tsuchi* (1) or *The Daughter of Samurai*, Collected Papers on Foreign Language and Literature at Teikyo University, Vol. 9, 2003, p. 133.
2. Yuji Segawa, Truth of *Atarashiki Tsuchi: Film Exportation of Pre-War Japan and Era of Madness*, Heibonsha, 2017, p. 170.
3. Ibid.
4. Tamaki Tsuchida, Concept of "Internationality" in Pre-war Japanese Film: Dream of Nagamasa Kawakita which could be seen in *NIPPON* (Senzenki no Nihon Eiga niokeru Kokusaisei no Gainen: *NIPPON* nimiru Kawakita Nagamasa no Yume), p. 28, Cre Biz, Vol. 7, Graduate School of Film Producing, 2012.
5. Chronological Table of *Atarashiki Tsuchi* (*Atarashiki Tsuchi*: Nenhyou), Theater Pamphlet of *Atarashiki Tsuchi*, Kinema-Jumpo-Sha, 2012, p. 42.
6. Junichiro Tanaka, *History of Development of Japanese Films* (Nihon Eiga Hattatsu-shi), Vol. II, Chuo Koron-Sha, 1957, p. 222.
7. Tadashi Iijima, Kimio Uchida, Matsuo Kishi, Tsuneo Hazumi (ed,), *Year Book of Japanese Motion Pictures 1936* (*Eiga Nenkan 1936*), Daiichi-Shobou, March 1936.
8. Ebisaka points out that this invitation was instigated by the German Ministry of Propaganda out of concern about Fanck's limitations – which it knew very well – rather than Fanck's personal initiative.
9. Toho Towa (successor of Towa Shoji) sealed the Itami version for a long time, and it is not easy to access it for viewing. No DVD is available. I managed to view it at the National Film Center (which became the National Film Archive of Japan in April 2018) in Tokyo by application for a special screening for researchers about ten years ago. In contrast, the Fanck version is available on DVD and was re-released in Tokyo in 2012, and there was a one-day special screening of Itami version at that time.
10. Takashi Ebisaka, "*Atarashiki Tsuchi* (2) or *The Daughter of Samurai*", *The Teikyo Journal of Comparative Cultures*, No. 17, 2003, pp. 46–47.
11. For the February screenings, the Japanese title of both version was simply *Atarashiki Tsuchi* (『新しき土』), but when Hibiya Theater decided to show Fanck's version from November 24, its Japanese title was changed to *Samurai no Musume* (『武士（サムライ）の娘』).
12. Yoshio Irie, *Atarashiki Tsuchi* (NFC Newsletter, National Film Center, The National Museum of Modern Art, Tokyo, Vol. II No.4 July–August 1996), p. 12.
13. Ebisaka, *Atarashiki Tsuchi* (2), p. 50.
14. Arnold Fanck, On the Exportation of Japanese Motion Picture Films, *Cinema Year Book of Japan 1936–1937*, Sanseido Co., Ltd., 1937, pp. 30–31.
15. Inuhiko Yomata, *Nihon no Joyuu* (Actresses in Japan), Iwanami Shoten, 2000, p. 45.
16. Chiyota Shimizu, *Atarashiki Tsuchi* no Kouseki (The Achievements of *Atarashiki Tsuchi*), *Kinema Jumpo*, March 1, 1937 (No.603), p. 13.
17. Donald Richie, *The Daughter of the Samurai*: a German-Japanese co-production, *Tokyo-Berlin/Berlin-Tokyo*, Mori Art Museum, 2006, Chapter 1.

18 *50 Years of TOWA: 1928–1978 (Towa no Hanseiki)*, Toho Towa Co., Ltd., 1978, p. 268.

Alhough the details of company M which Kawakita entrusted the distribution to are not certain, it is reasonable to assume that he must have visited the company's headquarters to arrange international distribution. The film companies headquartered in New York with names starting with M are Modern Film Corp. and Monogram Pictures Corp. There is also a possibility that it means Loew's Inc. the parent company of MGM. But Loew's Inc. was the biggest film company in the U.S., and two small companies are more likely for Towa Shoji to have contracts with, hence it seems that the Modern Film Corp., whose president at the time was Geo Barnett is most likely company M.

19 Jack Alicoate, (ed.), *The 1938 Film Daily Year Book of Motion Pictures*, 20th Annual Edition, The Film Daily, 1938, pp. 471–477 (Features Imported during 1937).
20 Tadashi Hirai, *Leni Riefenstahl (Leni Riefenstahl: 20 seiki Eizouron no tameni)*, Shoubunsha, 1999, pp. 78–81.
21 Frank Capra, *The Name above the Title: An Autobiography*, Vintage Books Edition, 1985, p. 346.
22 http://www.imdb.com/title/tt0796609/?ref_=fn_al_tt_1
23 Nagamasa Kawakita, "Eiga Yushutsu no Shomondai (Various problems of exportation of films)," *Nihoneiga*, December 1938, Special Issue, Vol. 3, No. 12, pp. 19–20.
24 Fanck, op.cit., p. 29. There is an abridged translation of the essay in Japanese in *Nihoneiga*, January 1937, Vol. 2, No. 1, but this is the author's translation.

9 The Mysterious Popularity of Japanese Films in Taiwan in the 1950s and '60s[1]

Mamie MISAWA

Introduction

This chapter analyzes the popularity of Japanese films in Taiwan in the 1950s and '60s.[2] Following half a century of Japanese colonial rule, Taiwan was requisitioned in 1945 by the Republic of China (hereafter ROC), led by the Chinese Nationalist Party (hereafter CNP), after the Japanese surrender ended WWII. With the memory of colonial rule and the war still fresh in their minds, the fact that Japanese movies were welcomed in Taiwan with great enthusiasm seems rather mysterious, and prompts a further question: why did Taiwan allow Japanese movies to be imported in the first place?

A common Japanese response to this question might be that "Taiwan is pro-Japanese." This and similar phrases have been used to counter negative accounts of Japanese colonization.[3] However, this defensiveness should also be regarded as an expression of Japan's colonialist attitude, which lingers in Japan.[4] Through the examination of documentary evidence, I offer an alternative explanation for the popularity of Japanese movies. That is, the geo-political context, which underpinned Japanese movies' popularity, could be seen as a result of negotiation between the ROC and Japan; even though this popularity was supported by a "pro-Japanese" tendency, Taiwanese people enjoyed Japanese movies in their own way, which might be seen as part of the process of de-colonization.

Previous literature and perspectives for this chapter

This chapter attempts to break new ground through analyses of historical records and a shift in perspective. For historical records, I have used archival resources such as reports by the local police in Taiwan, as well as surveys conducted by the Japanese embassy and the United States Information Service (hereafter, USIS), none of which have been previously considered in this field of academic research.

The 'shift in perspectives' results from focusing on two specific contexts: 1) continuity in Taiwanese movie history from the Japanese colonial period to the postwar period and 2) Japanese colonialism, which has endured even though Japan lost its colonies.

Academic research into the history of cinema in Taiwan appears to have neglected the colonial period until the 1990s. And when researchers did finally begin to consider this period, they rarely mentioned continuity with the postwar period. Yet, Taiwan's postwar movie history is a result of the intersecting and conflicting views of Taiwanese society and the government. For the ROC, regulation of movies similar to that in Mainland China was necessary for social harmony; whereas for the local Taiwanese society, there was continuity in how films were distributed and received by the public between the colonial period and the postwar period. In this sense, both the popularity and criticism of Japanese movies in Taiwan is notable when we consider the legacies of colonialism from the different perspectives of the government and the public. This chapter is an attempt to explain the tangled continuity by using historical records that have hitherto been overlooked.

In this chapter, "pro-Japanese" is used to represent goodwill towards Japan, referred to as "nostalgia" for Japan, and a "Japan Boom" by various commentators. But it is not always clear which "Japan" is being invoked. Especially in Taiwan, under strict information control policies, the word "Japan" sometimes indicates a vague conception of Japan, constructed by multiple and diverse layers of indirect or restricted information, or through personal experiences during the colonial period. It is therefore necessary to stress that the word "Japan" in this context represents particular and diverse perceptions of Japan imagined by individuals and institutions.

Some pioneering academic studies on Japanese elements in postwar Taiwan are worth considering here.[5] Huang Ying-zhe describes how the ROC government tried – immediately after the requisition – to eliminate Japanese influences such as books and movies as part of its program of cultural reconstruction for "Sinicization."[6] There has also been some excellent research focused on language problems relative to post-colonial

Taiwan, by He Yi-lin, Xu Xue-ji, and Morita Kenji.[7] They all point out that the ROC government sought to suppress the use of the Japanese language in their efforts to improve social integration. On the broader cultural policies of the ROC government, Xiao A-qin, Lin Guo-xian, and Sugano Atsushi researched "Taiwanese cultural nationalism," "Sinicization," "de-Japanization," and "localization (Taiwanization)" within their respective fields.[8] This chapter is indebted to previous research on Japanese images in postwar Taiwan. For example, Huang Chi-Huei highlights the complexity of Japanese images in Taiwan. She argues that those who directly experienced Japanese colonialism began, in the postwar period, to use the Japanese language as a means of resistance against the ROC government to demarcate themselves from their new oppressor: the ROC government.[9] This suggestion is crucial to understanding the popularity of Japanese movies in postwar Taiwan.

There are also two excellent anthologies on the reproduction of colonialism in postwar Japan: Igarashi Mako and Mio Yuko eds., *Sengo Taiwan ni okeru "Nihon": shokuminchikeiken no renzoku/henbo/riyo* ("Japan" in postwar Taiwan: the continuity/ transformation/ utilization of colonial experience) Tokyo: Fukyosha, 2006; Iwasaki Minoru, Ri Takanori, et al. eds., *Keizoku suru Shokuminchishugi : jienda minzoku jinshu kaikyu* (Continuing Colonialism: Gender/Nation/Race/Class) Tokyo: Seikyūsha, 2005. However, those researchers in the Igashi and Mio volume who explore the appearance of the "pro-Japanese" discourse do not adequately examine the socio-political structure in which these "pro-Japanese" sentiments arise; they focus instead on accounts of individual experiences which they collected through field work. In contrast, in the Iwasaki and Ri volume, those authors who seek to demonstrate that Japanese colonialism did, in fact, continue after the war, focus on socio-political concerns, but usually ignore the appearance of "pro-Japanese" sentiments and discourse, perhaps due to the inherent difficulty of discussing this issue when looking at Japanese colonialism on a broad spatial and chronological scale. Hence, while drawing insight from these studies, this chapter seeks to bridge the gaps they left unaddressed. To this end, I have relied on multi-archival (and multi-lingual) resources from the period, rather than retrospective individual accounts.

From this perspective, this chapter will examine the following points to analyze the popularity of Japanese movies in the 1950s and '60s: 1) the Japanese Movie Trade Fair, which was both incredibly popular and fiercely criticized in Taiwan, and the starkly different attitudes of the two governments (the ROC and Japan) towards the fair; 2) criticism of the fair, which reveals contradictory attitudes within the ROC government; 3) the relationship between the general popularity of Japanese movies and "pro-Japanese" tendencies found in surveys by USIS and the Japanese Embassy, and; 4) the various meanings of Japanese film consumption.

Japanese Movie Trade Fair: Two governments' perspectives

I will begin by analyzing reception of the Japanese Movie Trade Fair (hereafter, JMTF) held in Taiwan in 1960.

JMTF aimed to foster goodwill between Japan and Taiwan (ROC). It ran in Taipei for six days beginning March 10, 1960. There appears to be no academic literature about this event, except for the historical record of cinema in Taiwan.[10]

As the first international film festival in postwar Taiwan, the event was a rare entertainment opportunity for people living under the autocracy of the Chinese Nationalist Party (hereafter CNP). According to contemporary news reports from Taipei,[11] the sponsor (Japanese Embassy and the Motion Picture Producers Association in Japan Inc.) gave 3,400 free tickets out to those who applied by postcards, and 5,000 tickets were given to personnel of the ROC government. The number of application postcards reached 75,000 in two days. Even after additional screenings were scheduled, trying to get a ticket was compared to playing the lottery. Sold on the black market, these complimentary tickets reached a price of 60 New Taiwanese dollars, six times more than an ordinary cinema ticket at the time.[12] An article in a Japanese newspaper reported the event as follows:

> Local newspapers gave harsh criticism to this event despite it being quite popular among the public. For example, one newspaper wrote, "This movie fair praises militarism, effuses eroticism, and is full of inferior productions displaying swordsmen. That is because they look down on *Chinese people* as only being able to view such low-grade films. Furthermore, when those second-rate, even third-rate actresses came to Taipei, school-age girls and fans' reactions appeared to border on insanity. Japanese language cast a shadow over the event and one wondered if this audience showcasing 'disgraceful behavior' and chorusing Japanese songs happily in the theatre had forgotten their national identity. One even began to doubt what country it was.

> Surely, the "frenzy" which the *local Taiwanese* showed towards this fair was repulsive to the *Mainlanders*. Some young people were arrested because they threw stones and distributed flyers saying, "Have you forgotten the past?" There were also cases of harassing behavior such as remaining seated when the Japanese national anthem was played, and anonymous letters to newspapers that poured cold water on this fair. These criticisms and behaviors were undoubtedly caused by jealousy and resentment towards Japan. At the foundation, we can see the government hatred of the *Taiwanese* "nostalgia" for Japan which the fair revived. (emphasis added)[13]

As we can see, the event drew both sharp criticism and great enthusiasm, and the differences in opinion seem to be related to ethnic conflicts, as discussed in the next section.[14]

The ROC's motives for importing Japanese movies

Before analyzing responses to the JMTF, let us first examine the respective governments' motives for the JMTF, since the event required the permission of both governments.

After 1945, "the Taiwanese were able to shake off colonial rule at the hands of the foreign oppressor Japan and its thundering war cannons, however they were yet deeply involved in another less visible colonial system and another war, which had no roaring artillery but was still there."[15] With the CNP government's requisitioning of Taiwan, the Taiwanese citizenry became caught in the civil war between the CNP and the Chinese Communist Party (hereafter CCP), as well as the Cold War. Decrees of martial law and legislation for national mobilization kept Taiwan on a war footing until 1991.[16]

Moreover, those who took control of the government were "Mainlanders" (*waishengren*) who had come from mainland China with the CNP. The local Han Taiwanese (*benshengren*) who had experienced Japanese colonization felt that their expectations of the "Motherland" had been disappointed, because they were excluded from almost all areas of politics and the economy after the requisition. The new government encountered a series of problems, including deteriorating public safety and sanitation, food shortages and rapid inflation due to procurements for the civil war, and the inevitable corruption of a nepotist system favoring "Mainlanders," which left the locals increasingly unemployed. The locals resentment soon exploded into an anti-government uprising. This disturbance, known as the "2.28 Incident," was immediately and violently suppressed by the CNP. After the incident, the CNP government thoroughly purged those who had expressed objections to the regime, under the guise of "anti-communism." This "political education through terror"[17] forcibly silenced Taiwanese citizens.

We should pay careful attention to the different perspectives at the root of this ethnic conflict (*shengji maodun*) – perspectives which originated from different experiences: the local Taiwanese experience of colonial rule and the Mainlanders' experience of the war of resistance.

After requisitioning Taiwan, the ROC believed that "this province, colonized for 50 years, has the leftover poison (*Yidu*) of the enemy's (Japan's) cultural thought flowing deeply inside of it. For this reason, our task of cultural education (lit. "propaganda") is extremely important." Therefore, they tried to "remove the 'leftover poison' through publicizing government ordinances and controlling the mass media while promoting Chinese culture, in order to expedite an immediate effect."[18]

In the words of Chen Yi, the chief executive of Taiwan Province (*Taiwansheng xingzheng zhangguan*), cultural propaganda was meant to facilitate "Sinicizing" (*Zhongguohua*) as a solution to the "Imperialization" (*Kōminka*) conducted under Japanese colonization.[19] In this sense, "Sinicizing" in Taiwan inevitably implied "de-Japanization."

Therefore, the use of Japanese in newspapers and magazines was prohibited after 1946, because "the spread of Japanese (among the local Taiwanese), even greater than expected," was considered to be "evidence that the local Taiwanese had been made into *slaves* by Japanese colonization."[20] Japanese movies were provisionally banned, and Japanese books which contained "leftover poison" were prohibited.[21] Taiwan resumed importing Japanese movies, though, soon after normalizing trade with Japan – which was still occupied by the Allied Powers at the time – after the Korean War broke out in 1950.[22] When the ROC and Japan concluded a peace treaty in 1952, the ROC began to regard Japanese movies the same as other foreign movies, but they still limited both the number of imported Japanese films and days of their screening, unlike other imported films, through controlling distributors and censorship by the Movie Inspection Bureau (Dianying jianchachu).[23]

In other words, Japanese movies were still viewed by the ROC as "poison" that should be excluded fundamentally, but movies were imported nevertheless. No doubt this compromise was to a large extent because the ROC needed to strengthen its relationship with Japan, not only for national security concerns, but also for economic growth.[24] Importing Japanese movies was considered to be an effective way to foster bonds among those in the "anti-communist, liberal camp." Here we can see a clear connection to the articles referring to the "pro-Japanese" phenomena which were filed in the category "propaganda against Japan" by the ROC's Ministry of Foreign Affairs.[25] Indeed, it seems that, from the perspective of those close to the ROC government, importing Japanese films was regarded as a sort of "gift" to Japan, which was only incidentally a boon to national security and economic cooperation.[26] For example, an article in a Hong Kong newspaper in March 1959 stated,

> The ROC is looked down on by Japan, since there is no diplomatic trump card vis-a-vis Japan at the ROC's disposal, akin to the right to claim war reparations held by Korea, the Philippines, Indonesia, and Vietnam. There is no decisive means to punish Japan for what happened at the ambassadors' conference between Japan and the People's Republic of China and Japan's inhospitable treatment of the (ROC's) Foreign Minister Huang Shao-gu. Even though the ROC has offered *gifts* such as importing Japanese movies and Japanese publications in terms of economic cooperation between Japan and the ROC, the contribution from the Japanese side was little.[27]

In fact, in contrast with other goods (e.g., metal products and chemical fertilizers), Taiwan's biggest imports from Japan, movies were not a "necessity," that would negatively affect Taiwan's economy if they were banned. By the same token, allowing their importation seemed like an ideal "gift," as it had strong public support, yet could still be used as a bargaining chip at the negotiating table.

Japan's motives for exporting movies

From the other side, the Japanese government recognized that economic diplomacy and cultural diplomacy were the "most important tasks" for Japan's diplomatic policy after having "joined the United Nations and returned to the international community as a full-fledged member."[28] In 1957, Japan's Ministry of Foreign Affairs held a meeting on "cultural diplomacy," at which Kondo Shinichi, chief of the Public Information and Cultural Affairs Bureau (Jōhōbunkakyokuchō), stated that the Ministry of Foreign Affairs was "focusing on cultural exchange through film."[29] This remark attests to the revival of Japanese confidence in its film industry after Akira Kurosawa's *Rashomon* won the grand prize at the Venice International Film Festival in 1951. This victory was evidence that Japanese culture and entertainment had been approved by the international community.[30] After *Rashomon*'s success abroad, numerous agencies were established in both the public and private sectors to export and promote Japanese movies overseas.[31]

As part of its efforts to propel Japanese movies into the international market, the JMTF was first held in Rome in 1956. It was then held in New York twice and once in Berlin. Taipei in 1960 was the fifth JMFT.

Iguchi Sadao seems to have been integral in planning the event.[32] Iguchi, who had been the Japanese ambassador to Taipei in 1959 after having previously served as ambassador in the U.S. and Canada, was a member of the Japan-ROC Cooperation Committee[33] established in 1957. He was also the first vice-president of the Association for Promoting Japanese Film Overseas[34] established in 1957. The association provided the JMTF with a large sum to fund the event. The embassy of the ROC in Japan recorded that Iguchi visited in order to ask for relaxation of restrictions on Japanese books and movies.[35] Around the time Iguchi arrived in Taipei, the ROC repeatedly criticized Japan's expanding trade with the People's Republic of China (hereafter PRC).[36] It has been assumed that the Japanese representatives, such as Iguchi and Kondo, chief of the Information and Culture Bureau, who regarded exporting Japanese movies as "a tool of information and enlightenment for overseas," planned the JMFT in Taipei in order to ease the tension between Japan and the ROC.[37]

Furthermore, of the more than 45 countries importing movies at that time, Taiwan was the third largest importer of Japanese movies, after Okinawa and the U.S.[38] Although its market was even "more promising," it remained limited by ROC policy. Clearly the Japanese thought holding the JMTF in Taipei was an effective way to promote Japanese films and expand the market.

It is apparent that there was disagreement between the ROC, who reluctantly permitted importation of Japanese movies as a "gift" for bargaining, and Japan, who regarded exporting Japanese movies as a "practice" meant to foster a "Japan-ROC friendship," not only for economic benefit, but also for "cultural diplomacy." In other words, for the ROC, importing Japanese movies was permitted merely out of concern for their economic bonds and the "anti-communist" relationship with Japan in the context of U.S. military protection. Therefore, the decision to permit imports did not indicate a change of position on the idea that Japanese movies should be restricted in accordance with the ROC government's desired goal of "Sinicization" and "de-Japanization." Ultimately, in terms of Japanese movies, the ROC faced an incompatible double standard: *elimination* for the sake of "Sinicization" and "de-Japanization" set against *acceptance* of the goals of "anti-communism" and "reinforcement of the Japan-ROC relationship."

Thus, it has been suggested that the public "frenzy" for the JMTF and the popularity of Japanese movies in Taiwan were constructed against the ROC's reluctant acceptance of Japanese films and Japan's "arrogant" expectations "without reflection."[39] In a sense, this event can be regarded as a result of the two governments' hand-in-hand "pro-Japanese" performance, although their perceptions of Japanese movies were quite different.

Criticism of the Japanese Movie Trade Fair

Given that JMTF was the result of a "pro-Japanese" performance by both governments, as mentioned above, why did the CNP-controlled media criticize it so harshly? Here we need to examine the content of the criticism.

According to articles related to the 1960 JMTF, the following extract is typical of the tone found in these articles written in Chinese.

> The most despicable thing is that this time they showed the movie *Emperor Meiji and General Nogi* which is set against a backdrop of the Russo-Japanese War and flaunts the invasion of the northern part of China as valorous, that we might "appreciate" those massacres, presented under the guise of "cultural exchange!" The memory of an eight-year-long war of resistance and the smell of blood are still fresh, the massacre in Nanjing and the air raid on Chongqing are as vivid as if they had happened only yesterday. Despite this, in the end, crazed militarism fell to one knee and surrendered. Wake up! Do not simply conspire for your personal interest. Take a good look at reality. Serious reflection is demanded of you. Remember that our "president" showed you kindness and said, "Show kindness even when you have a strong reason

to hate someone," that the time of insanity is over, that you must no longer foolishly deceive yourselves and others with childish behavior.[40]

Similar opinions were published elsewhere, such as "A Wish for Understanding Chinese Culture" (*Gonglunbao* March 13,1960) and a four-frame comic strip that ridiculed a mayor for being infatuated with a Japanese actress.

Note that the media in Taiwan at the time was under a strict government information control regime afforded by the "war footing," and thus the biases seen in newspapers reflected the views of the ROC government to a strong degree.[41]

A police report from Taiwan Province

A report on the JMTF by the Police Department of Taiwan Province which was sent to the Ministry of Foreign Affairs more explicitly outlines the ROC government's views on the JMTF. This report lists four points summarizing the Police Department's complaints about the event as follows.[42]

1. The Japanese Embassy distributed free tickets to screenings, but there were too many people to be admitted. Many of those who did get in were able to understand Japanese, so they clapped their hands and exploded into laughter at the Japanese stars' humor and messages without waiting for the translation. We suspect the Japanese Embassy had political intentions.
2. The Japanese side had initially planned not to play the Chinese national anthem, just to play the Japanese National Anthem on the opening day of March 10. There was a special effort made to look down on our nation.
3. Almost all of the screened movies were commercialized works without any artistic value. In particular, the movie titled *Emperor Meiji and General Nogi* inflates their war record from when Japanese troops fought with the Russian Empire at Lüshun in northern China. The local Taiwanese who have never been to the mainland might fall into the misunderstanding that mainland China was originally a Japanese territory.
4. The attitudes of Japanese female stars were very arrogant. According to the news, they did not accept flowers at the airport when they came

to Taiwan from Japan, nor did they make any statement to praise Free China or show reverence to our Heads of State.

To comprehend this report, we should recall that originally the ROC government had two incompatible standards for importing Japanese movies. From this point of view, the JMTF was indeed an event where "Sinicization" and "de-Japanization" were compromised to "reinforce the Japan-ROC relationship." Moreover, the Police Department report tells us that the movies which were harshly criticized had been pre-screened and examined by ROC officials,[43] and reveals subtle differences among those officials. The Ministry of Education and General Headquarters of Security (*Jingbeizongbu*) thought movies such as *Emperor Meiji and the Great Russo-Japanese War* should be banned, while the Fourth Section of the Central Committee of the CNP (*Guomindang Zhongyangweiyuanhui di si zu*: responsible for information and propaganda matters within the country)[44] and the Information Office (*Xinwenju*) thought they were acceptable for screening.

Therefore, it can be concluded that the newspapers criticized the JMTF in order to impress upon the local Taiwanese the importance of "Sinicization" and "de-Japanization" which called for stopping importation of Japanese movies, as well as to rebuke the officials who had compromised on the logic of "Sinicization" and "de-Japanization."[45] Another aim might be to point out to Japanese officials and guests that they should not have been so arrogant with their film selections and general attitude, but should reflect on the invasion and era of colonial rule.[46] Archival materials at the Japanese Ministry of Foreign Affairs, however, indicate that the Japanese did not take those warnings seriously.[47]

Analyzing the popularity of Japanese movies

As we have seen, criticism of the JMTF can be understood in terms of the ROC's two contradictory standards. But, how do we account for the "frenzy" stirred by Japanese movies and the JMTF?

The Taiwanese correspondent for *Kobe Shimbun* attributed this phenomenon to "nostalgia for Japan." The authorities and the local press, though, stressed that this popularity was not unanimous but was mainly found among the local Taiwanese who had experienced colonization.

In 1960, when the local Taiwanese still shared memories of colonial rule, how could the people feel nostalgia for the old colonial era? One suggestion might be that life for the locals had been better under Japanese colonial rule than under the ROC's dictatorship. Previous studies, though, suggest quite the opposite: the Japanese army and police had killed many people during the colonial period,[48] producing no fewer casualties than the 2.28 Incident and the White Terror[49] under the ROC's dictatorial rule. Forced military enlistment also occurred. During World War II, more than 200,000 Taiwanese were conscripted as soldiers and as civilian-workers for the army. Many were wounded or died in combat, and many others were executed or punished as war criminals. Furthermore, the survivors suffered from a double standard of receiving lesser compensation than the "real" Japanese because they were seen as "non-Japanese" after the war.[50] Women were not exempt from appropriation during wartime. More than 300,000 unmarried young women were drafted to work at designated sites or joined in various mass organizations of labor.[51] All of these factors seem to belie suggestions of a positive assessment of Japanese colonial rule.

Nevertheless, separate surveys conducted in 1960 by Japan and the U.S. found that the local Taiwanese did, in fact, have some degree of "pro-Japanese" sentiments. I will return to these surveys below. For the moment, these seemingly contradictory interpretations call for a detailed analysis of how and why such "pro-Japanese" sentiments arose, considering the historical factors mentioned above.

In this section, I will first examine previous research addressing the popularity of Japanese movies in Taiwan, and then analyze the Japanese and U.S. surveys mentioned above. I will then propose a hypothesis to explain the "frenzy" over the JMTF and the popularity of Japanese movies, which is both compatible with the historical facts and contrary to the suggestion of a positive assessment of Japanese colonial rule.

Popularity of Japanese movies in postwar Taiwan

The JMTF surely had several attractions for the Taiwanese audience. It was the first international film event in Taiwan. It brought many foreign actresses to the island. And it was free entertainment with tickets distributed by the sponsor.

Beyond these factors, though, is the undeniable fact that Japanese movies were already quite popular in Taiwan at the time. We can see this, for example, in the recollections of a Japanese businessman who visited Taiwan in October 1958, who wrote: "The deeper we went into the back-country, the deeper their nostalgia for Japan seemed to be. As for a movie about the Russo-Japanese War and Emperor Meiji, I've heard that when the Emperor showed up in the movie, two-thirds of the audience stood and doffed their hats to show respect."[52] This account was filed among clippings sent to Japan's Ministry of Foreign Affairs by the ROC Consulate stationed in Osaka. Another article entitled "The Real Taiwan," published in the newspaper *Sankei Shimbun*, stated:

> I was surprised because there were signs of Japan (lit. "Japanese colors") all over the island. It was also the same in the theatre. In quantity, Japan can't compete with the U.S. which distributes 300 titles in a year. Nevertheless, theatres screening Japanese movies are always packed full. The biggest hit recently is *Emperor Meiji and the Great Russo-Japanese War*. We could also see how deep the Japan boom was, when we witnessed a poster of His and Her Imperial Highness pasted very reverently on the wall of a small shop.[53]

Moreover, research indicates that the most popular foreign films in Taiwan during the 1950s and '60s were Japanese.[54] Lü Su-shang provided statistics in his 1961 book, demonstrating that although fewer Japanese movies were imported than U.S. movies, the audience at each screening was twice as large, and therefore, the net income for each movie was greater. Hence, Japanese films were the more profitable of the two and remained the favorite from 1958–1960.[55]

Previous research has singled out two factors to explain the popularity of Japanese films. First, half the population of 8 million could understand Japanese,[56] and second, Japanese movies resonated more strongly with the Taiwanese lifestyles.[57] Huang and Wang suggested several additional factors: Japanese movies were technically more sophisticated than Mandarin movies; viewers associated a certain status with the act of watching Japanese movies; the viewers could readily relate to the experiences being portrayed on the screen, and; the younger generation had become interested in studying Japanese as trade with Japan began to flourish.[58] Generally speaking, it can be said that a "cultural and linguistic proximity" between Taiwan and Japan, which had been developed during the colonial rule and continued during the Cold War, played an important role.

Surveys by USIS and the Japanese Embassy in Taiwan in 1960

Hitherto, the literature on the attitudes held by the local Taiwanese towards Japan after the war has referred mainly to essays by Taiwanese intellectuals at the time, or to retrospective stories and accounts by external observers. The documents referred to below are quite different: they are surveys, in the form of a questionnaire administered to anonymous citizens by USIS (United States Information Service) and the Japanese Embassy in Taiwan in 1960.

The first document is a questionnaire, administered by USIS Taipei in August 1960, given to individuals who had participated in an orientation program for Taiwanese citizens wishing to study abroad.[59] After World War II, the U.S. developed a variety of public relations activities in Taiwan: inviting students to the U.S. to study was one of them.[60]

Respondents to the survey were graduates of universities such as the National Taiwan University and National Cheng Kung University. Around 75 people completed the questionnaire. (The group, 90% of whom were between 19 and 30 years old, included: 18 females and 57 males: 25 local Taiwanese and 50 Mainlanders). The questionnaire included questions about personal dispositions towards five countries and their citizens: the United States, Great Britain, Japan, India and the Soviet Union. The respondents had to choose between 'very good,' 'good,' 'normal,' 'bad,' and 'very bad,' to rate the target countries.

A highly favorable rating for the U.S. is unsurprising, given that the survey was conducted by USIS, and that the subjects were students who were applying to study in the U.S. For our purposes, there appears to be no factor which would result in the data being skewed in the case of Japan. In this regard, one can observe a clear dichotomy between the "Mainlanders" and the "Taiwanese," which is not found in the assessment of the other countries listed in the questionnaire. It seems safe to say that the local Taiwanese had a positive assessment about Japan, whereas the Mainlanders had a strongly negative assessment.

Another survey was conducted by the Japanese Embassy in Taiwan when it dispatched staff to the three cities of Taizhong, Tainan, Gaoxiong to carry out a census of the Japanese inhabitants of Taiwan, as an extension of the population census conducted in Japan in 1960. The embassy's survey, titled "Exploring Society," asked the local Taiwanese about their "feelings for Japan."[61]

On September 19, 1960, the Japanese Embassy published the following notice announcing its intentions in the newspaper *Central Daily News* (Zhongyang Ribao): "The Embassy will dispatch its agents specifically to carry out a census of the Japanese inhabitants in Taiwan. Those seeking consultation can send a letter directly to the following place during the given time period..." After publishing this advertisement, the staff investigated the feelings of the local Taiwanese for Japan through personal relationships and chance encounters.

According to the report, which was submitted to Japan's Ministry of Foreign Affairs, a disparity in feelings held towards Japan was largely dependent upon the age of the respondents. Those born before 1925 (over 35 years old at the time), some having done their military service in the Japanese army, mostly felt very close to Japan. A similar trend, though less strong, is noticeable in the generation born between 1925 and 1935 (age 25–35), who had completed their primary or secondary education during the colonial era. In contrast, those born after 1936 (less than 24 years old), most likely owing to the fact that they had been educated for nearly sixteen years under the ROC, had little interest in Japan. Officials dispatched by the Japanese Embassy interviewed several people, such as a bus driver (age 38), an employee of a hotel (age 32), a scooter driver (age 22), a third-year university student, and several intellectuals.

The scooter driver said he knew nothing about Japan, nor did he feel any specific urge to get to know it. The university student, expressing the younger generation's perspectives, said it was not right that his parents would think first of Taiwan and Japan before China. On the contrary, the bus driver (age 38, came to visit the embassy staff voluntarily) had fought alongside Japanese soldiers in the war and said that when he returned to Taiwan, "It was already occupied by Mainlanders. My language and my lifestyle, everything was Japanese. So, I couldn't get along with the ways of the Mainlanders... Is there any possibility that I can get Japanese nationality?" In addition, the hotel employee (age 32) who lit up and suddenly changed his attitude when he found that he was facing a Japanese speaker, stressed: "You can understand the longing for Japan by the reaction towards Japanese movies. If it's a Japanese movie, a theatre will always be packed, so we need to buy a ticket on the black market, while other foreign movies never fill up the theatres." In his words, the popularity of Japanese movies represented a longing for Japan. Of course, we must be cautious in interpreting the results of this survey. There is no doubt that the researchers' (Embassy officials) subjectivity came into play. And of course, the subjects surveyed were hardly representative of the range of opinions held by the Taiwanese at the time. It is nevertheless revealing that these opinions existed in Taiwan in 1960.

We should also note that individuals over the age of 25 were the primary consumers of entertainment, such as movies. The younger generation, born after 1936, comprised children, students and low-wage workers with little disposable income.

"Catharsis" through the reversal of center and periphery

The conclusion which can be drawn from these two official investigations is that the "frenzy" for Japanese movies was in part a result of "pro-Japanese" sentiments in Taiwan. We must therefore ask how these "pro-Japanese" sentiments, and more precisely, the affinity for Japanese movies, came about.

Previous research, as we have seen, already suggested a "cultural and linguistic proximity" might account for the attraction of Japanese films, film stars, and other "pro-Japanese" phenomena. I will focus instead on the "catharsis," or the excitement of extreme changes in spectators' emotions, resulting from a reversal in the center/periphery relationship in Taiwan to explain the "frenzy" for Japanese movies. To this end, we must consider the socio-political marginality of the Taiwanese who seemed to be most "pro-Japanese."

It is well known that anti-ROC intellectuals who fled the island launched a "Taiwanese independence movement." It was impossible to pursue this ambition within Taiwan. Under the dictatorship, the government vigilantly monitored the population for potential secessionist and independence movements. The government was cautious of "Taiwanese-ness" that might stimulate "Taiwanese nationalism," and was eager to integrate the Taiwanese citizenry into the Chinese language. Mandarin Chinese was the official language, and other languages such as Taiwanese Hokkien (mother tongue for about 73% of the population), Taiwanese Hakka (mother tongue for about 12% of the population), and the Taiwanese aboriginal languages were banned. Even in history classes, any reference likely to give rise to ideas of a unique "Taiwanese history" were carefully avoided. In other words, the regime sought to suppress both "Taiwanese-ness" and "Japanese-ness" in order to integrate the population into the Chinese language through "Sinicizing."

As we have seen, until 1949, the ROC government believed a "de-Japanization" policy was vital for Taiwan.[62] However, after 1950, they occasionally had to put on a "pro-Japanese" mask for the sake of strengthening the relationship with Japan in the interest of both economics and national security. In contrast, traces of "Taiwanese-ness" were initially tolerated, but from the late 1950s, they were increasingly marginalized. For example, Taiwanese Hokkien, Taiwanese Hakka, and the languages of Taiwanese aborigines used among native peoples of the island were prohibited in schools.[63] Consequently, by the time the JMTF was held in Taipei, Taiwanese society was oriented around a scheme of "Sinicization" with the "Chinese standardization" movement, whereas elements of "Taiwanese-ness" and those of "Japanese-ness" were both marginalized.

With this in mind, let us return to the university student interviewed during the Japanese Embassy's survey. Conceivably, his parents, who had grown up during the colonial era, grouped "Japan and Taiwan" as an expression of opposition to the ROC's "Sinicization" policies and practices. Both the Taiwanese and Japanese culture and language were marginalized in the same way by the ROC as the Taiwanese had been during the Japanese colonial era. Moreover, the student also mentioned that he had begun to feel negative sentiments toward the "Mainlanders" and had "started to re-evaluate his parents' ideas," after experiencing the unabashed nepotism of his Mainlander drill-instructor during his three-and-a-half-month-long military service. This indicates that the younger generation who had been educated under "Sinicization" and had experienced the "gap between the Mainlander and the local Taiwanese" might begin to sympathize with their parents' "pro-Japanese" sentiments.[64]

Hence, the JMTF, referred to by its critics as "an invasion by the Japanese language," can be seen as an inversion of the status quo, with the marginalized Taiwanese suddenly finding themselves as the primary audience, while the Mainlanders (most of whom were invited ROC government officials treated as VIPs) and Mandarin Chinese who usually monopolized the social-center were suddenly marginalized. In this time and space, the dominant center/periphery relationship of everyday life was inverted. Moreover, these circumstances were created by the government, in the interests of a "Japan-ROC friendship." This was why the local

Taiwanese appeared to embrace "pro-Japanese" sentiments fearlessly while Mainlanders experienced the situation as "disgraceful."

Let us return for a moment to the accounts of the Taiwanese audience standing and bowing when an image of the Japanese Emperor appeared on screen. Such behavior might be interpreted as internalized "Japanese-ness" unconsciously exposed through the audience's response to the film. The response to Japanese movies revealed how "Japanese-ness" was marginalized in two ways: on one hand, despite being an indelible part of the audience's identity, it was viewed as "leftover poison"[65] and was deemed by the ROC government and Mainlanders as evidence that people who had experienced the colonial rule had been made into "slaves."[66] On the other hand, the Japanese who had imposed their culture on the local Taiwanese forgot having done so, and then interpreted this behavior as "nostalgia" for the colonial era. In this situation, Japanese film gave a sense of being at the "center" to this doubly-marginalized "Japanese-ness" of the stigmatized local Taiwanese. Movies were mere entertainment, a space limited to a theatre, a time limited by the length of the film reel. That was why the government even under "war footing" could permit such excitement by the "reversal," and people could enjoy it without any fear.

Therefore, the "pro-Japanese" implications of the "frenzy" for the JMTF, the perceived "invasion by the Japanese language" and the popularity of Japanese movies in general, can be explained as a result of the marginalized Taiwanese seeking a sort of relief through the temporary "reversal" of entertainment. Their emotions on this occasion cannot be attributed to simple nostalgia, much less to a "positive assessment of Japanese colonial rule."

Bottom up de-colonization (de-Japanization) by appropriation?

Previous research has explored the meaning of using the Japanese language in Taiwan after World War II. Huang Chi-Huei pointed out that the Japanese language came to have an *a posteriori* mode of "resistance" under the ROC's rule.[67]

In this context, we must also note that in the second half of the 1950s, Japanese movies faced stiff competition from the local Taiwanese movies made in the Hokkien language (referred to hereafter as "Taiwanese Hokkien movies"). The golden age of Taiwanese Hokkien cinema began in 1956 with the movie *Xue Pinggui and Wang Baochuan* (*The Story of Xue Pinggui and Wang Baochuan*, Director He Jiming). This film enjoyed great success, displacing Japanese movies from the top place in net profit per film in the Taiwanese market.⁶⁸

The fact that the success of Taiwanese Hokkien movies had an impact on Japanese movies was also noted by the authorities of the island. At the time, the Commission For Assistance To The Film Business (*Dianying shiye fudao weiyuanhui*), the organization guiding local film production, expressed its concerns about the growing popularity of Taiwanese Hokkien movies in a document called the "Proceedings of the Seventh Committee" (January 30, 1957)⁶⁹ which raised the following points:

1. The production of Taiwanese Hokkien movies weakened the government's policy of recognizing Mandarin Chinese as the national language.
2. The content of Taiwanese Hokkien films did not correspond to the needs of the time.
3. Taiwanese Hokkien films lowered the standard for what was deemed art.

At the same time, it was also noted that "persons who are sympathetic to Taiwanese Hokkien films" expressed the view that "the number of screenings of Japanese films has fallen due to consecutive screenings of Taiwanese Hokkien movies. This is probably because the core audience is the same."⁷⁰ This indicates that, for the government, the success of Taiwanese Hokkien movies was seen as an obstacle to "Sinicization," while at the same time being a possible tool for "de-Japanization."

Both the government and the market recognized that the audience for Japanese and Taiwanese Hokkien movies overlapped, and were thus in competition. Therefore, it is possible that the popularity of Japanese movies was due to a gap in the market before Taiwanese Hokkien film burst onto the scene in the late 1950s.

Here we should note that film production in colonial Taiwan was highly experimental, not industrial. In this situation, Japanese movies could hardly be rejected, even by anti-Japanese groups like the Taiwan Cultural Association (*Taiwan wenhua xiehui*) when they conducted film screenings. But, in this setting, films were localized by employing a Taiwanese Hokkien-language narrator at the venue; essentially a process of appropriation. I have previously argued that this characteristic in the consumption of film could be called "hybridized localization on the spot."⁷¹

We might also view the success of Japanese movies after the war through the frame of this pre-existing consumer-appropriation mechanism.

Furthermore, it is worth noting that the Taiwanese remade many Japanese movies during the time of considerable growth for the Taiwanese Hokkien film industry during 1960s. This tendency to digest rather than reject Japanese films can be seen as a succession of pre-existing consumer-appropriation mechanisms. In other words, during the colonial period, they transformed Japanese movies into "their own Taiwanese movies" through "hybridized localization on the spot," and in the postwar era they produced "their own Taiwanese movies" by remaking Japanese movies. Therefore, rather than rejecting Japanese influences, they made them palatable for consumption by transforming them into local products.[72]

Conclusion

This chapter examined the popularity of Japanese movies in Taiwan in the 1950s and '60s in the context of the socio-political structure in Taiwan at the time, using diverse materials, while paying attention to two main contexts: the continuity between the colonial period and the postwar period of cinema history in Taiwan and the continuing legacy of Japanese colonialism.

In 1960, when the memory of the war and colonialism was still strong, the pre-conditions for Japanese movies' popularity were the cooperation and joint promotion by the two governments of Japan and the ROC in accordance with their shared "anti-communist" initiative and aim of a "Japan-ROC friendship." This led to a hand-in-hand "pro-Japanese" performance by the two governments.

However, the "pro-Japanese" mask of the ROC required not only suppressing memories of the war against Japan, but also compromising their "Sinicizing" and "de-Japanization" policies. The criticism of the JMTF was merely an expression of frustration about this compromise.

At the same time, there is no doubt that the so-called "frenzy" over the JMTF, as well as the general popularity of Japanese movies, was to some extent an expression of "pro-Japanese" sentiments among some segments of the Taiwanese population, as revealed by the surveys conducted by the Japanese Embassy and USIS. Nevertheless, it is now clear that these sentiments simply cannot be attributed to nostalgia for Japan. The "pro-Japanese" expressions were more complicated. They not only included an element of protest against the ROC's imposition of Chinese culture, but also had an aspect of the excitement, the temporal "catharsis" in the theatres made by a reversal of the "center/periphery" relationship in the general socio-political structure of Taiwan at that time.

Our elucidation of the competition between Taiwanese Hokkien film and Japanese film around 1960, reveals that to some extent, what appears to be "pro-Japanese" sentiments might be a result of appropriation by consuming Japanese cultural products, just like Taiwanese Hokkien film producers, who vigorously took elements of Japanese movies and weaved them into their own films.Of course, this does not entirely explain the appearance of "pro-Japanese" sentiments, but it does provide a more satisfactory explanation of the mystery than has been provided by previous research.

Finally, when we reconsider the accounts written by Japanese journalists at the time of the JMTF, it appears that they were unaware of how the Taiwanese had been marginalized by their post-colonial experiences, and thus assumed the appearance of "pro-Japanese" sentiments were nothing more than an expression of "nostalgia for Japan" or a display of "Japanese colors." In contrast, the local correspondent Wu, although depicting the "frenzy" of the JMTF, deliberately used both the word "nostalgia" and the phrase "disgraceful behavior" in quotation marks. There is a subtle but crucial difference between the Japanese journalists' perspective and Wu's. Here we might ask how the gaze of us who live in the 21st century is different from that of the Japanese journalists who penned those articles.

Local Taiwanese who experienced Japanese colonial rule were excited by the JMTF, welcomed Japanese movie stars and saluted the image of the Japanese Emperor on the screen not so long after the war. Surely, these facts cannot be denied. However, if we fail at imagining the connotations of the "pro-Japanese" facade, which were different at each phase, full of contradiction, and ultimately produced a form of bottom up de-colonization (de-Japanization) through appropriation, then the blind spot of Japanese colonialism remains unrecognized.

Note on the romanization of Chinese and Japanese words

As a general rule, this chapter uses the Pinyin system to render Chinese words into the alphabet, while it uses the Hepburn Romanization system for Japanese words. Proper names begin with family names followed by given names (e.g. Chen Yi, Iguchi Sadao).

The author would like to acknowledge KAKENHI funding support (Nos. 23510328 and 15K01893) for this project.

Abbreviations

CNP	Chinese Nationalist Party
CCP	Chinese Communist Party
ROC	Republic of China
PRC	People's Republic of China
JMTF	Japanese Movie Trade Fair
MFA-AH-T	Material of the Ministry of Foreign Affairs, owned by Academia Historica of the ROC
MFA-AS-T	Material of the Ministry of the Foreign Affairs, Academia Sinica of ROC
DA-MFA-J	Material of Diplomatic Archives of the Ministry of Foreign Affairs of Japan

Notes

1 This chapter was originally published in Japanese as "<Sengo> Taiwan deno Nihoneigamihonichi: 1960nen no nekkyo to hihan," and included in *Teikoku no Shikaku / Shikaku* (Perspective / Blind Spot of the Empire) (Sakano Toru, Shin Chang-gon eds., Tokyo: Seikyusha, 2010). It was translated into French and Chinese: "Aliénation ou acculturation coloniale? Taiwan et l' «énigme» d'un succès: le Festival du film japonais de Taipei" (1960), translated by Arnaud Nanta, Laurent Nespoulous, with help from Anne Kerlan on the Chinese, *Cipango – cahiers d'études japonaises*, numéro 18, vol. 2, 2012, pp. 13–53; "1960nian Taipei de ribendianyingxinshanghui suoyinqi de kuangre he pipan," translated by Wang Qiming, proofread by Zhong Shumin, *Taiwan yanjiu* (Research in Taiwan Studies), no. 17, October 2014, pp. 113–150. This English paper is a revised concise version of the original.
2 As mentioned, regarding the period after World War II as "postwar" is awkward when referring to Taiwan. In this chapter, the term "postwar" implies both the period after liberation from Japanese colonial rule and the period after World War II. Furthermore, the spatial term "Taiwan" indicates the area that was colonized by Japan after the Sino-Japanese War, and then requisitioned by the ROC after World War II.
3 The most famous case of this usage is Kobayashi Yoshinori's celebrated comic book *Taiwan-ron* (A View on Taiwan), Tokyo: Shogakukan, 2000.

4 Kobayashi's comics are criticized in East Asian Network of Cultural Studies eds. *Kobayashi Yoshinori Taiwan-ron o koete* (Overcoming Kobayashi Yoshinori's Taiwan-ron), Tokyo: Sakuhinsha, 2001. Mori Yoshio pointed out that in the background of the "Taiwan is pro-Japanese" discourse in contemporary Japan, there was a conversion of the strategy by Taiwanese independence activists in Japan, who advocated Taiwan's independence not only from NCP but also from PRC (*"Taiwan / Nihon, Rensa suru Koroniarizumu"* (Taiwan / Japan: Intertwined Colonialism), Tokyo: Inpakuto Shuppannkai, 2001). Furthermore, it was lingering Japanese colonialist attitudes since the postwar era that forced those Taiwanese activists to take this position. He thus revealed that the discourse had been mostly constructed by means of political purpose and they originated among people in the 1990s.

5 Wakabayashi Masahiro, "Gendai Taiwan no Nihon-Zō" (Concepts of Japan in Taiwan today) in Yamauchi Masayuki, Furuta Motoo, eds., *Nihon Imēge no Kōsaku* (Intertwining concepts of Japan), Tokyo: Tokyo Daigaku Shuppankai, 1997. Wakabayashi Masahiro, "Taiwan Nashonarizumu to 'Wasure-enu Tasha'" (Taiwanese nationalism and the unforgettable other), *Shisō*, no. 957, January 2004, pp. 108–125. Huang Chi-Huei, "Posuto Koroniaru Toshi no Hijyō (Sadness of the postcolonial city)," in Osaka University's Graduate School of Asian Culture and Urbanism, Hashizume Shinya, eds., *Ajia Toshi Bunka-gaku no Kanōsei* (Possibility of studies on Asian urban culture), Osaka: Seibundō shuppan, 2003, pp. 115–145. Huang Chi-Huei, "Taiwan ni okeru Nihon-kan no Kōsaku (Intertwined Japanese image in Taiwan)," translated by Suzuki Yōhei and Morita Kenji, *Nihon Minzoku-gaku* (Bulletin of the Folklore Society of Japan), no. 259, August 31, 2009, pp. 57–81. He Yi-lin, *Kuayue Guojing-xian* (Crossing the national borderline), Taipei: Douxiang chuban, 2006.

6 Huang Ying-zhe, *Taiwan bunka sai-kochiku1945–1947* (Reconstruction of culture in Taiwan 1945–1947), Saitama: Sōdosha, 1999.

7 He Yi-lin, *2.28 Jiken: 'Taiwanjin' keisei no esunoporiteikusu* (The 2.28 Incident: The ethnic politics which make the 'Taiwanese'), Tokyo: Tokyo Daigaku Shuppankai, 2003. Xu Xue-ji, "Guangfu chuqi de yuyan wenti (Language problems of Taiwan in the early postwar period)," *Si yu yan* (29–4), November 1991. pp. 155–184. Morita Kenji, *Tanitsugengoshugi to sono genkai: sengo Taiwan niokeru gengoseisaku no tenkai (1945–1985)* (Monolingual policy and its limits: Development of language policy in postwar Taiwan (1945–1985)), PhD dissertation, University of Tokyo, 2011.

8 Xiao A-qin (Hsiau, A-Chin), *Contemporary Taiwanese Cultural Nationalism*, London: Routledge, 2000. Lin Guo-xian, *"Zhonghua wenhua fuxing yundong tuixing weiyuanhui" zhi yanjiu (1966–1975)* (The research on "A committee for promoting revival of Chinese culture" (1966–1975)), Taipei: Daoxiang, 2005. Sugano Atsushi, *Taiwan no Kokka to Bunka* (Nation and culture in Taiwan), Tokyo: Keisoshobo, 2011.

9 Huang Chi-Huei, "Posuto Koroniaru Toshi no Hijyō." Huang Zhi-hui, "Taiwan ni okeru Nihon-kan no Kōsaku." For one thing, multiple ethnic groups comprise Taiwanese society, and each group has different historical experiences of the Japanese. For another thing, as she thinks Taiwan had been colonized by ROC after being freed from Japanese colonization, it was after democratization in

the end of 1980s that people in Taiwan could start to discuss their experience of Japanese colonization on their own initiative.
10 Lü Su-shang, *Taiwan dianying xiju shi* (A history of cinema and drama in Taiwan), Taipei: Yinhua chubanbu, 1961, p. 107.
11 "Zentou ni Bakuhatsuteki Ninki" (Massive popularity all over the island), *Kobe Shimbun*, evening edition, March 23, 1960. Filed in No.172–3 / 3023, Material of the Ministry of Foreign Affairs, owned by Academia Historica of the ROC (hereafter MFA-AH-T).
12 Ticket prices at the time were not uniform, but the average price for tickets from March 1959 and May 1960 are available. See Huang Jian-Ye, et al., eds., *Kua Shiji Taiwan Dianying Shilu 1898–2000* (The chronicle of Taiwanese cinema 1898–2000), Taipei: Wenjianhui, 2005, pp. 332, 377.
13 "Zentou ni Bakuhatsuteki Ninki" (Massive popularity all over the island), Reported by Wu in Taipei, *Kobe Shimbun*, evening edition, March 23, 1960.
14 In Taiwanese society, there are two major ethnic divisions: first, between Taiwanese aborigines (also called the Indigenous Taiwanese) (*Taiwanyuanzhuminzu*) and the Hans (*hanzu*); second, Hans are further divided into local Taiwanese (*benshengren*) (including the Hakka (*kejia*) and Hoklo (*fulao*, or *minnan*) people) and Mainlanders (*waishengren*). Ethnic tensions are thus multi-layered. Each of these groups has its own language. Most Mainlanders speak Mandarin, while the Hoklo and the Hakka each speak their own languages. The major language adopted for government use was Mandarin while over 80% of the population used Taiwanese (Hoklo) in everyday activity. It must be noted that the word "Taiwanese" (*benshengren*) in this chapter does not imply that this group alone represents the nation of Taiwan (*taiwanren*).
15 Wu Mi-cha, "Taiwanjin no yume to 2.28 jiken" (A Dream of the Taiwanese and the 2.28 Incident), in Ōe Shinobu and others eds., *Kindai Nihon to Shokuminchi 8* (Modern Japan and colonies 8), Tokyo: Iwanami Shoten, 1993, p. 63.
16 According to Lin Guo-xian, important laws that brought about the "war footing" in Taiwan "after the war" are as follows: national mobilization law (*Guojia zongdongyuan fa*) (1947–1991), martial law (*Jieyan fa*) (1949–1987), temporary regulations for the period of suppressing rebellions (*Dongyuan kanluan shiqi linshi tiaokuan*) (1960–1991). See Lin Guo-xian, "Zhanhou Taiwan de Zhanshi Tizhi" (War footing after the war in Taiwan), *Taiwan Fengwu*, no. 58–3, September 2008, pp. 135–165.
17 Wakabayashi Masahiro, *Taiwan: henyō shi chūcho suru aidenteitei* (Taiwan: Its changing and hesitant identity), Tokyo: Chikuma Shinsho, 2001, p. 73.
18 Huang Ying-zhe, *Taiwan bunka sai-kochiku 1945–1947*, Saitama: Sōdosha, 1999, p. 47.
19 *Renmin Daobao* (People's Leading Newspaper), February 10, 1946 (cited in ibid, p. 28).
20 Chen Yi and bureaucrats of the provincial government stated this officially, thus deepening their disputes with Taiwanese intellectuals. See, Huang Ying-zhe, *Taiwan bunka sai-kochiku 1945–1947*, p. 172. He Yi-lin, *2.28 Jiken: 'Taiwanjin' keisei no esunoporiteikusu*, Tokyo: Tokyo Daigaku Shuppankai, 2003, p. 197.
21 Huang Ying-zhe, *Taiwan Bunka Sai-Kochiku 1945–1947*, p. 46.

22 Liao Hong-qi, *Maoyi yu zhengzhi: Tai-ri jian de maoyi waijiao 1950–1961* (Trade and politics: Trading diplomacy between Taiwan and Japan 1950–1961), Taipei: Daoxiang Chubanshe, 2005. According to Liao, trade had already begun in 1947.

23 "Shin Sho-kan gaikobucho tono kaidanyō shiryō" (Reference material for the meeting with Shen Chang-huang, the Minister of Foreign Affairs), written by China Division in July 23, 1965, No. A'-422, Material of Diplomatic Archives of the Ministry of Foreign Affairs of Japan (hereafter, DA-MFA-J). Zheng Wanxiang, *Zhanhou Taiwan dianying guanli tixi zhi yanjiu 1950–1970* (Research on the movie control system in Taiwan after the war, 1950–1970), Master's Thesis at the National Central University (Taiwan), 2001, p. 47.

24 The Trade Agreement between Japan and the ROC was "undoubtedly a cardiac stimulant" for both countries' economic recovery. See Liao Hong-qi, *Maoyi yu Zhengzhi*, p. 25. In fact, from the resumption of trade until around 1960, for the ROC, Japan had been the leading country both in exports and imports. See ibid, pp. 2–3.

25 A letter from Taiwanese Distributors to the Deputy Minister of Foreign Affairs asks him to guarantee the number of imported Japanese movies. In the letter, the distributors request flexiblity, saying "for the purpose of sustaining anti-communism and resisting the Soviet Union, Japan is an ally that we must keep a firm grasp of." A letter to Shen Chang-huang, Deputy Minister of Foreign Affairs, March 11, 1954, No. 172–3,3005, MFA-AH-T

26 Councilors proposed resolving a foreign currency surplus problem created by the exportation of Taiwanese bananas through importing Japanese films. See Huang Ren and Wang Wei, *Taiwan Dianying Bainian Shihua* (One hundred years of Taiwan cinema) First Volume, Taipei: Zhonghua Yingpingren Xiehui, 2004, p. 595.

27 "Kokufu no tainichi gaikō ni kansuru shimbun kaisetsu kiji hōkoku no ken" (A report on the news related to the ROC's diplomacy towards Japan), March 11, 1959, from Andō Yoshimitsu the Consul general in Hong Kong to Fujiyama Aiichirō the Minister of Foreign Affairs, NO. A'-423, DA-MFA-J.

28 "Dai 1 kai bunka gaikō kondankai gijiroku" (The proceedings of the first Cultural Diplomacy Round-Table Conference), April 15, 1957, Public Information and Cultural Affairs Bureau, No. I'0011, DA-MFA-J. The proceedings show that the budget allotment for movies from this year forward was 15 million yen.

29 Ibid.

30 "Sekai no naka no nihon eiga" (Japanese movies in the world), *Kinema Junpō*, no. 235, June 15, 1959, pp. 48–62.

31 Examples include the Exporting Subcommittee of Motion Picture Producers Association of Japan, the Committee Overseeing the Federation for Exportation of Japanese Films, the Association for Promoting Japanese Film Overseas, and the Movie Subcommittee for the Board Overseeing the Exportation of Chemical Goods of the Ministry of International Trade and Industry.

32 Before the conclusion of the Peace Treaty with Japan, when the issue of Chinese participation arose, Iguchi, Vice-Minister of Foreign Affairs at the time, gave the opinion that "Japan does not hope the communist government participates as a signatory country, but is not concerned about the CNP government's

role." See Aiko Utsumi, "Sanfuranshisuko kōwajōyaku to higashi ajia" (The Treaty of San Francisco and East Asia), *Sengo nihon sutadeizu 40–50 nendai* (Studies on postwar Japan 1: 1940s–50s), Minoru Iwasaki et al. eds., Tokyo: Kinokuniya shoten, 2009, p. 141. Gaimushō jōyaku hōkika, *Heiwajōyaku no teiketsu ni kansuru chōsho 2* (Record of Treaty of Peace with Japan 2), Tokyo: Gaimusho, 1966, pp. 6, 71.

33 The Japan-ROC Cooperation Committee was a private organization established as a counterpart of the ROC-Japan Corporation Committee. They met regularly until 1972 to promote economic cooperation and cultural exchange. After the rupture of diplomatic relations in 1972, they stopped holding general meetings, but continued to exchange opinions and information among committee members for years. However, it is virtually defunct now.

34 The Association for Promoting Japanese Film Overseas was established in 1957 for "spreading and advertising Japanese movies abroad in order to promote exports, as well as strengthening international friendship and cultural exchange." See "Zaidanhojin nihon eiga fukyu kyokai setsuritsu kyoka shinseisho" (An application of permission for establishment of the Association of Promoting Japanese Film Overseas), from Fujiyama Aiichiro, the association's representative, to Mizuta Mikio the Minister of International Trade and Industry, May 1, 1957, owned by UNIJAPAN.

35 "Dianchen rifang xieliweiyuanhui Jingkou dashi laiguan suotan yaoqing wo qihui lai riji shukan jinkou yingpian zengjia bushu shiyou qijian heyou" (A telegram inquiring into the issue of Ambassador Iguchi. Member of the Japan-ROC Cooperation Committee's visit to our embassy to demand increased importation of Japanese books and movies), from the Embassy of the ROC in Japan to the Ministry of Foreign Affairs, October 24, 1957, "Zhong-ri hezuo cejin weiyuanhui" (The ROC-Japan Cooperation Committee), No. 031-3/0035, MFT-AS-T.

36 Shin Kawashima, Urara Shimizu, Yasuhiro Matsuda, Yang Yong-ming, eds., *Nittai kankeishi 1945–2008* (History of the relationship between Japan and Taiwan 1945–2008), Tokyo: Tokyo Daigaku Shuppankai, 2009, pp. 68–71.

37 "Riben dianying xinshanghui shishi jihua yaogang" (A summary of the implementation plan of the Japanese Movie Trade Fair), March 3, 1960, written by The Japanese Embassy, No. 172-3,3023, MFA-AH-T.

38 The ranking was as follows: 1) Okinawa, 2) USA, 3) Taiwan, 4) Hong Kong, 5) USSR, 6) PRC, 7) Brazil. See Noguchi Yuichiro, "'Eiga sangyo hokoku' naiyo to bunseki" (Contents and analysis of "The Report on the Movie Industry"), *Kinema Junpo*, no. 222, January 1, 1959, pp. 58–61.

39 In the *Young Warrior Newspaper* (*Qingnian zhanshi bao*) (March 10, 1960), the Japanese responsible for importing movies like *Emperor Meiji and General Nogi* under the guise of "cultural exchange" were told, "Serious reflection is demanded of you." They were reportedly "arrogant," according to the *Independence Evening Post* (Zili wanbao) (March 10, 1960).

40 Young Warrior Newspaper (*Qingnian zhanshi bao*) March,10, 1960.

41 The government restricted the media through laws such as "Measures to save paper resources pertaining to newspapers, magazines, and books" (Xinwen zhi zazhi ji shuji yongzhi jieyue banfa) (1947) and "Measures for controlling newspapers, magazines, books in Taiwan under the martial law" (Taiwansheng

jieyan qijian xinwenzhi zazhi tushu guanzhi banfa) (1949) etc. See Lin Guo-xian, "Zhanhou Taiwan de Zhanshi Tizhi."

42 A report by Police Department of Taiwan Province sent to headquarters, April 12, 1960. Transferred to the Ministry of Foreign Affairs and General Headquarters of Security in Taiwan. No.172-3,3023, MFA-AH-T.

43 A report by the Department of Information on March 11, 1960, sent to the Department of East Asian Affairs, No. 172-3, 3023, MFA-AH-T.

44 "Operational background: Notes on the Fourth Section of the Kuomintang" (From USIS Taipei to USIA, October 6, 1954), Record Group 84, Entry: UD2689, Box 2, The U.S. National Archives and Records Administration at College Park.

45 The judgment of the fourth section of the Central Committee (*Zhongsizu*) and the Information Office (*Xinwenju*) might stem from considerations of economic profit, which might have been linked to personal profit, through screening the movie, except for their consideration of "anti-communism." This is difficult to prove due to a lack of strong evidence, but it was well known that people who dealt with movies were involved in corruption. See the article "Pianshang chenqing jianyuan jiaoju dianjian wubi" (Movie distributors made a petition to the Control Yuan for correcting the problems of censorship), *Ziliwanbao*, March 8, 1960, p. 2. There are also reports that restricting imports of Japanese movies was motivated by "some government and army officials having investments in the local movie industry using other people's names." See the article "Nihon eiga seigen o haishi" (Abolition of the limitation on importing Japanese movies), *Asahi Shimbun*, July 20, 1953, p. 12. Thus, we must allow the possibility that government decisions were sometimes related to personal profits.

46 The movie selection process was criticized within Japan. See "Sekai no naka no nihon eiga" (Japanese movies in the world), *Kinema Junpo*, no. 235, June 15, 1959, pp. 48–62.

47 A memorandum about an article by the Associated Press said, "The Associated Press carried comments from the *Independence Evening Post* (Zili wanbao) that criticized the arrogant attitude of the embassy staff towards a Chinese journalist at the press conference of the Japanese Movie Trade Fair." The Associated Press article stated, "They apparently forgot they were on the territory of Free China, one of the victorious nations in World War II which has shown leniency towards the Japanese." See "Nihon Eigasai ni kanshi gaidenhousou no ken (Sending a foreign dispatch regarding the Japanese Movie Trade Fair)", from Endo, a chief of the China Division to Nakada, a councilor at the embassy in the ROC, March 14, 1960, No. I'-0069, DA-MFA-J.

48 For an account of the conquest of Taiwan, see Ōe Shinobu, "Shokuminchi ryoyu to gunbu" (Conquering colony and army), *Rekishigakukenkyu* (Journal of Historical Studies) 460, September, 1978, pp. 10–22, 41, and Xu Shi-kai, *Nihon tochika no Taiwan* (Taiwan under Japanese colonial rule), Tokyo: Tokyo Daigaku Shuppankai, 1972..

49 The White Terror in Taiwan refers to political suppression by the ROC government under martial law (1949–1987), following the 2.28 Incident. Political dissidents in Taiwan were imprisoned or executed as Chinese communist spies at that time, although there are claims that most of them were falsely accused..

50 It was not until 1988 that the Japanese government started to pay compensation based on Act No. 105 of 1987, "Act on Condolence Payment, etc. for Surviving Family of War Dead Who Lived in Taiwan." However, the amount was far less than that provided to the "real" Japanese.
51 Ts'ai, Hui-yu Caroline, *Taiwan in Japan's Empire-Building: An institutional approach to colonial engineering*, London and New York: Routledge and Academia Sinica, 2008, p. 181. Taiwanese "comfort women" were also forced into sexual slavery by the Imperial Japanese Army, although their plight remained unknown for a long time after the war. See Funü jiuyuan jijinhui (Women's rescue foundation of Taipei) eds., *Taiwan weianfu baogao* (Report on comfort women in Taiwan), Taipei: Taiwan shangwu yinshuguan, 1999.
52 Tamura Taro "Taiwan Manpo" (Walk slowly in Taiwan), *Imahashi News*, August 1959, p. 72. Filed in "Propaganda against Japan," No.003 / 0001, Material of the Ministry of Foreign Affairs, Academia Sinica of the ROC (hereafter MFA-AS-T).
53 "Taiwan no Sugao" (The real Taiwan), *Sangyo Keizai Shimbun,* August 9, 1959. Filed in "Propaganda against Japan," No.003 / 0001, MFA-AS-T.
54 Liu Xian-cheng, *Taiwan dianying: Shehui yu guojia* (Taiwanese cinema: Society and state), Taipeixian: Shijue chuanbo yishu xuehui, 1997, p. 77. Li Tian-duo, *Taiwan dianying: Shehui yu lishi* (Taiwanese cinema: Society and history), Taipeixian: Shijue chuanbo yishu xuehui, 1997, p. 115.
55 Lü Su-shang, *Taiwan dianying xiju shi*, p. 107.
56 Lü Su-shang, *Taiwan dianying xiju shi*, p. 53.
57 Liu Xian-cheng, *Taiwan dianying: Shehui yu guojia*, p. 77.
58 Huang Ren and Wang Wei, *Taiwan Dianying Bainian Shihua* (One hundred years of Taiwan cinema), pp. 211–212.
59 "The Image of America and Things American" (A Survey of Opinions Among Participants in the American Studies Orientation Program at USIS Taipei, August 1960), Record Group 306, Entry 38, Box 5, the U.S. National Archives and Records Administration at College Park.
60 Wu Lin-Chun, "Sengo Taiwan ni okeru rokkufera zaidan no enjojigyo" (The Rockefeller Foundation's assistant project in postwar Taiwan), in Yuka Tsuchiya and Toshihiko Kishi, eds., *Bunka reisen no jidai* (De-centering the cultural Cold War: U.S. and Asia), Tokyo: Kokusai Shoin, 2009.
61 "Moto taiwanjin no tainichikan ni kansuru ken" (A report of the Taiwanese feelings for Japan), from Iguchi Sadao, Ambassador extraordinary and plenipotentiary in the ROC to Kosaka Zentarō, Ministry of Foreign Affairs, October 13, 1960. No. A'-423, DA-MFA-J.
62 The government allowed exceptional use of the Japanese language as a tool for specified political affairs. See Xu Xue-ji, "Taiwan guangfu chuqi de yuyan wenti" (Language problem in Taiwan in the early days of retrocession), *Si yu yan*, no.29–4, November 1991, pp.181–182.
63 He Yi-lin, *Kuayue Guojing-xian,* p. 217 calls attention to the fact that the conflicts between the Chinese language and the Japanese language and that of the Chinese language and the Taiwanese languages were separated by the time lag.
64 A reevaluation of the apparent "pro-Japanese" sentiments of the older generation and compassion for them can be seen in the work of Wu Nian-zhen, who portrayed his father's life in postwar Taiwan in the movie *A Borrowed Life*

(1994), as well as in the research pursuits of Taiwanese researchers born in the postwar period. Hence, we may conclude that this kind of reevaluation was not particular to the interviewee but was rather a general tendency of those who had been educated under the "Sinicization" policy and whose parents were apparently "pro-Japanese."

65 It is important to recognize that Japan, through concluding a peace treaty with the ROC and being its ally as part of an "anti-communist" bloc, has tended to forget its role as invader and oppressor. In this context, the bus driver's question, "Is there any possibility that I can get Japanese nationality?" may arise less from nostalgia for Japan than from having been driven into a corner. However, this is only one of many possible interpretations.

66 Huang Ying-zhe, *Taiwan bunka sai-kochiku 1945–1947*, pp. 172–182. He Yi-lin, *2.28 Jiken: 'Taiwanjin' keisei no esunoporiteikusu*, pp. 193–196.

67 Huang Chi-Huei approached the Japanese language and concepts of Japanese in postwar Taiwan, using the concept of the "double-layered relationship of a colony." See Huang "Taiwan ni okeru Nihon-kan no Kōsaku (Intertwined Japanese image in Taiwan)."

68 Lü Su-shang, *Taiwan dianying xiju shi*, p. 101. On the contrary, when Japanese movies resumed imports after a one-year suspension, excepting theatres which screened U.S. movies, almost all theatres were monopolized by Japanese movies, so that Taiwanese as well as Mandarin movies had fewer opportunities to be shown. See Liu Xian-cheng, *Taiwan dianying: shehui yu guojia*, p. 78.

69 "Jiaoyubu dianying shiye fudao weiyuanhui di qi ci weiyuanhui huiyilu" (Proceedings of the Seventh Committee of the Commission for Assistance to the Film Business), January 30, 1957, No. 172–3, 2987, MFA-AH-T.

70 Ibid.

71 See Misawa Mamie on the concept of "hybridized localization on the spot": "Shokuminchiki taiwan niokeru eiga fukyu no 'bunsetsuteki keiro' to 'konseiteki dochakuka'" (Hybridized nativization through divided routes of the cinema popularization in colonial Taiwan) *Ritsumeikan Studies in Language and Culture* 15:3 (February 2004) pp. 39-52; "Zhimindi shiqi taiwan dianying jieshou guocheng zhi hunheshi bentuhua" (The 'hybridized localization' of movie diffusion in colonial Taiwan), Masahiro Wakabayashi and Wu Mi-cha, eds., *Transcending the Boundary of Taiwanese History: Dialogue with East Asian History*, Taipei: Bozhongzhewenhua, 2004, pp. 243–270 (Chinese, translator: Chen Wen-Song); and *"Teikoku" to "Sokoku" no hazama: Shokuminchiki Taiwan eigajin no kōshō to ekkyō* (Between "The Empire Of Japan" And "Motherland China": Collaboration and boundary crossing of Taiwanese film activists in the colonial period), Tokyo: Iwanami Shoten, 2010.

72 The characteristics of movie perception in colonial Taiwan leave room for the possibility of Mandarin movies having been localized as well.

Personal Names Index

Bergher, Michael 62–67, 71
Buck, Pearl S. 185, 195

Ch'oe In-gyu 157, 159, 162–163, 170, 172, 175–177, 179–180
Chiang Kai-shek 95

Doihara Kenji 84

Fanck, Dr. Arnold 184–188, 190–194, 197–200

Goebbels, Paul Joseph 186, 192
Guo Moruo 89

Hara Setsuko 188, 191–192
He Jiming 221

Iguchi Sadao 210
Imai Tadashi 106, 174
Itami Mansaku 185, 188–194, 198

Kawakita Nagamasa 68, 180, 186–188, 192, 194, 199–200
Kim Il Sung 115, 123, 126, 128, 130, 133, 140, 145, 147–148
Kim Jong-il 7, 115, 122–124, 131, 140, 148
Kim Jong-suk 7, 115, 128
Kurosawa Akira 210

Lober, Louis 64

Mayer, Charles C. 66
Milliken, Carl E. 67–69

Ohkawa Hiroshi 102–104

Park Chung-hee 176–177

Riefenstahl, Leni 185, 194

Tatebayashi Mikio 10, 17, 20
Tezuka Osamu 110
Toyoda Shiro 174

Vespa, Amleto 83

Yang Hansheng 87

Yi Chang-yong 159, 160–161, 165–166, 179–180
Yi Gwang-su 173–174, 182
Yoo Hyeon-Mok 180
Yu Hyôn-mok 178, 183
Yuan Congmei 86

Zhang Zuolin 83

Subjects, Film Titles and Geographical Names Index

2.28 Incident 208, 214

American cultural diplomacy 60
American imperialists 134
anti-American 46
anti-communism / anti-Comintern Pact 185–186, 208, 211
anti-Soviet 46
Astro Boy 107, 110
Atarashiki Tsuchi (Der Tochter des Samurai; The Daughter of the Samurai) 184–186, 188–189, 191–194, 196–200
Axis alignment 186

Buddhist 143, 150 *see also* neo-Buddhist
business licensing system 22

caricature 139
"catharsis" through reversal 218–223
censorship 4–5, 38, 94–95, 157–161, 165, 168, 174–175, 179, 181, 208
Censorship Regulations of Moving Pictures or "Films" (*Katsudo shashin "firumu" ken'etsu kisoku*) 11–12, 14–15
Central Bank of China 60, 67, 73, 77
Central Motion Picture Exchange (CMPE) 65–66, 68, 70
China 41
  People's Republic of China (PRC) 209–210
China Film Co., Ltd. 186
Chinese Communist Party (CCP) 207
Chinese Nationalist Party (CNP) 203, 206–208, 211, 213
Chongqing 82

Christian/Christianity 142, 150
Cold War 5, 38–39, 46, 119, 133
collective imaginary 116
colonialism 175, 204–205, 222–223
communism/communist 116, 127–128, 151
  anti-communism/anti-Comintern Pact 185–186, 208, 211
  anti-Soviet 46
Confucian 129–131, 136, 142, 147, 149–151 *see also* neo-Confucianism
Constitution (of Japan) 39, 46, 49
Constitution (of North Korea) 147
consumerism 51–52
cultural diplomacy 209–210
cultural imperialism 59, 77
cultural (or creative) industries 1–3
cultural policy 1
cultural politics 9
cultural studies 2

de-colonization 203, 220, 223
decree authority 24
de-Japanization 205, 208, 211, 213, 220–223
Department of State (US) 58, 60, 63, 65–66, 68–70, 73, 75, 77–78
domestic production 100, 107–109, 112

economic recovery 112
Eight Man 110
Emperor Meiji and General Nogi 211–212
Emperor Meiji and the Great Russo-Japanese War 213, 215

234

Subjects, Film Titles and Geographical Names Index

film companies 3, 8
film industry 1, 5–6, 8, 10–11, 17, 21–22, 37, 53, 58–60, 76–77, 101–105, 159–161, 176, 180–181, 210, 222
Film Law 10ff.
film production committee 36, 53
first piece of cultural legislation 11, 14, 20
Five Company Pact 108
Five Scouts (Gonin no Sekkohei) 24–25
Frankfurt School 2

Gigantor 110
government 1–5, 8
government policy 3, 6 *see also* cultural policy, policy
government propaganda 9

Home Ministry's Police Bureau (*Naimusho keihokyoku*) 12
Homeless Angels 157–165, 170–179, 181
hybridized localization on the spot 221–222

imaginary 116, 119, 145, 150, 152
imperialist/imperialization/imperial Japan 68, 101, 139, 143, 150, 173, 208 *see also* American imperialists, cultural imperialism, Japanese imperialism/imperialists

Japan's Self-Defense Forces (JSDF) 36ff.
Japanese colonial rule 203
Japanese Embassy 204, 206, 212, 216–217, 219, 222
Japanese imperialism/imperialists 4–5, 122, 134, 157, 176, 178
Japanese Movie Trade Fair 205–206, 211
Japanese Spy 82ff.
Juchean 130, 150
Juche-led world 137

Know Your Enemy: Japan 198
Korea 49
 Korean tradition 135
 Korean War 76, 122, 179
 North Korea/North-Koreans 41–42, 46–48
 South Korea/South Korean 41, 118, 129, 138, 140–141, 145, 149, 152

Love and Fealty 180

Manchuria 10, 22, 49, 83, 160, 179–181
Manichean 117
Marxism/Marxist 144, 147, 182
masculinization 143, 150 *see also* re-masculinization
media
 cultural industry 2–3
 mass media 40, 53
 media companies 2
 media conglomerate 2
 media industries 8
 modern/modernity 9, 117, 141, 147, 149, 166, 173, 176, 179, 182–183
 traditional modern 117
motherhood 126, 133, 135, 143, 147, 152
Motion Picture Association (MPA) 67–68, 73–75, 77
Motion Picture Export Association of America (MPEA) 66–68, 78
Mushi Production 110
My Japan 184–185, 195, 197–198

national defense films 82
national film policy 12, 16 *see also* cultural policy/politics, government (cultural) policy
national identity 50, 140, 158
nationalism 8, 36–37, 43–44, 50–53, 176, 183, 205, 218
neo-Buddhist 130, 143, *see also* Buddhist
neo-Confucianism 141 *see also* Confucian

neo-liberalism 8, 39, 52, 54
neo-nationalism 40, 54
North Korea / North-Koreans 41–42, 46–48, 179

Oath of Imperial Subjects 164, 169, 172, 182
Office of War Information (OWI) 62–66, 185, 195
others/otherness 137, 145

patriot/patriotism 48
People's Republic of China (PRC) 209–210 *see* China
policy 1, 8, 14–16, 23, 32, 40, 63–65, 117, 141, 148–149, 165, 168, 178, 180, 182, 221
  cultural policy 1
  government policy 3, 6
postwar 5, 8, 46, 60, 62, 66, 72–73, 100–101, 105, 109, 112, 115, 183, 204–205
pre-censorship system 27 *see also* censorship
pro-American 46
production companies 3
pro-Japanese 203–205, 209, 211, 214, 218–220, 222–223
propaganda 4–5, 7–9, 38, 51, 82, 97, 116, 123, 129, 152, 181, 186, 198, 209, 213
Proposition Concerning Establishment of a National Film Policy 16 *see also* Film Law
Public Information and Cultural Affairs Bureau 209–210

qualitative improvements 17

racism 50
Rashomon 105–106, 210
recommendation system 11, 21, 26, 30–32
registration system 1–13, 21, 26–27, 32, 76
re-masculinization 151, 158, 163, 170, 179 *see also* masculinization

representation 90, 116–117, 143, 166, 169, 174
Republic of China (ROC) 203–220, 222–223

sacrifice 36, 42–45, 48–49, 53–54, 150, 152
self-sacrifice 8, 36, 38, 43–45, 50, 53–54, 126, 129, 142
Shen Bao 70–71, 73
Sinicization 204–205, 211, 213, 219, 221–222
Sino-Japanese War 17, 20, 82, 179, 182
socialist 7, 122–123, 133, 149, 151
South Korea/South Korean 41, 118, 129, 138, 140–141, 145, 149, 152
Soviet Union *see* Union of Soviet Socialist Republics (USSR)
State Department *see* Department of State (US)
Suicide Squad of the Watchtower 174
Sunshine Policy 139, 141, 145, 149

Taiwan 49, 203–219, 220–223
Taiwan Cultural Association (*Taiwan wenhua xiehui*) 221
Taiwanese Hokkien films/movies 220–223
Technicolor films/pictures 64, 70–71
Television Corporation of Japan (TCJ) 108, 110–111
Thatcherism 39
Toei 102–107, 111–112
Toei Animation 102–105, 108, 110–111
totalitarian 116, 152
traditional modern 117 *see also* modern
Treasury Department 185
Tripartite Pact 186
Tuition Fee 157–159, 162, 172, 179

United States (US) 8, 37, 40–43, 45–46
  United States Information Service (USIS) 180, 204, 206, 216, 222
Union of Soviet Socialist Republics (USSR) 39, 147, 149–150

Subjects, Film Titles and Geographical Names Index

war movies 37–38
White Snake Tale 102–103, 105, 107
White Terror 214
Wolf Boy Ken 110
World War II 5, 39–40, 46, 48–49, 51–52, 101, 109, 112
  WWII propaganda 53

Xue Pinggui and Wang Baochuan (The Story of Xue Pinggui and Wang Baochuan) 221

Young Looks 174